TRAINS, VIDEO GAMES, & SUPERHEROES

AUTISM IN CONTEXT

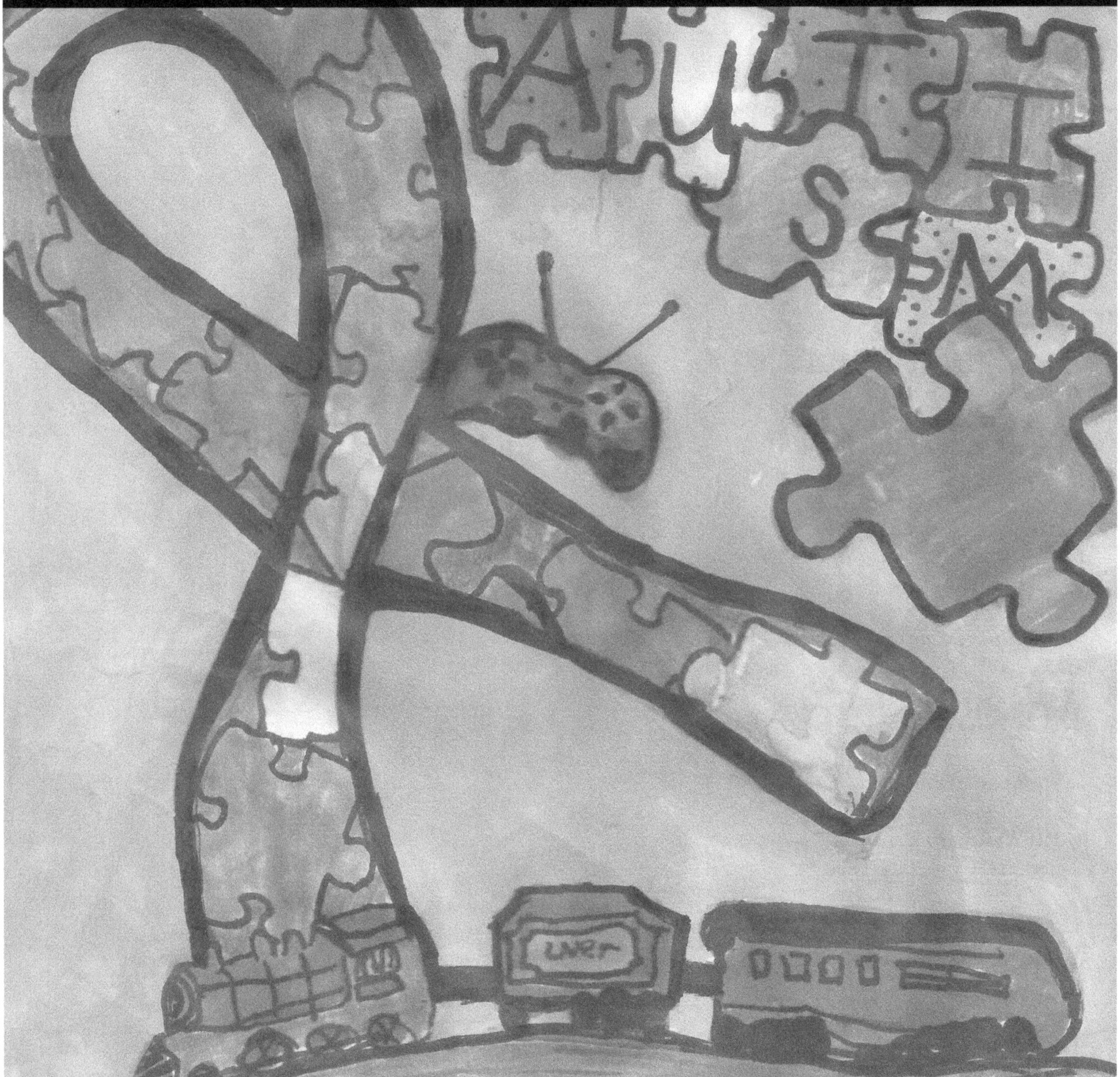

Raschelle Theoharis * Michael Fitzpatrick

Kendall Hunt
publishing company

Cover image courtesy Clancie Glennon. Used with permission.

Kendall Hunt
publishing company

www.kendallhunt.com
Send all inquiries to:
4050 Westmark Drive
Dubuque, IA 52004-1840

ISBN 978-1-4652-6642-2

Printed in the United States of America

CONTENTS

1 Overview of the Book

Chapter 1 Subject Index:

1. Autism

2. Special Education

INTRODUCTION

This chapter serves as an introduction to both Max and the content of this book, which covers **special education** (SPED) concepts through one specific disability, **autism spectrum disorder**. For example, while learning about the assessment process, readers are exposed to specific characteristics related to autism and provided scenarios related to SPED topics. In addition, to the content, chapters also include Scenarios (shared by Max's mom and family members), Professional Analysis (from professionals in the field), and first person testimonials (shared by professionals, friends, and family members). Finally, there are a few excerpts from Max where he shares what it is like to have autism and his experiences in SPED.

This book will be useful in helping readers make connections between what they are learning in class and real-life situations (i.e., transferring knowledge to application of educational concepts and principles). Further, the text promotes critical thinking, inquiry, and reflection related to specific SPED theories and topics through case studies. It is important to note, scenarios have become more valued as a beneficial tool for pre-service and in-service teachers allowing an opportunity to critically analyze situations in which they might find themselves.

Throughout this text, readers are allowed the opportunity to synthesize information from class, textbooks, field experiences, and background knowledge to inform their decisions about highly probable situations presented in the scenarios. Using these scenarios should help to formulate a strategic plan of action after evaluating the facts, thinking through the pros and cons of possible solutions, and selecting the best options most likely to produce maximum benefits for all involved.

Finally, it should be noted not all chapters are parallel. For example, some chapters may only have a Professional Analysis whereas others do not. Further, Chapters 3 and 8 were written by guest authors who are well-versed in the topical areas. Now it is time to get to the good stuff and meet Max…

MEET LAWRENCE MAXWELL THEOHARIS: WHO IS THIS KID?

Max was born December 7, 1999. He seemed to be developing normally until around the age of 2. This is when; I noticed some language delays (being in the education field I was noting all of his developmental milestones). He was diagnosed with autism at age 2½. He began extensive therapy in all areas. This is where his journey began. There have been celebrations and challenges through the years and some of these are discussed in the scenarios throughout the chapters. Currently, Max is about to begin high school. He has had many educational and life transitions, from which, we both have learned a lot.

I think I am a pretty amazing guy! I am super amazing at life and other stuff. I am learning to drive, and really like hitting the mud puddles in the parking lots. I like spending time with my dad, and playing Star Wars Monopoly, because he is the only one who likes Star Wars and Monopoly. I love my sisters, but they can be really loud, and I don't like loud noises. I have fun playing games with them, and showing them funny YouTube videos. I don't really like school, but I really get good grades. My favorite class last year was social studies, but I did not like Spanish or music. I like social studies, because Mr. Putt brought snacks to class, told really interesting stories, and watched movies. I consider myself cheap, in fact I cut the electric bill in half; however, I drove my family crazy with turning off the lights and A/C! I figure there is no reason to spend money unnecessarily when you can save it to buy really cool stuff.

I am not really sure what I want to do when I grow up. I really like the thought of being a stuntman, fixing cars, inventing things, being an American Picker, or repo man. I have thought about college, and I know my mom really wants me to go, but I do not really want four more years of school. We will see. I enjoy getting to do research studies, because I get paid. Sometimes they just draw blood, have me throw a ball at the wall with one hand, or try new technologies involving sensations. It is pretty cool, but I still like getting paid. Plus I get out of school, and get to spend the day with my mom. I like taking vacations to Missouri to visit my family. This summer I was able to work with my Uncle Andrew, and made some money, so now I can save it or buy new Play Station games. I taught my cousins some new video games, and enjoyed the time I got to spend with them.

I am not much into adventure, but I have started riding more roller coasters at Hershey Park. I wanted to ride the new water slide at Schlitterbahn Water Park in Kansas City. It is the tallest in the WORLD!!! I rode Great Bear with Aunt Crystal, and it is now my new favorite!

My school has a program I am involved in that helps me to learn social skills. We take a lot of field trips around the area. We have gone kayaking, zip-lining, eating at a fancy restaurant, skiing, and hiking. I just really enjoyed getting out of school, although my family seems to see a difference in me. They tell me they notice me talking to other people more, am able to look people in the eyes more, and able to explain what I want or need without feeling shy. All in all I think I am just a pretty amazing guy!

An 8th grade English assignment adds some insight into Max's personality and philosophies.

Change

By

Max Theoharis, 8th grade

I believe that changes are never permanent. The world itself is frequently changing. So why are so many people afraid of change? I think that everyone should embrace change instead of being afraid of it. Why, if nothing ever changed, life would, in a sense, be the very same each and every day. So, should not people as a whole embrace the changes in our lives instead of fearing them?

One of the major changes in my life was when I moved from Kansas City to North Carolina, then from North Carolina to Maryland, and from there to Pennsylvania. These changes have not only helped me to meet new people, but also to make new friends. At first when I moved from North Carolina to Maryland I did not like it. But then I learned that it was not such a bad thing. I got to meet new people, and make new friends.

Change, therefore, is not always a bad thing. Change is what we make of it, and if we make the best of it then change is not hard to deal with. The way to accept change is to change our attitude towards it. Why then, is change looked on as a negative thing? The way we look at change determines our attitude towards it. I believe that if you look at the positive side of change, then it is easier to cope with change. However, if you look at the negative side of change it is much more difficult to cope with change. Sometimes, though, things do not always change for the better. But your attitude towards change makes all the difference. So if you change your attitude towards change, change becomes easier. I believe in change.

I find this philosophy paper Max wrote to be an interesting one for two reasons. Children with autism often have a difficult time with change. When Max was much younger, he experienced challenges with changes. As he has gotten older he does better dealing with changes in routine, schedules, and transitioning to classes or starting a new school year. That said, I found the topic and his perspective of change unexpected.

This journey has been filled with wonderful professionals, teachers, family, and friends who have got to know Max. They have supported him, loved him, and guided him through his journey. The next two scenarios will help to introduce you to Max as others see him, share the types of friendships he has made, and illustrate how important a support network is to families and students with disabilities.

FIRST PERSON TESTIMONIAL

Coming out of his Shell

By

Courtney Rickabaugh, *English Language Arts Teacher Big Spring Middle School, Newville, PA 17241*

I was Max's 7th grade English Language Arts teacher for the 2012–2013 school year upon his move to Pennsylvania. When Max arrived in Pennsylvania after his 7th grade year had started, he came as a quiet, shy, introverted young man who hardly made eye contact with any of us. But when he left 7th grade to move onto 8th grade, he walked down the hallway with his head held high, making eye contact with his peers and teachers, participating in the daily workings of his classes, and smiling, genuinely smiling! He had come out of his shell!

Meeting Max for the first time was not unlike meeting other students with autism I had worked with in my 18 years of teaching, but what was different was that there was a curiosity about Max that I noticed as he looked all around the classroom. You have to first understand my room is not the typical classroom in its decoration style, so I thought that maybe he was overwhelmed, but as I watched his eyes move from decoration to poster to decoration to art work, he would randomly smile, as if what he had just seen or read intrigued him. Max was placed in my homeroom, which is also my 3/4 period class that also comes back to me at the end of the day for a glamorized Study Hall called Resource, so we saw a lot of each other daily.

One of the first things that I realized about Max is that he was more comfortable talking to me than to his peers. He would speak to me as he walked into the classroom, would quietly ask me questions about our work, and always said parting words to be as he left the classroom, either for another class or another day. His manners and kindness were evident in all of his interactions.

As the weeks progressed and he got more and more acclimated to our school and the students, I waited for him to find a buddy, someone he could connect with in our classroom. When I did not see that happening on its own, I created some group work so that he would have the chance to get to know other students and more importantly, they would get to know Max. As the group worked together, I was pleased to see Max smiling and if I happened to look at just the right moment, I could see him participate.

Max's mom and I were in frequent email contact and one of the emails shared the details of how Max had really gotten into the lessons that he was learning in Health class. I had noticed that Max was slimming down, but that process is pretty common in 7th grade boys, as this is a year where they hit a pretty steep growth spurt. His mom shared that he was eating more consciously and had set a goal for himself and their family for the remainder of the school year. This information became a great place where Max and I connected, as I started to ask him questions about his exercise and what he was eating that day. In fact, most days, we would check in with each other about our breakfasts and report what we had eaten before coming to school.

As spring approached and the world started to wake up from the winter slumber, Max began to really emerge from his shell. He had created some strong bonds with a few students who he sat with at lunch, he was participating in class on a frequent basis, and the class got to see his dry sense of humor on occasion, which they really enjoyed, as did Max. On the last day of school, as we signed yearbooks and said our summer goodbyes, I hugged Max and told him I would miss him and that I was proud of him, and he thanked me. I thanked him in return, as he had taught me probably more than I had taught him.

FIRST PERSON TESTIMONIAL

WHY WE LOVE MAX ...

By

Tawanna Curry

The first time I met Max, I loved him. After all, he made my son, Brandon smile and for the first time I felt Brandon had a friend who really understood him. Our *play dates* were never very long and did not involve elaborate plans but the boys enjoyed each other and while they did not always express it right then and there, their requests for more time together let Raschelle and I know that we were on to something positive. Bowling, movies, Skyzone, mini golf, our homes, and the mall have been the backdrop for our times together and even years later, I can remember something special about each visit. Max is someone that our family loves to talk about as if he is truly part of our family.

Three years ago he changed everything for us and we will forever be grateful. His calm manner and quick wit is a perfect match for my son and their love of shirts with comical sayings bonds them together. Max has never been afraid to share what is on his mind and seems so comfortable in the skin he is in. Unknowingly he has done what I had been trying for years to accomplish with Brandon. He made Brandon feel like he could have friends and he could have fun with people other than his family.

The day I told my son that Max was moving was one of the few times I have seen my son show emotion for someone. It was also the first time I saw him cry about someone he cared for. Brandon does not show emotion very often but for hours he cried and repeatedly said "it hurts for Max to go." I was unsure what would happen to their friendship and could not imagine Max not being a part of our lives. We have not seen each other as much as we like but when Max and his family have made it to Maryland I have seen a different young man each time. Max is maturing and growing and taking on new interests that I did not imagine he would be drawn towards. He still says little but when he does it brings an automatic smile to our faces. I have noticed that Max inspires Brandon. Brandon listens intently to Max and what he is accomplishing and in the weeks following, Brandon makes strides of his own.

I hope that their friendship is one that lasts a lifetime. I am tearing up as I think about how different life would be not just for Brandon, but our whole family if Max were not a part of it. Max is an amazing young man with a quite coolness that draws you in and keeps you captivated. I cannot wait to see what the world holds for this young man.

PROFESSIONAL ANALYSIS

Understanding Max: A Great Example of What is Possible!

By

Dr. Paul G. LaCava, Associate Professor of Special Education, Rhode Island College

The introduction provides an empowering account that is a positive and realistic portrayal of an individual with autism; indeed, it is a counter-story to historically unrealistic views of disability (Cohen-Rottenberg,

2014). We read about the strengths, personality, struggles, and adventures that Max has and it helps us to realize both the similarities and differences in our lives and humanely connect with Max and his family. The stories in this introduction and throughout the text from teachers, family, friends, and Max himself, weave a rich narrative and hence make the SPED content more meaningful.

We know family-professional partnerships (e.g., frequent communication, trust, etc.; Turnbull et al., 2012.) and self-determination (e.g., having casual agency, setting goals, making choices, etc.; Wehmeyer, 1998) are key to improving outcomes and quality of life for individuals with disabilities. This chapter initiates these in the introduction of Max, his family, and other stakeholders as Max clearly states his goals, preferences, likes, etc., while his family and other stakeholders benefit from everyone's knowledge, opinions, and expertise.

It was great to read how Max describes change and why it is so important; change is a constant in education and our world and special educators need to learn how to be civic professionals to guide transformation in our schools (Boyte & Fretz, 2010). The above vignettes illustrate this civic professionalism by showing how teachers did not view Max and his family as clients who would blindly accept the expertise they had, but rather as partners collaborating to do what was best for Max. Likewise, Max is seen as an evolving self- advocate with an active role in the co-creation of his education plan and future.

The different perspectives presented also support the idea of collaboration and how teamwork is essential when solving the problems that face students with disabilities. Further, the importance of appropriate, positive supports is shown via a teacher testimonial; Ms. Rickabaugh understood Max's needs and then provided supports to help him be successful. Max and those around him also understand his strengths and interests and seek to capitalize on them. It is refreshing that the chapter displays an individual with autism in a positive light who can and does make changes in his life as well as contributions to society. Ms. Curry's words are inspiring as we hear the impact of Max's friendship on her son.

Finally, this chapter illustrates the importance of relationships. Yes, you will learn about many significant historical events, laws, disability characteristics, teaching methods, and other important concepts in this text. And yes, teaching children with disabilities the essential skills of reading, social interaction, math, problem solving, etc. is critical; however, none of this is possible without building strong relationships! Enjoy your journey with Max as you learn about special education...

SUMMARY & CONCLUSION

The purpose of this chapter was to provide readers a concise overview of the text and introduce Max. Subsequent chapters will reflect historical-to-current literature and research related to students with autism and the authors will make connections to both Max and SPED.

References

Boyte, H. C., & Fretz, E. (2010). Civic professionalism. Journal of Higher Education and Engagements, 14, 67–90.

Cohen-Rottenberg, R. (2014). *Strategies for creating counter-narratives in disability representation.* (Unpublished master's thesis). Union Institute & University, Cincinnati, OH.

Turnbull, A. P., Turnbull, H. R., Wehmeyer, M. L., & Shogren, K. (2012). Exceptional lives: *Special education in today's schools* (7th ed.). Upper Saddle River, NJ: Merrill/Prentice Hall.

Wehmeyer, M. L. (1998). Self-determination and individuals with significant disabilities: Examining meanings and misinterpretations. *JASH, 23,* 5–16.

2

Cases, Policies, & Characteristics

Chapter Objectives

After studying this chapter readers should be able to:

- Understand how each of the selected landmark cases pertain to students with ASD.
- Discuss how the six principles and four stated outcomes of IDEIA (2004) impacts students with ASD.
- Explain the similarities and differences between the five disorders of ASD.
- Identify stereotypies behavior they may observe individuals display in the *natural environment*.

Chapter 2 Subject Index:

1. Aggression and Self-Injurious Behavior
2. Americans with Disabilities Act
3. Applied Behavior Analysis
4. Appropriate Education
5. Asperger's Disorder
6. Authorization of Assistance
7. Autism
8. Autism Spectrum Disorder
9. Autistic Disorder
10. Autistic psychopathology
11. Centers for Disease Control
12. Childhood Disintegrative Disorder
13. Children Ages 3 to 5
14. Children Ages 6 through 21
15. Communication and Language
16. Diana v. State Board of Education (1970)
17. Economic Self-Sufficiency
18. Education for All Handicapped Children Act
19. Equal Opportunity
20. Four Stated Outcomes
21. Free And Appropriate Public Education
22. Full Participation

23. IDEIA Part B
24. IDEIA Part C
25. Independent Living
26. Individualized Education Program
27. Individuals with Disabilities Education Act
28. Individuals with Disabilities Education Improvement Act
29. Intellectual Functioning
30. Larry P. v. Riles (1972)
31. Least Restrictive Environment
32. Local Education Agencies
33. Multidisciplinary Teams
34. No Child Left Behind Act
35. Nondiscriminatory Evaluation
36. Parental Participation
37. Pervasive Developmental Disorder Not Otherwise Specified
38. Procedural Due Process
39. Race to the Top
40. Repetitive and Unusual Behavior Patterns.
41. Rett's disorder
42. Sameness and Perseverance.
43. San Antonio School District v. Rodriquez (1973)
44. Savant Syndrome
45. Section 504 of the Rehabilitation Act
46. Sensory
47. Six Core Principles
48. Smith v. Robinson, 1984
49. Socialization
50. Special Education
51. Splinter Skills
52. Stereotypies
53. Timothy W. v. Rochester, New Hampshire (1989)
54. Use of Funds
55. Zero Reject

INTRODUCTION

The authors made the following generalizations while writing Chapter 2. First, unless this text is being used in an introduction course, this *is not* the reader's first exposure to historical, litigation, legislation, and general information specifically related to **special education** (SPED). Therefore the intent of this chapter was to provide a truncated refresher rather than delving into the intricacies that are often associated with introduction to SPED courses. Readers who are interested in additional information should consider reviewing these textbook resources (a) Arnett, Fitzpatrick, and Theoharis (2013); (b) Hallahan and Kauffman (2006); (c) Kirk, Gallagher, Anastasiow, and Coleman (2006); (d) Friend (2011); (e) Snell and Brown (2011); and (f) Turnbull, Turnbull, Wehmeyer, and Shogren (2010) for a thorough analysis of each of the topics discussed throughout. The focus of this chapter provides an overview of (a) landmark cases, (b) reforms and legislation, (c) six principles and four stated outcomes of the **Individuals with Disabilities Education Improvement Act** (IDEIA, 2004), (d) **autism spectrum disorders** (ASD), (e) definition of autism, (f) historical overview, (g) disorders, and (h) characteristics.

LANDMARK CASES

Below are a summary of pertinent landmark cases in which the decisions that were rendered had resounding implications for students with disabilities receiving SPED services.

Diana v. State Board of Education (1970). Diana was a Latino student who experienced academic difficulties. In alignment with district policies, she was administered an IQ test in English which was not her primary (i.e., native) language. Results indicated she was mildly mentally retarded. The court ruled assessments cannot be discriminatory (discussed below).

Larry P. v. Riles (1972). Larry was an African-American student who was inappropriately classified as having an intellectual disability based on a culturally biased assessment. Similar to Diana, the courts ruled that the test was biased and placements were discriminatory. The courts struck down the use of an IQ test to solely determine a student's eligibility for disability classification (discussed below).

San Antonio School District v. Rodriquez (1973). The court ruled that education *was not* a right afforded protection under the U.S. Constitution. Conversely, in subsequent cases, it is evident courts have endorsed the notion that states are responsible for ensuring the quality of education to their students. Specifically for SPED, which was initially focused on access and has transformed to outcomes driven (discussed below), students with disabilities are entitled to a **free and appropriate public education** (FAPE) and fairness, not equality.

Timothy W. v. Rochester, New Hampshire (1989). According to court documents, Timothy was a student who was profoundly mentally retarded and suffered complex developmental disabilities including (a) spastic quadriplegia, (b) cerebral palsy, (c) seizure disorder, and (d) cortical blindness. School personnel asserted that due to the severity of Timothy's condition he was not benefiting from the educational services the district could provide him. The court upheld the *zero-reject* provision (discussed below) and declared that states are not afforded the discretion to determine who is educable and must provide FAPE to every student regardless of ability level.

REFORMS & LEGISLATION

Section 504 of the Rehabilitation Act (P.L. 93-112, 1973) was the first piece of federal legislation that focused on providing rights to individuals with disabilities. Essentially, Section 504 helps prevent discrimination and offers protection for *all* individuals with disabilities while accessing federally funded programs.

Education for All Handicapped Children Act (P.L. 94-142, 1975) introduced a series of educational reforms which provided students with disabilities greater access to the general education curriculum. Although access did not necessarily equate to outcomes, this act opened the proverbial door to a population who were traditionally either underserved or not receiving appropriate educational services in the K-12 school environment.

In 1990 P.L. 94-142 was reauthorized and renamed the **Individuals with Disabilities Education Act** (IDEA, 20 U.S.C. § 1400 et seq.) and amended again in 1997. The primary thrusts of these two reauthorizations continued to focus on increasing access for students with disabilities. However, in 2004

IDEA was updated and renamed the IDEIA which shifted the emphasis from access to improving the educational outcomes of students with disabilities.

IDEIA Part B (20 U.S.C. Secs. 14111419) extended services to children between the ages of 3 through 21 and included the following four prongs:

1. **Authorization of Assistance**. Part B authorized federal funds to state and **local education agencies** (LEA) to educate students between the ages of 3 and 21.
2. **Children Ages 3-to-5**. Part B granted states the opportunity to choose whether or not to educate students between the ages of 3 through 5. If a state opted to provide SPED services, they must comply with IDEIA provisions (Turnbull, Stowe, & Huerta, 2007)
3. **Children ages 6 through 21**. IDEIA authorized federal aid to state and LEA to serve students between the ages of 6 through 21. It should be noted certain states have extended this age range, for example, Michigan currently provides SPED and transitional services for students with specific disabilities until they are 26.
4. **Use of Funds**. States and LEA receiving IDEIA funding must comply with *all* IDEIA provisions.

IDEIA Part C (20 U.S.C. Secs. 1431-1444) extended provisions to include early childhood services for infants and toddlers (AKA 0-3). Similar to Part B's second prong (i.e., *Children Ages 3 to 5*) states and LEA have the option of choosing to provide educational services to this student population (Turnbull et al., 2007).

The **Americans with Disabilities Act** (ADA, P.L. 101-336, 1990,) is a federal mandate intended to stop discrimination and extends nondiscrimination protections to employment, transportation, state and local government programs, private businesses, and telecommunications. ADA provides individuals with disabilities reasonable accommodations, accessibility, and avoidance of undue hardships.

The **No Child Left Behind Act** (NCLB, P.L. 107-110, 2002) is another significant law impacting students with disabilities. The significance was clearly evident when considering NCLB (2002) increased educators' responsibilities to ensure *all* students achieved academic success (Abedi, 2004; Berry, 2004; Linn, 2003; Rose, 2004) especially students with disabilities (Fitzpatrick & Knowlton, 2007; Fletcher, Coulter, & Reschly, 2004; Jones, Zirkel, & Barrack, 2008). Additionally Zirkel (2007) reported that IDEIA (2004) reinforced the requirements of NCLB (2002). Although **Race to the Top** (2010) has updated the precepts of NCLB, the implications of these acts are entrenched in holding schools and school districts accountable for their students' educational outcomes (Abedi, 2004) and require them to achieve adequateyearly progress for *all* of their students (Abedi, 2004; Berry, 2004; Fitzpatrick & Knowlton, 2007; Linn, 2003; & Rose, 2004).

SIX PRINCIPLES & FOUR STATED OUTCOMES OF IDEIA

According to Turnbull et al. (2007) IDEIA (2004) has the following **six core principles**:

1. **Zero Reject**. *All* students receiving SPED services are entitled to receive FAPE regardless of the severity of their disability (see Timothy W. v. Rochester, New Hampshire, 1989).
2. **Nondiscriminatory Evaluation**. In order to determine the existence of a disability **multidisciplinary teams** are mandated to use racially and culturally appropriate testing protocols, evaluation materials, and procedures. For example, no single test can be used for identification purposes and the assessment process should be in the student's native language and (see Diana v. State Board of Education, 1970; **Larry P. v. Riles**, 1972).
3. **Appropriate Education**. The student receives individualized instruction, programs, and services that benefit him/her while working toward achieving national policy goals.
4. **Least Restrictive Environment**. To the maximum extent possible, students with disabilities are to be educated in the *traditional classroom* with their nondisabled peers.

5. **Procedural Due Process.** This provision allows parents, legal guardians, or others acting in this capacity to hold schools accountable for their child's educational outcomes while simultaneously allowing schools to hold parents accountable for their child (see **Smith v. Robinson**, 1984)
6. **Parental Participation**. This provision helps ensure that parents, legal guardians, or others acting in this capacity are active participants on the multidisciplinary team and have direct input about their child's education.

According to Turnbull et al. (2007) IDEIA (2004) has the **four stated outcomes** discussed below:

1. **Equal Opportunity**. Students with disabilities are provided equitable access to the general education curriculum to the maximum extent possible.
2. **Full Participation**. Students with disabilities should not be excluded from extracurricular activities (e.g., chess club, band, sports teams) to the maximum extent possible.
3. **Independent Living**. Individuals with disabilities should be integrated into society, including quality of life and leisure activities, to the maximum extent possible.
4. **Economic Self-Sufficiency**. Individuals with disabilities should be employable to the maximum extent possible.

AUTISM SPECTRUM DISORDERS

ASD is the fastest-growing developmental disability in the world (Autism Society of America, 2003). Similar to other disability classifications (e.g., learning disabilities), there is no cure, only compensation (Arnett et al., 2013). The following sections provide a comprehensive introduction to students with ASD which consists of the definition, historical overview, descriptions of various disorders associated with ASD, and characteristics.

DEFINITION OF AUTISM

Congress added autism as an IDEA disability category in 1990 and defined the condition as:

> *Autism* means a developmental disability affecting verbal and nonverbal communication and social interaction, generally evident before age three, that adversely affects a child's educational performance. Other characteristics often associated with autism are engagement in repetitive activities and **stereotypies**, resistance to environmental change or change in daily routines, and unusual responses to sensory experiences. Autism does not apply if a child's educational performance is adversely affected primarily because the child has a serious emotional disturbance as defined in paragraph (c) (4) of this section. A child who manifests the characteristics of autism after age three could be identified as having autism if the criteria in paragraph (c) (1) (i) of this section are satisfied (34 CFR, Part 300 300.8 [c][1][i-iii]).

HISTORICAL OVERVIEW

Bleuler (1911) is often credited for coining the terms *autism* and *autistic* which are derivatives from the Greek word *autos*, meaning *self.* Originally, he used the terms to describe aspects of individuals with schizophrenia because they would become withdrawn from the outside world. However, autism was not universally recognized until the 1940s when Kanner (1943)—a psychologist at John Hopkins—described the disability while working with 11 children. Unlike Bleuler, Kanner's work differentiated between children with schizophrenia and those with autism.

In 1944, Asperger—a pediatrician in Vienna—used the term **autistic psychopathology** to describe a group of older children and adolescents who displayed autistic characteristics. Intuitively there were many dynamics during the 1940s which prevented Kanner and Asperger from discovering each other's research and findings. Interestingly, Asperger's work was significantly underreported in English-speaking countries until Wing (1981)—a psychiatrist from London—coined the term Asperger's syndrome in her seminal article entitled *Asperger's Syndrome: A Clinical Account.*

Rimland (1964)—a father of a child diagnosed with autism—published a book entitled *Infantile Autism: The Syndrome and Its Implications for Neural Theory of Behavior.* According to Sincile-Kira (2004), the crux of his argument was autism was not a consequence of neglectful parenting, rather was the result of neurological functioning and genetic factors. As an aside, Rimland is credited for founding the Autism Research Institute which helped advance the field of autism for more than 40 years.

Unfortunately in 1967 the field of autism encountered a significant setback when Bettelheim fraudulently authored the book *The Empty Fortress.* Bettelheim claimed to be a student of Freud and was awarded a faculty position at the University of Chicago based on his apparent credentials, accolades, writing skills, and personality. Subsequently he was appointed to serve as a director of Orthogenic School that specialized in working with children with autism and their families (Jepson & Johnson, 2007).

Bettelheim theorized that parents of children with autism were cold and unfeeling and is credited for coining the term *refrigerator mothers.* Essentially the manifestation of the parent's disorder (e.g., inattentive, uncaring, etc.) created a child with autism because they did not receive the love, nurturing, or support they required from their caregivers. Although both parents and children received therapy, he did so separately. For example, children would attend residential school while parents participated in therapy sessions to cure their psychopathology and his treatments became accepted and implemented nationally and internationally (Sicile-Kira, 2004). However, in the 1970s his theory and treatments were proven ineffective and he resigned his faculty position at the University of Chicago and directorship at the Orthogenic School (Jepson & Johnson, 2007).

In 1987, Lovass—psychologist—created a treatment known as applied behavior analysis. Rather than attempting to find a cure, Lovass made a significant impact in the history of autism because he focused on understanding autism, developing effective treatments, and improving the lives of children with autism.

DISORDERS

As noted above, in 1990 the **Education for All Handicapped Children Act** (1975) was reauthorized and renamed IDEA. This reauthorization made **autism** a separate disability classification and included related disorders that are identified under ASD. In alignment with the provisions outlined in IDEA (1990—and its subsequent reauthorizations—students can be diagnosed with one-of-five related pervasive developmental disorders including: (a) **autistic disorder**, (b) **Asperger's disorder**, (c) **Rett's disorder**, (d) **childhood disintegrative disorder** (CDD), or (e) **pervasive developmental disorder not otherwise specified** (PDD-NOS).

While each of the aforementioned disorders is identified under ASD, they are uniquely defined according to age of onset, severity, and manifestations of characteristics (discussed below). It should be noted that of the five disorders, autism currently has the highest prevalence rates and serves as the primary focus of this textbook.

Autistic Disorder. Autism is a neurobiological disorder that causes individuals to process information differently and can be seen on a continuum from mild to severe. Individuals with autism typically experience the inability to: (a) use language and communicate with others, (b) relate with others and build positive relationships, (c) respond to sensory stimuli, and (d) employ nonverbal behaviors. According to the DSM-V (2011), the onset of autistic disorder occurs prior to age three and is defined by characteristics in the following three areas: social interaction, communication, and stereotypies.

Asperger's Disorder. The American Psychiatric Association (2011) reported that Asperger's disorder is a neurodevelopmental disorder that is similar to autistic disorder. However, unlike autism, individuals with Asperger's often have average to superior IQ and possess good verbal skills. Additionally, children with Asperger's must not demonstrate any significant delays in self-help or adaptive behaviors. According to Howlin and Asgharian (1999) individuals with Asperger's are typically diagnosed around the age of 7 with the mean age of 11. However, despite their abilities, they tend to have (a) delays in expressive and receptive language development and (b) experienced difficulties using language in meaningful ways. For example, their language appears to be more formal and they are known to speak in long monologues focused on specific areas of interest. Moreover, they often experience difficulties interacting appropriately in social settings because they misinterpret social cues.

Rett's Disorder. Rett's disorder is an X-linked dominate disorder and is primarily found in girls. Despite normal functioning having been reported during the first 18 months, the onset occurs around the age of 2 and developmental declines continues as a child ages. Around age 10, at least two of the following skills have been negatively impacted (a) expressive or receptive language, (b) social skills, (c) motor functioning, and (d) bladder control. Similar to autism individuals with Rett's have stereotypic and repetitive behaviors.

Childhood Disintegrative Disorder. CDD is a rare disorder, affecting 2-in-100,000 children, and is more common in boys than girls. Children may display characteristics of CDD between the ages of 3-and-10. However, prior to onset, the child experiences typical development in regards to language, social skills, and adaptive behaviors. Upon onset, the child experiences significant losses across these domains. Moreover children with CDD often experience additional medical conditions.

Pervasive Developmental Disorder Not Otherwise Specified. According to the American Psychiatric Association (2011) both the medical community and families are continually confused with the term PDD-NOS because the diagnostic criteria are vague. Essentially it states autism has a later onset and includes atypical symptomatology but this definition fails to provide adequate detail.

CHARACTERISTICS

According to the American Psychiatric Association (2000) the defining characteristics of ASD are related to language, communication, social skills, and behavior. In alignment with their definition, the following sections will focus on (a) communication and language, socialization, (b) aggression and self-injurious behavior, (c) repetitive and unusual behavior patterns, and (d) intellectual functioning.

Communication & Language. The National Research Council (2001) reported children with autism have language abilities across a broad range from non-or-limited to complex verbal communication skills. Children with autism often have difficulties communicating in the following (a) areas focusing on one topic, (b) using natural gestures to support dialogue, (c) pronoun reversals, (d) echolalia, and (e) expressive and receptive language deficits. According to Prazant (1983) it was believed only half of the children diagnosed with autism would develop the ability to communicate. However, Koegel (2000) suggested 85-90% of children with autism learn to speak meaningfully because of early interventions and research-based teaching strategies.

Socialization. Socialization is typically difficult for individuals with autism. For example, it is not uncommon for individuals with autism to experience difficulties expressing emotions, forming relationships, and understanding the emotional state of others. The American Psychiatric Association (2000) developed the following criteria based on struggles individuals with autism often experience (a) nonverbal behavior, (b) peer relationships, (c) spontaneous shared interest with others, and (d) reciprocity. Interestingly, each of the functions of socialization is closely related to deficits individuals with autism experience under communication and language.

Aggression & Self-Injurious Behavior. *All* behaviors send messages. However, for individuals with limited language abilities—especially those with autism—have difficulties expressing their wants and needs. Therefore, it is important for parents, teachers, and caregivers to be aware of the various types of behaviors they engage in. For individuals with autism it is common for them to act out aggressively and display self-injurious behaviors.

It is important to note that both aggression and self-injurious behavior can cause extreme damage. While aggressive behaviors are directed towards others, self-injurious behaviors are a direct attack on themselves. Self-injurious behaviors can include but are not limited to head banging, biting, or scratching and Hyman and Towbin (2007) reported these behaviors can continue into adulthood.

Repetitive & Unusual Behavior Patterns. Individuals with autism often exhibit repetitive and unusual behavior patterns. As briefly noted above, they may engage in stereotypic which includes repetitive self-stimulating behaviors such as humming, rocking, or flapping of hands. Additionally an individual with autism may be distracted for copious amounts of time by engaging in extraneous behaviors. According to Loftin, Odom, and Lantz (2007) these behaviors often create a social stigma which inhibits others from interacting with an individual with autism.

Sameness & Perseverance. Individuals with autism often adhere to strict routines and insist on sameness, predictability, and structure which help provides a sense of security. Disruptions in their *normal routine* can cause individuals with autism to become anxious and stressed. For example, what may appear to be an insignificant change in schedule can create a *major meltdown* for some. Similarly before proceeding with a task (e.g., homework), they may require specific locations for individuals and objects such as trinkets, toys, books, etc.

Sensory. Harrison and Hare (2004) reported between 70% and 80% of individuals with autism exhibit unusual reactions to sensory stimuli. They may be either (a) hypersensitive (i.e., over responsive) or (b) hyposensitive (i.e., under responsive) to sensory input from their environment. For example, individuals who are hypersensitive often have difficulties blocking out sounds, tasting foods, touching textures, and smelling aromas. Conversely individuals who are hyposensitive are often unresponsive and appear oblivious to sensory stimulation that would typically gain a reaction from others

Intellectual Functioning. Intellectual abilities of individuals with ASD span across a full range. However, Coolican, Bryson, and Zwaigenbaum (2008) reported that epidemiological surveys show that between 70% and 80% of individuals with autism meet the criteria for intellectual disabilities. Additionally **splinter skills** and **savant syndrome** are somewhat common among this population. Individuals who display splinter skills demonstrate relatively superior performance in a given area that would be unexpected based on their cognitive abilities. It is estimated that 10% of individuals with ASD have savant syndrome. Heaton and Wallace (2004) described individuals with savant syndrome as those who possess extraordinary abilities in a specific area (e.g., musical skills, mathematical abilities, etc.) while simultaneously functioning in the intellectual disability range in all other areas.

MAX'S SCENARIO

Living the 6 Principles: The Spirit of IDEA

When Max was diagnosed with autism at age 2.5, it began our journey through IDEA touching each of the six principles (Zero Reject, FAPE, **Least Restrictive Environment** (LRE), Non-Discriminatory Evaluation, Parent and Student Participation, and Due Process). For the most part our experiences with each have been within the spirit in which they were intended under IDEIA, 2004. While I recognize this has been our experience (and only our experience up until this point in Max's education), I understand this is not true for all families with children with disabilities. In the past, I have attended support groups where families and school district have agreed the child needed services, but the services were not provided for various reasons, and heard from other families about difficulties with **Individualized Education Program** (IEP) meetings, assessments, placements, and/or services. Thus far, for the most part Max's experiences have been positive.

Zero Reject is a provision that recognizes that all children can learn and benefit from an appropriate education program regardless of severity or type of disability (Arnett et al., 2013). When Max was first diagnosed with autism, he displayed many of the *typical* characteristics which negatively impacted his ability to communicate verbally and nonverbally (Schepis, Reid, Behrmann, & Sutton, 1998), transition from one activity to another (Marks, Shaw-Hegwer, Schrader, Longaker, Peters, & Powers, 2003) and socialize appropriately (Filipek, Accardo, Ashwal, Baranek, Cook, & Dawson, 2000; Lord & McGee, 2001). With all Max's needs when he was first diagnosed and all of the services he required to meet his needs, expectations were held high and it was always presented by professionals that he could learn and that appropriate education would provide benefit.

FAPE mandates that school districts provide access to general education and specialized education services. In addition, it also requires children with disabilities receive support free of charge the same as their non-disabled peers. This has been true for Max throughout his educational career, however each year it has looked different and reflected his needs. Annually, Max's multidisciplinary team meets to develop an IEP that aligns with his needs. This document includes modifications, accommodations, and supports services that have allowed Max access to the general education curriculum and to participate in the LRE with success.

The general education classroom has not always been the LRE for Max. At the time of diagnosis, Max began receiving most of his services at home or in a special preschool program. At age 3, he transitioned to the local school district (and from an IFSP to an IEP), where he was in a special education classroom with two peer models. Many of the services he needed took place in the classroom. Max transitioned to kindergarten to a building across town that had the services to best meet Max's needs. During his kindergarten and 1st grade years, his teachers provided him with access to the general education curriculum and many opportunities to be with his non-disabled peers. Each year after, max spent less time in the resource room and more time in the general education classroom with support.

Every three years (sometimes it was not quite three years, outlined below), Max participated in a 3-year re-evaluation. This nondiscriminatory evaluation was conducted in Max's native language, considered appropriate mode of communication, were validated for the purposes in which they were being used, and were administered by trained personnel (Arnett, Fitzpatrick, & Theoharis, 2013). Finally, multiple assessments were given by a multidisciplinary team to determine the appropriate education for Max. This non-discriminatory evaluation principle has two purposes, and Max has seen both: (a) determine if a disability is present and (b) if there is a disability determined whether the student requires special education and if they do which services will be needed. One of Max's 3 year re-evaluations (I mentioned above followed a different time line), was going to fall after the start of his 6th grade year. The elementary IEP team with some discussion of members of the future IEP team at the middle school determined it would be best for Max to be evaluated during his 5th grade year. This was based on many factors. The primary rationale was that he was familiar with the teachers and professionals at the elementary school as well as the school environment. Allowing Max to be evaluated during his 5th grade year in a familiar environment with familiar adults, it was thought, would best illustrate Max's abilities and needs on the assessments.

IDEA (1990) recognized parents (family members) as having a significant role in the education of children with disabilities (Arnett et al., 2013). This included parents serving as advocates, giving permission for testing, and participation in decision making (including eligibility, services, goals, and placement) (Arnett et al.). I have participated in Max's education in each of the described ways. In addition, IDEIA (2004) also states, the student may be a part of the IEP team or attend their IEP meetings whenever appropriate—if they may have something vital to contribute to planning his or her educational program and future. Specifically, IDEIA (2004):

- Provides that the public agency must include the child with a disability at the IEP meeting "whenever appropriate," and
- Requires that the child be invited to attend the meeting "if the purpose of the meeting will be the consideration of the postsecondary goals for the child and the transition services needed to assist the child in reaching those goals" [§ 300.320(b)].

Thus far, Max has participated in the IEP process in minimal ways (I hope this increases in the near future, but he has just turned 14). The past two years, Max has completed questionnaires about what he would like to do in the future. This information was shared and used during his IEP meeting, though he was not there to share the information. The first year, Max indicated he would like to be a superhero, (when prompted for something more realistic) racecar driver, or gold digger. The following year, Max indicated he would like to do something in auto repair. This past year, Max's IEP also included a paper he wrote indicating why he needed the services he was receiving and how he saw the benefit. While I did not read the paper, the description of what he provided at home illustrated he sees benefits in the services he receives, though he is missing some connections on why he receives them and why they are needed. As more participation is added during his final years of school, I think these connections will become more evident.

Our family has not personally had an example that aligns with the principle of procedural due process. That said, I recognize its purpose and value. It helps to ensure that families have a voice in the decisions made by the school and that I am an equal partner and decision maker in Max's education.

PROFESSIONAL ANALYSIS

An Evolving Understanding of Autism Spectrum Disorder

By

Dr. Brenda Swaggart, Olathe School District #233

A Changing Definition. Autism spectrum disorder was first recognized as a separate disability category under Pervasive Developmental Disorders (PDD) in the Diagnostic and Statistical Manual-3 (DSM-3) in 1980 when it was called *infantile autism*. In 1987, the label was changed to *autistic disorder*. Asperger syndrome was added as a pervasive developmental disability in the DSM-IV, published in 1994. Arguably, the most sweeping revision to the manual's PDD section occurred in the 2013 publication of the DSM-V. In this update, Autistic Disorder, Asperger syndrome, and PDD-Not Otherwise Specified are presented as a single disability category, ASD. In other words, the addition of the word *spectrum* to the disability name reflects the already understood notion that autism is characterized by a group of symptoms and qualities that are highly variable. Advocacy groups and parents worried that children with higher skills would be denied services and that monies would be allocated to individuals demonstrating the most severe level of the disability. Researchers, also, had reservations, citing that studies prior to and in conjunction with the revision would not be comparable (Kaufmann, 2012). While the DSM is not a legal authority, it is revered as an evaluative guide for various developmental and mental health issues (Cohen, Dickerson, & Forbes, 2014).

In response to the rising number of children with ASD and the continued emphasis on inclusion, school districts are compelled to develop necessary programs, policies and supports (Murdick, Garten, & Fowler, 2014). The provisions of FAPE and LRE are applied to students with ASD just as they are to students with other disabilities. How to provide appropriate services for students with ASD is an area of SPED that is likely to see continued litigation. It is imperative that all educators be trained on strategies and evidence-based interventions (Murdick et al., 2014). The law, in fact, mandates that established interventions be employed (Schetter & Stabel, 2010). Further, IDEA (1997) required that education personnel create an individualized education plan (IEP) to meet the unique learning needs of each student with a disability requiring special education services (§ 1400 (d) (1) (A)). "Educating children with ASD often requires even higher levels of differentiation and individualization than for students with other disabilities" (Murdick et al., 2014, p. 257).

ASD is a neurodevelopmental disorder defined as a specific set of behaviors, not origins. It is commonly described as having both a genetic and an environmental component. That is, "environmental factors may trigger the expression of certain genes" (ncsl.org/research/health/autism-policy, retrieved 05-05-14). But unlike Rett syndrome, for example, which was removed from the PDD section of the DSM, there is no clear genetic marker and there are no medical tests to definitively identify ASD. Diagnosticians must instead rely on observation, history and parent report to make a diagnosis.

As discussed above, features of the disorder include impairments in communication, social skills, and behavior. Moreover, it is often associated with developmental regression with a wide range in the timing and nature of skill loss. Persons identified with ASD must currently or by history meet criteria A, B, C, and D. The DSM-V necessitates that symptoms begin in early childhood but acknowledges that full manifestation may not be evident until adolescence when social demands exceed capacity (Kaufmann, 2012). Moreover, the diagnosis necessitates that one of three functioning or severity levels based on need for support be identified (Cohen et al., 2014).

Special Education & ASD. ASD is a lifelong disorder that requires sustained support. Appropriate identification is critical for early intervention and special education services, as early intervention typically results in improved outcomes for the individual. For educational purposes, the IDEIA (2004) "only requires communication and social deficits, with the presence of restricted or stereotyped behaviors noted to be 'often associated' with the disorder" (34 C.F.R. § 300 [c] [1] quoted in Sullivan, 2013). Moreover, IDEIA permits states to amend the federal definition, which may have implications for identification, educational practices, and incident rates (Sullivan, 2013). For example, a school district may require a medical diagnosis in order to access specialized programming or that a qualified person (e.g., an employee with advanced training in ASD) be a part of the multidisciplinary team.

In addition to differences among state definitions and changes to diagnostic practices, variables such as professional and public awareness, referral patterns, availability of services and age at diagnosis have likely contributed to a dramatic increase in prevalence estimates (Haines, 2012). In March 2014, the **Centers for Disease Control** (CDC) announced that 1:68 children is identified with autism, a 30% increase from 2012 (Park, 2014). If prevalence rates remain steady, the number of school-aged children with ASD is projected to rise 44% by 2013 (Autism Society, April 19, 2013 cited in Cohen et al., 2014). And, with an average per pupil expenditure for a student with autism at over $18,000 in the 1999-2000 school year, as estimated by the Special Education Expenditure Project (Sullivan, 2013), school districts will experience a significant financial responsibility. Moreover, given that well over half of the children diagnosed with ASD do not have an intellectual disability and besides the ASD diagnosis could be taught in general education settings, districts will need to prepare educators to meet these students' educational needs (Murdick et al., 2014).

The courts have been clear in addressing program individualization. In Deal v. Hamilton County Board of Education (2004), for example, the court ruled that the school district had violated IDEA by providing a one-program-fits-all approach to meet the needs of students with ASD. Rather than looking at the child's specific needs and considering the parents' request for a specific **Applied Behavior Analysis** program, the district invested in one methodology and used it will all children with ASD. The court made a similar ruling in Henrico County School Board v. R. T. (2006) when it affirmed the parents' position that their young child had not been afforded FAPE when the school district proposed that the child continue in the school-based program that utilized a structured teaching model after having not progressed. In yet another example of the need for individualization, the court ruled in favor of the parents when their child with autism was denied use of his service dog at school. The dog was tethered to the boy and stood ground if the child tried to run, thus, helping to keep the boy safe. Moreover, parents noted that the dog was soothing to their child and allowed for more natural peer interactions than would be possible with a paraeducator (K. D. v. Villa Grove Community Unit School District, 2010). Increased emphasis will likely be placed on appropriate transition plans and services, as well. "Assuming that prevalence stays flat in the future, the population of adults with autism is expected to rise 625 percent by the year 2030" (Autism Society, April 25, 2013, cited in Cohen et al., 2014).

Beyond issues related to FAPE and LRE, litigation is likely to continue to address other areas, including bullying (Cohen et al., 2014; Murdick et al., 2014). Children with ASD are five times more likely to be bullied than their peers. Furthermore, children with less severe presentations of characteristics (e.g., level 1) are more likely to be bullied because their social awkwardness is more noticeable and because they are more likely to be included in general education settings than students with more involved ASD. A case in point is Hernandez v. Los Angeles Unified School District (2007). The school district was found negligent when a young boy with autism sustained serious injury after being kicked in the groin by a classmate when the boy's one-on-one associate left him alone.

Federal Response. Regardless of whether or not the dramatic rise in the number of persons diagnosed with autism is real or the result of variables such as increased awareness and early diagnosis, the federal government has taken much needed action in recent years. In 2007, the United Nations General Assembly passed a resolution declaring April 2 as World Autism Awareness Day. In 2011, President Obama followed suit citing the tremendous impact of autism on millions of Americans" (Cohen et al., 2014). In addition, the Combating Autism Reauthorization Act (P.L. 112-32) was enacted and released 693 million dollars to continue the federal investment initiated in 2006 through the 2014 fiscal year. In 2013 Obama recognized World Autism Awareness Day by announcing the launch of a $100 million initiative, Brain Research through Advancing Innovative Neurotechnologies (BRAIN). An additional federal initiative is seen in conjunction with passage of the Patient Protection and Affordable Care Act in March 2010. Currently, 34 states provide for some form of coverage for behavior treatments for persons with ASD (Cohen et al., 2014). Further, the 2000 Children's Health Act established the National Center on Birth Defects and Developmental Disabilities at the CDC and authorized the establishment of Centers of Excellence at both the CDC and the National Institutes of Health to promote research and to monitor efforts related to the causes, diagnosis, early detection, prevention and treatment of autism (National Archives and Records Administration, 2000).

SUMMARY & CONCLUSION

This chapter presented a series of court cases; policies; and synopsis of the definition, history, disorders, and characteristics related to individuals with ASD. It is important to note despite having commonalities, no two individuals diagnosed with ASD are the same. Finally, throughout the remainder of this textbook, it should be evident how each of the topics discussed in this chapter are interwoven in relation to Max's Scenarios, First-Person Testimonials, and Professional Analyses.

References

20 U.S.C. § 1400 et seq. (1990). Individuals with disabilities education act.

20 U.S.C. § 1400 et seq. (1997). Individuals with disabilities education act.

20 U.S.C. § 1400 et seq. (2004). Individuals with disabilities education improvement act.

Abedi, J. (2004). The No Child Left Behind Act and English language learners: Assessment and accountability issues. *Educational Researcher, 33*(1), 4–14.

ADA (1990).42 U.S.C. 12101 et.seq. (1990). Americans with Disabilities Act.

American Psychiatric Association. (2000). *Diagnostic and statistical manual of mental disorders* (4th ed.). Washington, DC: American Psychiatric.

American Psychiatric Association: DSM-V Development. (2011). 299.00: Autism Spectrum Disorder: Proposed Revision. Retrieved May 13, 2014 from http://www.dsm5.org/ProposedRevisions/Pages/propsedrevision.aspx?rid=94

Americans with Disabilities act of 1990 (ADA) (P.L. 101-336), 42 U.S.C Secs. 12101 *et seq.*

Arnett, S., Fitzpatrick, M., & Theoharis, R. (2013). *Foundations of special education: Understanding students with exceptionalities.* Dubuque, IA: Kendall Hunt.

Autism Consortium. (2012). DSM-5: The new diagnostic criteria for autism spectrum disorders. Retrieved May 5, 2014 from http://autismconsortium.org/symposium-files/WalterKaufmannAC2012Symposium.pdf

Autism Society of America.(2003). New autism facts. Advocate, *36*(1), 1.

Autism Speaks. (2014). DSM-V diagnostic criteria. Retrieved May 5, 2014 from http://www.autismspeaks.org/what-autism/diagnostic-criteria

Berry, B. (2004). Recruiting and retaining "highly qualified teachers" for hard-to-staff schools. *NASSP Bulletin, 88*, 5–27.

Cohen, J. A., Dickerson, T. A., & Forbes, J. M. (2014). A legal review of autism, a syndrome rapidly gaining wide attention within our society. Albany Law Review, *77*(2), 309–423.

Coolican, J., Bryson, S. E., & Zwaigenbaum, L. (2008). Brief report: Data on the Stanford-Binet Intelligence Scales (5th ed.) in children with autism spectrum disorder. *Journal of Autism and Developmental Disabilities, 38*, 190–197.

Diana v. State Board of Education, CA 70 RTF (N.D. Call. 1970).

Education for All Handicapped Children Act of 1975 (P.L. 94-142), 20 U.S.C Secs.1400(d).

Education of All Handicapped Children Act of 1975. PL 94-142.

Filipek, P. A., Accardo, P. J., Ashwal, S., Baranek, G. T., Cook, E. H., & Dawson, G., (2000). Practice parameter: Screening and diagnosis of autism [Electronic version]. *Neurology, 55*, 468–479.

Fitzpatrick, M., & Knowlton, E. (2007). No Child Left Behind's implementation in urban school settings: Implications for serving students with emotional and behavior disorders. *American Academy of Special Education Professionals.* http://aasep.org/aasep

Fletcher, J. M., Coulter, W. A., & Reschly, D. J. (2004). Alternative approaches to the definition and identification of learning disabilities: Some questions and answers. *Annals of Dyslexia, 54*(2), 304–331.

Friend, M. (2011). *Special Education: Contemporary Perspectives for School Professionals* (3rd ed.). Upper Saddle River, NJ: Prentice Hall.

Haines, C. (2012). Silently seizing. Shawnee Mission, KS: AAPC Publishing. Retrieved May 5, 2014 from http://clinton4.nara.gov/WH/new/html/Wed_Oct-18_101652_2000.html

Hallahan, D. P., & Kauffman, J. M. (2006). *Exceptionallearners: An introduction to special education* (10th ed.). Upper Saddle River, NJ: Pearson.

Harrison, J., & Hare, D. J. (2004). Brief report: Assessment of sensory abnormalities in people with autistic spectrum disorders. *Journal of Autism and Developmental Disorders, 34*, 727–730.

Heaton, P., & Wallace, G. L. (2004). Annotation: The savant syndrome. *Journal of Child Psychology and Psychiatry, 45*, 899–911.

Howlin, P., & Asgharian, A. (1999). The diagnosis of autism and Asperger Syndrome: Findings from a survey of 770 families. *Developmental medicine and Child Neurology, 41*, 834–839.

Hyman, S. L., & Towbin, K. E. (2007) Autism spectrum disorders. In M. L. Batshaw, L. Pellegrino, & N. J. Roizen (Eds.), *Children with disabilities* (6th ed). Baltimore: Paul H. Brookes.

Jepson, B., & Johnson J. (2007) *Changing the course of autism.* Boulder, CO: Sentient Publications.

Jones, R. E., Zirkel, P. A., & Barrack, R. D. (2008). Special education and regular education: Achieving high school success with the NCLB and the IDEA. *Catalyst for Change*. *35*(2), 19–24.

Kirk, S. A., Gallagher, J. J., Anastasiow, N. J., & Coleman, M. R. (2006). *Educating exceptional children* (11th ed.). Boston, MA: Houghton Mifflin.

Koegel, L. (2000). Interventions to facilitate communication in autism. *Journal of Autism and Developmental Disorders, 30*(5), 383–391.

Larry P. v. Riles, 730 9 F. Supp. 969, 1984 U.S. App. LEXIS 26195 (1984).

Linn, R. L. (2003). Accountability: Responsibility and reasonable expectations. *Educational Researcher*, *32*(7), 3–13.

Loftin, R. L., Odom, S. L., & Lantz, J. F. (2007). Social interaction and repetitive motor behaviors. *Journal of Autism and Developmental Disorders*, *38*, 1124–1135.

Lord, C. & McGee, J. P. (2001). Educating children with autism. National Academy Press.

Marks, S. U., Shaw-Hegwer, J., Schrader, C., Longaker, J., Peters, I., & Powers, F. (2003). Instructional management tips for teachers of students with autism spectrum disorders (ASD) [Electronic version]. *Teaching Exceptional Children*, *35*, 50–54.

Murdick, N. L., Gartin, B. C., & Fowler, G. A. (2014). *Special education law* (3rd ed.). Boston: Pearson.
National Research Council. (2001). *Educating children with autism.* Washington, DC: National Academy Press.
NCLB (2002) 20 U.S.C. 6301. No Child Left Behind.
No Child Left Behind Act (P.L. 107-110). (2002). Retrieved May 13, 2014 from http://www.ed.gov/nclb
Park, A. (2014, March 31). U.S. autism rates jump 30% from 2012. Time, 68.
Prazant, B. M. (1983). Language acquisition and communicative behavior in autism: Toward and understanding of the "whole" of it. *Journal of Speech and Hearing Disorders, 48*, 296–307.
Rehabilitation Act of 1973 (P.L. 93-112), 29 U.S.C Secs. 504.
Rose, L. C. (2004). No child left behind: The mathematics of guaranteed failure. *Educational Horizons*, *82*(2), 121–30.
San Antonio School District v. Rodriquez 411 U.S. 1 (1973).
Schepis, M. M., Reid, D. H., Behrmann, M. M., & Sutton, K. A. (1998). Increasing communicative interactions of young children with autism using a voice output communication aid and naturalistic teaching [Electronic version]. *Journal of Applied Behavior Analysis, 31*(4), 561–578.
Schetter, P. & Stabel, A. (2010). Evidence Based Practices in Autism Spectrum Disorders. Retrieved May 5, 2014 from UC Davis MIND Institute. Retrieved May 5, 2014 from http://www.ucdmc.usdavis.edu/mindinstitute/videos/video_autism.html
Sicile-Kira, C. (2004). *Autism spectrum disorders: The complete guide.* New York, NY: Berkeley Publishing.
Smith V. Robinson, 468 U.S. 992 (1984)
Snell, M., & Brown, F. (2011). *Instruction of Students with Severe Disabilities* (7th ed.). Boston, MA: Pearson.
Sullivan, A. L. (2013). School-based autism identification: Prevalence, racial disparities and systemic correlates. *School Psychology Review*, *42*(3), 298–316.
Timothy W. v. Rochester, 875 F.29 954 (1989).
Turnbull, A. P., Turnbull, H. R., Wehmeyer, M. L., & Shogren, K. (2010). Exceptional lives: Special education in today's schools (6th ed.). Upper Saddle River, NJ: Merrill/Prentice Hall.
Turnbull, H. R., Stowe, M. J., & Huerta, N. E. (2007). *Free appropriate public education*: *The law and children with disabilities* (7th ed.). Denver, CO: Love.
Wing, L. (1981). Asperger's syndrome: A clinical account. *Psychological Medicine*, *11*, 115–130.
Zirkel, P. (2007). An IDEA for general educators? *Catalyst for Change*, *34*(1), 16–18.

3 Assessment

Chapter Objectives

After studying this chapter readers should be able to:

- Identify the two different perspectives for assessing students for autism.
- Summarize the importance of observation when assessing students for autism.
- Explain the educational assessment protocols used for identifying students with autism.
- Discussed the importance of early identification.

Chapter 3 Subject Index:

1. Adaptive Physical Education
2. Assessment
3. Assistive Technology
4. Autism
5. Autism Spectrum Disorder
6. Autistic
7. Individualized Education Program
8. Individuals with Disabilities Education Improvement Act
9. Multidisciplinary Team
10. Occupational Therapy
11. Parallel Played
12. Response to Intervention
13. Sensory Integration
14. Sensory Processing Issues
15. Special Education
16. Specific Learning Disability
17. Speech-Language Pathologist

INTRODUCTION

There are two ways to identify children with **autism spectrum disorder** (ASD): medically and educationally. Traditionally, students on the severe-to-profound end of the spectrum are diagnosed prior to entering the public school setting. Therefore, the author opted not to use the procedures and protocols that medical professionals use to diagnose this group of children. Rather the focus of this chapter will include **special education** (SPED) **assessment** procedures in accordance with *the* **Individuals with Disabilities Education Improvement Act** (IDEIA, 2004). Additionally as the demographics of the American family is changing the definition of *parent* in IDEIA (2004) reflects this trend (Turnbull, Stowe, & Huerta, 2007). Throughout this chapter, the word *parent* refers to a natural, adoptive, foster parent, guardian, grandparents, stepparent, or other relative with whom the child lives or surrogate parent (20 U.S.C. Sec. 1401(23)).

It should be noted there are similarities and differences between the eligibility criteria in the DSM-V and the criteria in IDEIA (2004). According to Hammond, Campbell, and Ruble (2013) the two models are similar in eligibility criteria for **autism**. On the other hand, these authors pointed out "The key distinction between the psychiatric and educational definitions of autism is the emphasis on educational impact for students to be eligible for services within public education settings. There is no requirement of educational impairment for a psychiatric diagnosis of autism to be rendered" (p. 36). However, many members on the **multidisciplinary team** benefit from knowing a pre-existing diagnosis by expediting the educational diagnosis and SPED and related services.

This chapter will focus on assessment protocols and procedures for making an educational diagnosis of autism. Educational assessments help the multidisciplinary team determine whether or not the student meets the criteria in IDEIA (2004) to receive the educational diagnosis of autism and if so use the results of the results to develop an appropriate **Individualized Education Program** (IEP). Please note it is beyond the scope of this chapter to provide step-by-step directions for various assessment procedures; rather the authors provide a summary of the various instruments used when identifying students who qualify according to Federal, State, and Local regulations. Further, in some districts students are required to undergo a formal educational evaluation even if they have a medical diagnosis of ASD.

IDENTIFICATION & CONCERNS

Consider for a moment a time in which you were in the natural environment (e.g., shopping center, church, transportation terminal, etc.). Can you recall a time when you observed well-behaved children? Perhaps you told your significant other, someone in your group, or complimented the parent "*These kids are well-behaved.*" How often has this happened compared to the number of times you have witnessed kids throwing temper tantrums, defiant behaviors, and apparently unwarranted outbursts based on the context of the setting?

For example, what is your typical reaction when dining out and your dinner is interrupted by a patron—typically a child—who becomes increasingly disruptive to a level you believe warrants intervention? Do you (a) ignore it, (b) attempt to ignore it, (c) become frustrated, or (d) take action (e.g., intervene, leave, etc.).

You may be wondering, *What do these scenarios have to do with teaching, or more importantly assessment of a student suspected of having autism?* The author would argue this simple exercise has everything to do with assessment because observations are critical to the assessment process.

EDUCATIONAL EVALUATION

In the educational setting, if educators observe behaviors that suggest a student is **autistic**, the same legal requirements in IDEIA (2004) must be followed. It is beyond the scope of this chapter to include a detailed explanation of these requirements. However, an overview is included to help readers understand the general process before specifics are provided for evaluating a child with autism.

The requirements in IDEIA (2004) stipulate that evaluations must be "multidisciplinary, multifaceted, and unbiased" (Turnbull, et al., 2007, p. 120). Further, evaluations must (a) be comprehensive, (b) include a variety of assessments, (c) use technically sound instruments that may assess the relative contribution of cognitive and behavioral factors, in addition to physical or developmental factors, and (d) are not discriminatory based on racial or cultural basis (IDEIA, 2004). Another important requirement in IDEIA (2004) is that parents must be informed of their rights and give informed consent to that specific evaluation and "that consent shall not be construed as consent for placement for receipt of special education and related services" (20 U.S.C. Sec. 1414(a)(1)(D)).

It is important multidisciplinary teams provide parents with the specific assessments that will be administered and protocols must be given in the student's native language or other mode of communication unless it is clearly not feasible. Further, the tests must be "most likely to yield information on what the child knows and can do academically, developmentally, and functionally" (Section 300.304(c)(1)(ii)).

RESPONSE TO INTERVENTION

Response to intervention (RtI) was included in the 2004 Amendments to IDEIA. Educators are required to implement an RtI for students suspected of having a **specific learning disability** (SLD) before a student is referred for special education evaluation (34 CFR 300.8(c)(10)). Although RtI is *not* required in IDEIA for students suspected of having autism, Hammond et al. (2013) argued that RtI model is helpful for assessing and serving students with autism.

To date, no empirical studies were found on RtI specifically related to assessing students with autism. However, case study research by Bayat, Mindes, and Covitt (2010) suggested RtI was an effective strategy in a preschool classroom, which included students with autism. The researchers concluded that the "use of RtI in preschool can be specifically beneficial to address social-emotional issues in children, and to provide appropriate positive behavior support for the child" (para. 34).

TOOLS TO IDENTIFY STUDENTS WITH AUTISM

Once the parent gives informed consent, formal evaluations can be conducted. Please note that the following assessments are listed in alphabetical order but can be administered concurrently.

ACADEMIC ACHIEVEMENT

Individual academic achievement tests must be administrated in the evaluation. Many standardized individual achievement tests are available. Examples include but not limited to: BRIGANCE Early Childhood Developmental Inventory III, Kaufman Test of Educational Achievement™ (3rd ed.), Woodcock-Johnson® III Normative Update (NU) Tests of Achievement, and Wechsler Individual Achievement Test® (3rd ed.).

ADAPTIVE PHYSICAL EDUCATION

Students with autism have neurological differences, which may affect their physical functioning, coordination, and skill level in many activities. Therefore, the multidisciplinary team should consider an **adaptive physical education** (APE) evaluation (Doyle & Iland, 2004). Students in **physical education** (PE) classes are graded on ability and often citizenship and sportsmanship. The social and communication aspects of PE may not be immediately associated with autism. Doyle and Iland (2004) recommend that the PE teacher collaborate with the occupational therapist, speech-language pathologist, other faculty, and parents to look at the social aspects in PE.

The purpose of an APE is to determine the child's ability to participate in PE (with or without modifications), identify areas of needs that can be improved through PE, and determine how the student will participate in group games. Other social and communication skills that can be targeted in PE are "sportsmanship, taking cues and signals from others, understanding and functioning of teams, taking turns, waiting, and cheering for others" (Doyle & Iland, 2004, p. 211).

Members of the multidisciplinary team may use observations and checklists to document these behaviors during the evaluation. Surveys from educators and parents are also useful tools to determine if APE is necessary (Doyle & Iland, 2004).

ASSESSMENTS FOR EVALUATING AUTISM

Several standardized and informal screening and diagnostic assessments are available to evaluate students for autism. Ratings should be completed by multiple people who have knowledge about the student including health care professionals, teachers, coaches, family members, and if capable, the student. Raters are asked to score the student on the core characteristics of autism—Social, Communication, Behavior, and Academic Performance. Readers will find a truncated list of published instruments that are used to evaluate individuals for autism at the end of this chapter.

ASSISTIVE TECHNOLOGY ASSESSMENT

If the multidisciplinary team determines the student needs an **assistive technology** (AT) device, an AT assessment is completed (Doyle & Iland, 2004). Since there is no licensure in AT, the assessment is often completed by a speech-language pathologist, an occupational or physical therapist, or someone who is recognized as a provider of AT. Other possible evaluators are AT specialists or practitioners or engineers who have a technology background.

In order to determine which device will provide the maximum benefit, the student should be evaluated with the device in a natural environment. The assessor should document the degree "to which the device produces the desired outcomes" (Doyle & Iland, 2004, pp. 223–224).

COGNITIVE FUNCTIONING (IQ ASSESSMENTS)

A psychometrist or other qualified professional must administer individual intelligent quotient (IQ) tests. The publisher of the instrument determines the level of qualifications a person must have before he or she is allowed to give the test. The Stanford-Binet Intelligence Scales (5th ed.), the Wechsler Preschool and Primary Scale of Intelligence™ (4th ed.), the Wechsler Intelligence Test for Children® (5th ed.), and the Wechsler Adult Intelligence Scale (4th ed.) are commonly used to measure intelligence. If a student is nonverbal, the *Test of NonVerbal Intelligence*™ (4th ed.) or Raven's Progressive Matrices™ may be appropriate.

OBSERVATIONS

Observations are required in formal evaluations and must be considered by the multidisciplinary team to determine whether the child qualifies for SPED and related services. The observations are completed by teachers and related service providers in the school setting (20 U.S.C. 1414(c)), Sec. 300.305). Other observations may be warranted based on the nature and/or severity of the behavior. For example, if the student has difficulties with social interactions, it may be appropriate to observe the student on the playground, cafeteria, or other social setting in the school.

A behavior must be observable and measurable (Doyle & Iland, 2004). Behaviors that can be observed and measured (i.e., can be counted) include but not limited to hitting, pushing, rocking, yelling, and writing.

Behaviors that are not measurable are (i.e., that cannot be counted) include but are not limited to anger, sadness, happiness, and frustration (see Clancy's Observation below). Jacobsen (2008) recommended the observer organize observations by clearly stating the observable behaviors. For example, *the student left his/her chair 7 times in 10 minutes*. She also suggested that observers record their impression about what the behavior might mean and what it might mean to the student. Finally, Jacobsen urged the observer to include suggestions, recommendations, and questions that the multidisciplinary team can address.

OCCUPATIONAL THERAPY & SENSORY INTEGRATION ASSESSMENT

The multidisciplinary team may recommend and **occupational therapy** (OT) and **sensory integration** (SI) assessment because many individuals on the spectrum have **sensory processing issues** (SPI; Parents Guide to Symptoms and Diagnosis, 2014). Kranowitz (2005) defined sensory integration as "the inability to use information received through the senses in order to function in daily life" (p. 9). Dunn (2008) suggested that "sensory processing is a person's way of noticing and responding to sensory events that occur in everyday life" (p. 140).

The purpose of an OT and SI assessment is to determine a student's ability to function during the day in his or her environments (Doyle & Iland, 2004). The results of the assessment will identify areas that can be improved through individual or group therapy.

A student is evaluated in several areas including but not limited to adaptive skills, self-reliance and self-organizational skills, body posture and position, and gross and fine motor skills. Several published and standardized assessments are available including but not limited to Peabody Developmental Motor Scales-2, School Function Assessment, Sensory Profile™ 2, and Test of Visual-Motor Skills-3.

SPEECH & LANGUAGE ASSESSMENTS

Communication is one of the core deficits that characterize individuals with autism and it is essential that the student be evaluated his or her speech and language development (Doyle & Iland, 2004). A **speech-language pathologist** (SLP) normally conducts these assessments.

In 1991, Frith translated Hans Asperger's 1944 paper (Attwood, 2008). Asperger described children who had language impairments including the inability to understand pragmatics—the social aspects of speech (as cited in Attwood, 2008). Barron-Cohen (2001) asserted that "almost every aspect of pragmatics involves sensitivity to speaker and listener mental states, and hence mindreading though it is important to note that pragmatics also involves using context" (p. 11). As such, the SLP should include an evaluation of pragmatics when evaluating students.

Asperger also described impairments in semantics, which is the meaning of words or phrases and prosody, which is the pitch, tone, and rhythm of speech (as cited in Attwood, 2008). Therefore, the SLP should assess these aspects of the student's language development during the evaluation. Examples of published instruments include but are not limited to Communication and Symbolic Behavior Scales Developmental Profiles™, Language Use Inventory, and Oral and Written Language Scales II®. The SLP may also assess for articulation errors if the multidisciplinary team believes this child may need this related service (Doyle & Iland, 2004). Several of the published assessments listed at the end of the chapter have a language component.

CLANCY'S OBSERVATION

It is possible to identify autism in children at 18 months or younger, (Attwood, 2008), and a clinical diagnosis of ASD could be made at ages 24-36 months with 100% accuracy (Moore & Goodson, 2003). These findings support the research completed by Lord (1995). In contrast, the average age of diagnosis is between 48–61 months (Center for Disease Control, 2014; Pinto-Martin & Levy, 2004; Shattuck et al., 2009).

Equally important are the results of a study by Maenner et al. (2013). These researchers found "the median age at ASD identification was inversely associated with the number of documented behavioral features, decreasing from 8.2 years for children with only seven behavioral features to 3.8 years for children with all 12" (para. 3) behavioral symptoms included in the *DSM-IV-TR*. Researchers suggest that early intervention for students who are diagnosed with autism have better outcomes (McEachin, Smith, & Lovaas, 1993; Rogers, 1999).

Recognizing that early intervention improves outcomes, Mrs. Patterson the administrator of a preschool agreed to allow me to observe Clancy because she and his teacher, Ms. James believed that he exhibited symptoms of Asperger's syndrome. They wanted additional information on his behaviors from an outside observer to provide additional information. Pseudonyms are used throughout this analysis to protect anonymity.

BACKGROUND

Clancy is a 3 year-old male enrolled in a private, Christian preschool in the Midwest. His biological parents are married, and he has one brother who is about 8 months old. His father is a member of one of the US Armed Forces and his mother is employed on a military installation. No birth or medical information was available.

Clancy's mother shared with Mrs. Patterson that her father (Clancy's maternal grandfather) had symptoms of Attention Deficit Hyperactivity Disorder (ADHD). Clancy's mother noted that Clancy also exhibits ADHD behaviors at home. However she added, "Clancy's actions are not the same. They are somehow different."

OBSERVATIONS

I observed Clancy in his preschool classroom, an outdoor activity, and outdoor playground. Clancy has eight classmates ranging from almost 3 years of age to almost 4 years of age. After the observations, I discussed the observations with the administrator, teacher, and teaching assistant. I grouped the observations into the four main dimensions that professionals use to measure and diagnose autism: Social, Communication, Behavior, and Academic Performance. However, some of the observed behaviors could be included in a different category than assigned.

SOCIAL DIMENSION

At the beginning of school, one student did not want to separate from his father and was sobbing. Clancy walked over to him, watched for a short time until Mrs. James reassured him that Matt was *Ok*, and then kindly redirected him back to his seat. Clancy complied without resistance. Individuals on the spectrum have "difficulties with emotion and mental-state recognition (Barron-Cohen; Hobson, both cited in Golan & Barron-Cohen, 2008), in turn underlie the social difficulties that are a part of the ASD diagnosis" (Golan & Barron-Cohen, 2008, p. 235).

Clancy did not display any emotions when he closed the door on another student's head (the description is in the Gates & door section). Although Mrs. Patterson, Mrs. James, and Ms. Kelly all agreed that Clancy was not malicious, they also asserted that Clancy rarely showed emotion when he accidently hurt another student. This behavior is another indicator that may have autism.

During free time, Clancy **parallel played** with his classmates at times. On the other hand, he interacted appropriately with me in associative play pretend time using the toys in the play kitchen after watching other students interact with me. These stages are age appropriate for three year old children (Sikich, 2014). On this account, Clancy did not exhibit characteristics of autism.

COMMUNICATION DIMENSION

During many of the activities, Clancy only used two-or-three word sentences such as *I help*, which are described in context in other dimensions. On the other hand, when he communicated with me during free time, he spoke in sentences that were more complete. I noted, however, that he usually spoke without intonation. Asperger described his patients as having "unusual prosody that affected intonation, pitch, and rhythm" (as cited in Attwood, 2008. p. 23) In regards to the two or three word phrases, Mrs. Patterson and Mrs. James indicated that Clancy usually spoke in age appropriate sentences but had unusually flat intonation.

Clancy mostly used the appropriate pronouns during my observation period, but did say *Me help* on one occasion. Researchers found that some students on the spectrum do not use pronouns correctly (Jordan; Lee, Hobson, & Chiat; Tager-Flusberg all cited in Hobson, Lee, & Hobson, 2009). The apparent implication is that Clancy does not demonstrate pronoun reversals that characterize many individuals with autism.

BEHAVIOR DIMENSION

Clancy demonstrated several off task behaviors during the observation. The descriptions in this section are divided by activity rather than set in chronological order

Prayer Time. The teacher asked students to fold their hands in prayer to start school. Clancy did not fold his hands and walked to the puzzle storage area (see description in Academic Performance). He returned to his seat when redirected. Ms. Kelly, the teacher's assistant helped him fold his hands. Later, the teacher asked the students to fold their hands to pray before snacks. Clancy did not fold his hands or participate in the song others sang for grace.

Free Time. Clancy played appropriately with a toy jeep (e.g., pushing it on the floor, opening and closing the doors, and making jeep noises). Doyle and Iland (2004) suggested children on the spectrum do not play with toys "in a way that shows they know what the toy represents" (p. 16). In this regard, Clancy did not exhibit a characteristic of autism.

Miscellaneous. A student dropped her puzzle before formal activities began. Clancy said, *I help* and went to the student but he could not fit one piece into the puzzle. On another occasion, he said, *I get it* when something else dropped. He went back to his seat without protest when redirected in both incidents.

During free play, Clancy ran the jeep into another student who was lying on the floor. He did not apologize but repositioned the toy and pushed it in another direction. On another occasion, he jabbed a Duplo block into another boy's arm. When this child told the teacher, Mrs. James intervened and asked Clancy to apologize. Clancy complied but it was a rote almost echolalic apology. She later told me that this was common and without apparent remorse.

Music Time. Ms. James played several age appropriate songs and students danced and sang along with the CD. Clancy stood and danced about 10 seconds. Twice he went to the sand table. He also went to the calendar and placed the number on the calendar line. On this occasion when he was redirected, he said he needed to use the bathroom and walked to the door. When he returned, he stopped at the science table and began playing with a toy. The teacher redirected him to the activity but he once again went to the sand table then into the toy storage area. When he was redirected to his seat, he picked up his name tag and moved it to an empty chair.

Doors & Gates. During transition to a rest room break, Clancy tried to pull the doorstop out to close the door. The teacher redirected him twice by asking him to keep his hands in his pocket. When they returned from the break, Clancy closed the door even though he was not the last in line. When the students lined up for the outside activity, Clancy closed the door and it hit another student in the head. During snack time, Clancy went to the closed back door and locked it. Ms. Kelly unlocked the door and explained why it was important to keep the door unlocked and redirected him to his seat. During free time on the outdoor play equipment, Clancy tried to open the safety gate.

Individuals on the spectrum often have a fascination with an object that is unique to that person (Kluth & Schwartz; Winter-Meissiers, both cited in Kluth, 2010). Mrs. James said Clancy is fascinated with doors and compulsive about closing or locking them. Another explanation might be that Clancy does not understand the consequences of his actions. Doyle and Iland (2004) stated students with autism may "persist in doing dangerous things even when told or shown what else to do" (p. 16). Another explanation is that Ms. Kelly was not at her usual position at the gate on the playground. Persons with autism have a need for sameness (Doyle & Iland. 2004), which may be the reason Clancy decided to open the gate.

ACADEMIC PERFORMANCE

This section is divided by activities rather than chronological order. As noted above, some descriptions could be included in other dimensions, particularly the communication, and behavioral dimensions. I discuss the implications for these activities in the Summary section.

Puzzles. After finding his seat at the beginning of school, Clancy began working the wooden knob puzzle that was on the table in front of his chair. Unlike most of his classmates who finished at least one puzzle (with or without a knob), Clancy had much difficulty placing the pieces in the correct position. Ms. Kelly stopped at his seat the help him. Clancy did not accept her assistance but continued his trial and error method of placing the pieces in the board. The teaching assistant completed the puzzle and Clancy returned the puzzle to the correct place after the teacher said it was time for the next activity.

During free time, Clancy brought a wooden puzzle of the right and left hands to me. The thumb, fingers were numbered and the palms marked left or right. Clancy could not find the correct positions but did not accept my help. When free time was over, he put the pieces in anywhere they fit; I completed the puzzle after he transitioned to the next activity.

Weather Bear. Mrs. James led the children in a weather related learning activity by asking what the weather was outside and how should the weather bear be dressed. Clancy said twice, *I put on hat*. The teacher indicated that the bear did not need a hat today. When she asked a student to put on the bear's shoes, Clancy said, *I do it*. The teacher redirected and assured him he could help dress the bear. Later she asked Clancy to put on his vest and he dressed the bear with the vest in the appropriate position.

Calendar Time. Mrs. James took a pointer for the calendar activity. Clancy jumped out of his chair and went to the easel that had the calendar number on it and exclaimed, *I do it*. He was redirected to his seat. Clancy did recite the numbers with the other students.

Alphabet Time. Next, Mrs. James asked another student to lead the calendar activity. Clancy got out of his seat and said, *I do it*. Ms. Kelly reminded him that he had helped dress the weather bear. Clancy did not recite the alphabet with the other students.

Outside Activity. Mrs. James read a story about seeds and plants to the students while still in the classroom. Then the teacher and Ms. Kelly accompanied the students outside to a raised garden plot that was prepared and then distributed seeds to them. Clancy planted his seeds as instructed.

OBSERVATION SUMMARY

Based on my observations, Clancy may be on the spectrum because he demonstrated several deficits in the core characteristics. These include observed discrepancies in social, behavioral, and communicative dimensions. Conversely, since Clancy is in preschool, it is difficult to ascertain if the lack of participation in the academics was a result of lack of background knowledge or experience, or the possibility of being on the spectrum. My hypothesis is that further observations and perhaps a formal evaluation (i.e., assessment) are justified.

PROFESSIONAL ANALYSIS

The Value of Early Identification

By

Angela Heishman, Big Spring School District

Reflecting on my graduate training and early experiences in my career as a school psychologist, there were very few children in the public school setting being identified with autism and those who were tended to be diagnosed by a physician usually by the age they were enrolled in preschool.

As students entered the school system with services already in place from their involvement with early intervention, specialized programming was able to be carefully planned prior to their first day in the classroom. Transitions into the public school system during this time did not always go very smoothly as there was still much to be learned about how to best address the unique needs of individuals on the autism spectrum.

Despite the attention given to the development of the initial IEP, various factors often emerged affecting their transition as they had to adjust to a new environment with different teachers, peer groups, expectations, and schedules. Although we know that the sounds, smells, and textures of a room can have a drastic impact on the success of the transition for individuals with ASD, it generally cannot be predicted regarding what stimuli could impact a specific individual.

For example, I know one student, who appeared to experience a great deal of angst in response to hearing the sound of the teacher's shoes on the floor, which led to regular meltdowns in the classroom until the source of his discomfort was discovered. After an examination of possible triggers in the environment, it was discovered that the behavioral difficulties dissipated when the teacher began to wear a different pair of shoes.

As there has been an increase in the number of individuals identified with Autism prior to entering school, schools generally have become more equipped to address the needs of these students through the provision of employing autism specialists and creating specialized classroom and interventions.

Another issue that also needs to be considered by schools is how to help the families who have a school-aged child yet to be diagnosed with autism. A disorder that was once rarely known by individuals in the general population has become a common term in many people's lives as family members of individuals with indented with ASD advocates have been able to use media channels to educate others about the struggles that children with autism and their caregivers face on a daily basis in just completing everyday life activities. As more people have achieved some degree of understanding on the characteristics linked with autism, more parents are likely finding themselves questioning whether their child may fall on the autism spectrum and consulting their doctors for the answers.

Although family physicians and pediatricians have been active in the role of screening and diagnosing autism, not all children may fit into a specific mold and thus the diagnosis may be deferred, or not even considered. For example, because of delays in development in communication or motor skills it is—at times—difficult to differentiate between various disorders, particularly for individuals who may not consistently exhibit stereotypical behavioral symptoms linked with ASD.

Although these individuals are often referred for early intervention services in order to conduct a comprehensive evaluation and design a plan to address their developmental needs, the tendency is for these children to be identified with a developmental delay or speech or language impairment as the professionals involved also need to rule out factors that may be contributing to the presentation of symptoms. Another factor that needs to be considered in diagnosing autism in young children is the influx of people in the general population learning about ASD, the waiting lists to see the experts in the field can be quite long, making it difficult for parents to schedule an evaluation.

Despite the significant attention directed towards providing awareness of autism to the general population and the increase availability of community services for children that fall on the spectrum, there are children who have been observed by their teachers fairly early in their school years as displaying various characteristics linked with ASD, but have yet to be identified. There are various challenges that appear to have affected families' ability to have their children evaluated or diagnosed prior to entering school.

One factor I have observed is that some parents do not recognize that their child's manner in which he or she interacts with the world is developmentally different than his or her peers, particularly if this is their first child and he or she is not involved in a day-care or preschool program. When considering routine physicals are required during early childhood development, the data used by the medical community relies significantly on parental observations, thus a parent unaware of what is considered normal may not report symptoms that are seen as delayed or not typical to others.

I have also worked with parents who have reported that they thought their child was going through a phase and that it will pass. Others have indicated that they were concerned about looking like a bad parent as they felt inadequate in managing their patience and frustration with the more challenging behaviors displayed by their child.

I have also worked with many families who have reported that their child is just a little quirky, as they add that he or she reminds them of one of their own siblings or of an aunt or uncle. With the prevalence of children being raised by their grandparents, I have also worked with individuals raising grandchildren who initially attributed the developmental delays and behaviors to other factors such as the emotional dishevelment in the child's life.

While working with individuals living in poverty, I have also had experience with families who may not have realized that there were resources available to them to assist in addressing the behavioral, motor, and communication concerns they observed during their child's early years of life. Additionally, there are transient families and do not have the consistent experience with a physician to help guide them in addressing the needs of children identified with ASD. These are among the various scenarios that have contributed to children on the Autism spectrum not being identified until entering school.

Educational professionals are finding themselves on the frontline in having to discuss the possibility with parents that their child display characteristics linked with autism and that further evaluation is needed. Some families may be appreciative of the resources schools can provide them in completing a multidisciplinary evaluation to help them understand their child's needs while others may be distraught and frustrated that their child is being labeled with autism.

Once identified, understanding early interventions and addressing the needs of individuals with autism provides the student with increased opportunity for success in the future. Thus, it is imperative for educators and families to work together to ensure that individuals with autism are not falling through the cracks and are being provided with the support they need as early in their elementary years as possible. Moreover, it is important for the multidisciplinary team and members of the medical community to work collaboratively to help ensure there continues to be ongoing awareness of autism and to keep abreast of the recent changes in diagnosis criteria and review the research on how best to address the needs of these students. Finally, it is vital to build and maintain collaborative relationships in order for students with autism to be successful during their school years and prepared for the transition to adulthood.

SUMMARY & CONCLUSION

In this chapter, readers were introduced to the various aspects of assessing a child who is suspected of having autism and the importance and legal basis for properly identifying them. The author discussed several assessments that the multidisciplinary team should consider including in the formal evaluation. The results of the assessments will help the team to determine if the child meets the criteria (definition) in IDEIA (2004) for an educational diagnosis of autism. If the multidisciplinary team determines that the student qualifies, the results will guide them as they develop the objectives and goals for the IEP.

Selected Instruments Used to Evaluate Students Suspected of Having Autism

Instrument	Ages
• Assessment of Basic Language and Learning Skills®-Revised	3–12 years
• Adaptive Behavior Assessment System® (2nd ed.) (ABAS II®)	Birth to 89:11 years
• Asperger Syndrome Diagnostic Scale (ASDS)	5–18 years
• Autism Diagnostic Observation Schedule™ (ADOS™)	Toddlers to adult
• Autism Diagnosis™ Interview-Revised (ADI™-R)	Children and adults with a mental age above 2.0 years
• BRIGANCE Early Childhood Developmental Inventory III,	Birth through 7 years
• Checklist for Autism in Toddlers (CHAT)	18 month developmental check-up
• Childhood Autism Rating Scale™ (CARS™)	2 years and up
• Communication and Symbolic Behavior Scales Developmental Profiles™ (CSBS DP™)	Children with functional communication age of 6 to 24 months and a chronological age of 6 months to 6 years.
• Communication and Symbolic Behavior Scales Developmental Profiles™ Infant-Toddler Checklist	12 months
• Gilliam Autism Rating Scale (3rd edition) (GARS)	3 through 22 years
• Kaufman Test of Educational Achievement, Third Edition (KTEA™-3)	4 to 25:11 years
• Language Use Inventory LUI	18–47 months
• Modified Checklist for Autism in Toddlers™ (M-CHAT-R™)	16–30 months
• Oral and Written Language Scales™, Second Edition (OWLS™-II)	3 years 21 years
• Peabody Developmental Motor Scales (2nd ed.) (PDMS-2)	Birth to 5 years
• Raven's Advanced Progressive Matrices (APM)	12:0–16:0 years 17:0 years and older
• Raven's Coloured [sic] Progressive Matrices (CPM)	5 through 11 years, elderly persons, and mentally and physically impaired persons
• Raven's Standard Progressive Matrices Plus (SPM Plus)	6:0–16:0 years 17:0+ years
• Sensory Motor Profile™-2	Birth through 14:11
• School Function Assessment (SFA)	Birth through 5 years
• Social Communication Questionnaire (SCQ)	Over 4.0 years, with a mental age over 2.0 years
• Stanford-Binet Intelligence Scales (5th ed.) (SB5)	2 years–85+ years
• Test of Nonverbal Intelligence (4th ed.) (TONI-4)	6:0 years–89:11 years

Instrument	Ages
• Test of Visual Perceptual Skills-3	4.0 years–18:11 years
• Wechsler Individual Achievement Test® (3rd ed.) WIAT®	4.0 years–50:11 years
• Wechsler Adult Intelligence Scale (4th ed.) WAIS-IV	16.0 years–90:11 years
• Wechsler Intelligence Scale for Children® (5th ed.) (WISC®-V)	6.0 years–16 years
• Wechsler Preschool and Primary Scale of Intelligence™ (3rd ed.) (WPPSI™ -III)	2:6 years–7.3 years
• Woodcock-Johnson® III Normative Update (NU) Tests of Achievement	2 years–90 years

References

Attwood, T. (2008). An overview of autism spectrum disorders. In K. D. Burton, & P. Wolfberg, (Eds.), *Learners on the autism spectrum: Preparing highly qualified educators* (pp. 19–43). Shawnee Mission, KS: Autism Asperger.

Barron-Cohen, S. (2001). Theory of mind in normal development in autism. *Prisme, 34*, 174–183.

Bayat, M., Mindes, G., & Covitt, S. (2010). What does RtI (response to intervention) look like in preschool? *Early Childhood Education Journal, 37*, 493–500. doi 10.1007/s10643-010-0372-6

Centers for Disease Control. (2014). *Autism spectrum disorder (ASD).* Retrieved October 5, 2014 from http://www.cdc.gov/ncbddd/autism/data.html

Doyle, B. T., & Iland, E. D. (2004). *Assessment diagnosis . . . & more.* Arlington, TX: Future Horizons.

Dunn, W. (2008). Sensory processing: Identifying patterns and support strategies. In K. D. Burton & P. Wolfberg, (Eds.), *Learners on the autism spectrum: Preparing highly qualified educators* (pp. 138–159). Shawnee Mission, KS: Autism Asperger.

Golan, O., & Barron-Cohen, S. (2008). *Systemizing emotions: Using interactive multimedia as a teaching tool.* In K. D. Buron & P. Wolfberg (Eds.), *Learners on the autism spectrum: Preparing highly qualified educators* (pp. 234–253). Shawnee Mission, KS: Autism Asperger.

Hammond, R. K., Campbell, J. M., & Ruble, L. A. (2013). Considering identification and service provision for students with autism spectrum disorders within the context of response to intervention. *Exceptionality: A Special Education Journal*, *2*, 34–50. doi: 10.1080/09362835.2013.750119

Hobson, R. P., Lee, A., & Hobson, J. A. (2010). Personal pronouns and communicative engagement in autism. *Journal of Autism and Developmental Disorders, 40*, 653–664. doi: 10.1007/s10803-009-0910-5

Individuals with Disabilities Improvement Act (2004), U.S.C.A. Sec. 20 U.S.C. 1414 *et seq.* 34 CFR Secs.300.301 *et seq.*

Jacobsen, P. (2008). The education team: Positive, effective, interdisciplinary collaboration. In K. D. Buron, & P. Wolfberg (Eds.), *Learners on the autism spectrum: Preparing highly qualified educators* (pp. 278–305). Shawnee Mission, KS: Autism Asperger.

Kluth, P. (2010). *You're going to love this kid!* (2nd ed.). Baltimore, MD: Paul Brookes.

Kranowitz, C. A. (2005). *The out-of sync child: Recognizing and coping with sensory processing disorder* (Rev. ed.). New York, NY: Skylight Press.

Lord, C. (1995). Follow-up of two-year-olds referred for possible autism. *Child Psychology and Psychiatry, 6*, 1365–1382.

Maenner, M. J., Schieve, L. A., Rice, C. E., Cunniff, C., Giarelli, E., Kirby, R. S., . . . & Durkin, M. S. (2013). *Journal of the American Academy of Child and Adolescent Psychiatry*, *52*, 401–413.

McEachin, J. J., Smith, T., & Lovaas, O. I. (1993). Long-term outcome for children with autism who received early intensive behavioral treatment. *American Journal on Mental Retardation, 97*, 359–372. Retrieved October 5, 2014 from http://dddc.rutgers.edu/pdf/mceachlin_et_al.pdf

McEachin, J. J., Smith, T., & Lovaas, O. I. (1993). Long-term outcome for children with autism who received early intensive behavioral treatment. *American Journal on Mental Retardation, 97*, 359–372. Retrieved October 12, 2014 from http://dddc.rutgers.edu/pdf/mceachlin_et_al.pdf

Moore, V., & Goodson, S. (2003). How well does early diagnosis of autism stand the test of time? Follow-up study of children assessed for autism at age 2 and development of an early diagnostic service. *Autism, 7*, 47–63. doi: 10.1177/1362361303007001005

Pinto-Martin, J., & Levy, S. E. (2004). Early diagnosis of autism spectrum disorders. *Current Treatment Options in Neurology, 6*, 391–400.

Rogers, S. (1999). Intervention for young children with autism: From research to practice. *Infants and Young Children, 12*(2), 1–16.

Shattuck, P. T., Durkin, M., Maenner, M., Newschaffer, C., Mandell, D. S. Wiggins, L. . . . & Cuniff, C. (2009). The timing of identification among children with an autism spectrum disorder: Findings from a population-based surveillance study. *Journal of the American Academy of Child and Adolescent Psychiatry, 48*, 474–483. doi: 10.1097/CHI.0b013e31819b3848

Sikich, K. (2014). *The four stages of play.* Retrieved October 5, 2014 from http://www.district196.org/ec/Teacher-Curriculum/KaySikichTheFourStagesofPlay.cfm

Turnbull, H. R., Stowe, M. J., & Huerta, N. E. (2007). *Free appropriate public education: The law and children with disabilities* (7th ed.). Denver, CO: Love.

4

IEP

Chapter Objectives

After studying this chapter readers should be able to:

- Identify the various components of the IEP.
- Understand the value and importance of the multidisciplinary team plays when developing an IEP.
- Compare and contrast the similarities and differences between the eight components and five special factors that need to be addressed when developing an IEP.
- Explain the link between home and school.

Chapter 4 Subject Index:

1. Autism Spectrum Disorders
2. Due Process Safeguards
3. Education for All Handicapped Children Act
4. Free and Appropriate Public Education
5. Individualized Education Program
6. Individuals with Disabilities Education Improvement Act
7. Least Restrictive Environment
8. Local Education Agency
9. Multidisciplinary Team
10. Present Level of Performance
11. Self-Determination
12. Special Education

INTRODUCTION

Children with **autism spectrum disorder** (ASD), live in a world where most people think and communicate differently than they do (Buron & Wolfberg, 2008). They often have areas of strength and areas that are challenges including cognitive, communication, social, behavior, and sensory (Attwood, 1998; Klin, Volkmar, & Sparrow, 2000). To help support these challenges, these students benefit from **special education** (SPED) services, therapies, and interventions (Bate, 2004; Wiss, 2004). While it is no surprise each service has a unique focus, it is important to note that everyone working on behalf of the child can benefit from collaboration through the **Individualized Education Program** (IEP) process. From this perspective, there are many factors that should be considered when developing an effective IEP.

According to the **Education for All Handicapped Children Act** (P.L. 94-142) of 1975, students with disabilities are entitled to an individualized, **free and appropriate public education** (FAPE). As mandated by SPED law, when a student with ASD qualifies for SPED services a **multidisciplinary team** is established. The IEP serves as the cornerstone of SPED. It is important to remember that this is a legal document, not a simple piece of paperwork, that is the set of content, instruction methods, assessment, and long-term planning that will be used with an individual student. The requirements for IEPs continue to evolve with each reauthorization. However, the underlying principles remain critical components of the IEP and include collaborative planning, selecting educational goals that build on the student's strengths, and evaluating student progress annually. This chapter addresses the purposes of meetings, participants, preparation, tips for success, and evaluating the IEP.

INDIVIDUALIZED EDUCATION PROGRAM

One of the key responsibilities of the multidisciplinary team is to develop the IEP for students with disabilities. The IEP serves as a map for the student with disabilities-providing a clear understanding of where they are currently, where they need to go, and how they are going to get there. The IEP is required a legal document that outlines, defines, and guides the educational process and helps ensures the student is receiving an appropriate education (Arnett, Fitzpatrick, & Theoharis, 2013). It is this legal document that is developed and modified together with families and professionals who will be working with the student. As a result full understanding of the IEP process is critical for teachers, other professionals, and family members. In thinking about the IEP, it is important to remember two basic propositions of SPED. First, individualization is the hallmark of SPED practices (Turnbull, Turnbull, & Wehmeyer, 2010). Second, the **Individuals with Disabilities Education Improvement Act** (IDEIA, 2004) requires a student's IEP to ensure involvement with and progress in the general education curriculum and helps ensure that it addresses the student's unique learning needs (Turnbull et al., 2010).

The IEP is a written record of the decisions reached by the multidisciplinary team (Pierangelo & Giuliani, 2007). This document serves several different purposes including but not limited to: (a) a communication tool between families and the school; (b) allows families to be equal participants and jointly decide how to best meet the student's needs; (c) accounts for differences between families and the school to be met through the IEP meeting and if necessary through procedural due process established under SPED law; (d) establishes commitment—in writing a—of resources necessary to support the student with a disability with SPED and related services; (e) serves as a management tool that helps ensure each student with a disability is provided appropriate services to meet their educational needs; (f) is a compliance and monitoring document; and (g) an evaluation system to determine the extent of progress toward meeting the learning and behavioral outcomes, defines and mandates an effective process that engages families and school district officials in meaningful conversations about the student's educational needs (Pierangelo & Giuliani, 2007). Additionally the IEP is not a performance contract or guarantee by the district or teacher that a student will progress at a specified rate. The school district must provide all services that have been stated in the student's IEP. It is also obligated to make good-faith efforts to assist the student in attaining the determined IEP goals (Pierangelo & Giuliani, 2007). For these reasons, the IEP is the foundation of the student's SPED program.

It is important to recognize that SPED law does not require a specific IEP form to be completed, rather IDEIA (2004), like other federal policies, is written with grey areas so that states and school districts can tailor the process to meet the needs of the students and respond to the changes in practices developed through the most current research in the field (Thoma & Wheman, 2010).

MAX'S IEPS: THE MEETINGS & DOCUMENT

Every year, for the past 12 years, I have attended an IEP meeting (in the early years it was an IFSP) to discuss the services Max would receive, the annual goals he would work towards, and the educational placement options. Some years there were multiple meetings (usually because he was progressing slower or faster than expected—one year the plan was to meet every six months verses annually). Some meetings have been routine, while others have included significant debates about services and placement. Each of these meetings are one hour (sometimes longer—Max's have always tended to be longer) is my one hour where we talk about all the things Max needs to work on (minus the 5 minutes where we discuss his strengths).

Prior to attending an IEP meeting, I have always asked a friend or colleague to attend with me. Not because, I expect something to go wrong, rather because I often need someone to retell me what happened during the meeting. Let me explain further, with the focus of the meeting being about something of great importance to me, Max, and it being about things he cannot do, it can be rather emotional.

After I leave the meeting if you asked me to explain what happened during the meeting, I might tell you Max continues to have problems with holding his pencil and using the correct grasp. Then, you would ask, what they are going to do to work on that, my focus was on the problem. I might not be able to tell you in-depth what happened next or what the plan is or the annual goal related to the area of weakness. That is where having someone attend the meeting with me is extremely helpful. My friend is better able to grasp the whole picture of what happened during the meeting. While there are notes and the IEP document itself, it is nice to go for coffee with a friend after the meeting and have them tell me the things I missed. This often makes it seem not as bad because of the individual pieces I can get hung upon.

These meetings have been hosted in a variety of spaces—classrooms, conference rooms, teachers' workrooms with round tables, rectangle tables, and student desks pushed together. Each school has had different professionals leading the meeting—SPED teacher, school psychologist, or school counsel, or has been my experience. While schools work to make the environment less intimidating and more inviting for parents (and having led IEP meetings and attended as a parent), it is evident the professionals always outnumber the parents—which usually results in an overwhelming feeling—even with the best intentions. That being said, the best meetings are those where a professional shares a story about Max--something that really lets me know they have gotten to know him and they value having them in their classroom. It does not have to be much, but makes the start of the meeting more relaxing. For example, when Max was in first grade, his teacher brought in pictures Max had drawn and she shared the stories Max told about our family while he was drawing them–this provided a light moment before beginning the meeting.

Typically, the meeting begins with introductions and parental rights. Then, the meeting moves to the questions. I give a lot of thought to prior to the meeting to these standard queries. What are Max's strengths? What areas does he need to improve? What are your hopes and dreams for Max's future? I find answering these questions to require thought and skill. I do not want the professionals sitting across the table staring at me to think I am overly negative, but I do want to make sure all of Max's needs are addressed in his IEP and the document truly reflects his abilities. My hopes and dreams for the future—well I would like my toddler with no expressive or receptive language skills to go to college seems a little silly to say out loud, but I hate to look like I do not have high expectations for him. And what I really want to say is I want him to be happy and enjoy life—being an active participant in society however possible with whatever supports needed.

The meetings continue from there to a review of last year's goals and his progress to present levels of performance. Then, we discuss the goals for the upcoming year and where is the best placement for Max to reach the goals. As Max has gotten older, he has spent less time in self-contained and resource classrooms and more time in the general education classroom. For students with disabilities this is typically not the case, states report a tendency to serve a larger percentage of students with disabilities ages

6-11 in regular classrooms; that percentage decreases for students ages 12-17 and 18-21. They also report this pattern is true across the disability groups (http://www2.ed.gov/pubs/OSEP96AnlRpt/chap3b.html). The only exception that has been seen is for students with learning disabilities (see Fitzpatrick, 2010). In addition, research confirms that efforts to integrate younger students have generally been more successful than efforts with older students. This may be attributed, in part, to the departmentalized structure of secondary schools, the academic demands of the secondary curriculum, or the competitive culture that exists in many secondary schools. During this time, the gap for students with disabilities becomes wider. Finally, a significant number of elementary school students with disabilities have speech or language disorders, which can often be addressed in general education classrooms resource. Many of these students do not require SPED and related services in secondary school (http://www2.ed.gov/pubs/OSEP96 AnlRpt/chap3b.html).

The multidisciplinary team also reviews assessments that will be administered during the year and what accommodations will be needed, transportation, assistive technology, and related services. At the end of the meeting, a paper is passed around the table and attendees all sign the form stating we were in attendance—the next school day Max has a new IEP in place.

The IEP meeting, working together to develop the IEP document, requires trust—confidence in each other's word, being reliable, using sound judgment, maintaining confidentiality, and trusting yourself (Turnbull et al., 2010). In addition, this trust continues as services are provided, goals are worked on, data is collected, and relationships are built. Each quarter, when grade cards come home, I receive a progress report that lets me know how Max is progressing on each of his goals. If ever I feel another meeting is needed, as a member of the IEP team, I can request a meeting (just like any other member of the IEP team).

IEP PARTICIPANTS

According to IDEIA (2004), the multidisciplinary team must include at least one general education teacher, SPED teacher, representative of the **local education agency** (LEA) (typically the SPED director or the building principle), someone who can interpret evaluation results (this may be someone serving in another role such as the school psychologist) related services provider(s), transition specialist for students age 16-21, parents, and when appropriate the student. IDEIA states, "A member of the IEP team shall not be required to attend an IEP meeting, in whole or in part, if the parent of a student with a disability and the local educational agency agree that the attendance of such member is not necessary because the member's area of the curriculum or related service is not being modified or discussed in the meeting" (20 U.S.C. 1414 (d) (1) (C) (i)). Additionally, "if the member will miss the meeting or will be asking to leave early for those reasons, the parent and the LEA must consent to the excusal and the member needs to submit in writing to the parent and the IEP team input into the development of the IEP prior to the meeting" (20 U.S.C. 1414 (d) (1) (C) (ii)). Finally, "the parents agreement to the individual's request must be in writing" (20 U.S.C. 1414 (d) (1) (C) (iii).

It is important all participants attend the IEP meeting, but also participate and contribute to meaningfully in order to ensure the student has an IEP that best meets their academic, behavioral, emotional, and social needs. In order to do so, participants must understand their duties in writing an IEP. Turnbull et al. (2010) outline four general duties of multidisciplinary team members:

- Confirm mandatory participation from individual team members.
- Follow IDEIA's process for developing an IEP using the student's strengths, including parents' concerns, aligning the results of non-discriminatory evaluations to annual goals, incorporate the student's academic, developmental, and functional needs.
- Include all of the required components of an IEP.
- Specify the student's educational placement, using the principle of **least restrictive environment**.

In addition, to the broad responsibilities, there are specific roles and responsibilities each member should follow to ensure the best outcomes for the student. The specific roles are described below.

General Education Teacher. General education teachers play a key role in the education of students with disabilities. In addition, they are the member of the IEP team with expertise in the general curriculum and the general education grade level classroom. General education teachers know the expectations, teaching strategies, and approaches already used in the classroom.

Given the added emphasis on participation and progress in the general education curriculum and IDEIA (2004) mandates, the general education teacher's roles and responsibilities on the IEP team have increased. A general education teacher must participate in the development, review, implementation (if appropriate), and revision of the student's IEP. This information is helpful when the IEP team makes decisions about necessary supports needed to ensure that the child will be able to make progress toward his or her annual goals.

It should be noted, the general education teacher is not required to participate in all decisions as part of the meeting or be present for the entire meeting. They should be in attendance to participate in discussions and decisions that involve how to modify the general education curriculum in order to ensure student success and achievement. Parents should be involved in the discussion regarding if a general education teacher will not be present during any part of the IEP meeting.

SPED Teacher. The special educator on the team can be either the student's SPED teacher or a service provider (e.g., speech language pathologist). This individual may be the person who serves as the student's case manager and facilitator during the meeting. The special educator contributes important information about evidence-based practices for educating students with disabilities. Since his or her training is in educating students with disabilities, the SPED teacher can speak about modifying the general education curriculum to meet the student's needs, identify aids and services, and share accommodations that would be appropriate for assessments (Thoma & Wehman, 2010).

Representative of the LEA. The representative of the LEA could be the principal of the school building, SPED director, or another school district representative. This person must be: qualified to supervise the specially designed instruction designed to meet the needs of students with disabilities, be knowledgeable about the general education curriculum, understand the availability of community resources, and have the authority to commit agency resources and ensure the services stated in the IEP can be provided (64. Fed. Reg. 12, 4777 [March 12, 1999]).

Interpreter of Evaluation Results. During meetings where there are assessments and data that need to be interpreted and the instructional implications of the evaluation results, there needs to be an interpreter. Often this person is the school psychologist, but the responsibility could be given to the general education teacher, SPED teacher, LEA representative, or another person on the multidisciplinary team, as long as the person can interpret the instructional implications of the evaluation results (Pierangelo & Giuliani, 2007).

Related Services. If a student's evaluation indicates the need for a specific related service or the student already receives related services, the provider of the service should be a member of the multidisciplinary team and in attendance at the IEP meeting. They need to provide information related to the nature, frequency, and the amount of related service that is provided to the student (Pierangelo & Giuliani, 2007).

Transition Service Providers. When the student reaches the age of 16 (some school districts provide transition services prior to the age of 16), a transition specialist must also be a part of the multidisciplinary team. This individual can assist with planning services the student will need for transition; explain different funding options; share the criteria for qualification to receive services; and provide information related to the laws, rights, and responsibilities (Thoma & Wheman, 2010).

Parents. Parents are important members of the multidisciplinary team and have significant information to offer. They can verify the accuracy of information, provide information and observation, share information regarding their child's ability to generalize skills and concepts in the home and community environments, and give information about the student's medical history and current status (Pierangelo & Giuliani, 2007). Parents can also share aspects of their child's life outside of school that might have an impact on the child's performance or behavior at school.

Parents know their child well and talk about their child's strengths and needs and incorporate this information into assisting with enhancing their child's educational plan. They can offer insights into how the way their child learns best and the child's interests. Parents can participate in developing educational goals and objectives based on present level academic and functional performance. They can share their goals for the future and assist with determining SPED services that may be needed and identifying an appropriate program for their child. While the intent of IDEIA (2004) parents be equal contributing members on the multidisciplinary team, it is important to remember IEP meetings and the developing the IEP is a new experience for most families (Pierangelo & Giuliani, 2007).

Student. The student may be a participant in the IEP meeting or a member of the multidisciplinary team. If transition services are being included in the discussion of the IEP, then the student must be invited to attend. When students take a role in their IEP meeting, are taught the process, and begin participating, they can learn to advocate for themselves and about **self-determination**.

Others. The parents or the school district may invite other individuals to attend the multidisciplinary team meeting. Invitees may have knowledge about the student or have an expertise in a specific area. The decision about whether or not the invited individual has the knowledge or expertise is left to the persons extending the invitation. The school district official must tell the parents about their right to invite others to the meeting and is appropriate for the district to ask if they intend to bring others to the meeting. The presence of lawyers at an IEP meeting is strongly discouraged for both parents and the school because it creates an atmosphere that is not necessarily focused on collaboration, trust, and working for the best interests of the student (Pierangelo & Giuliani, 2007).

IEP MEETING PREPARATION

IEP meetings must be held under the following circumstances: (a) within 30 days of determining eligibility for SPED services, (b) on or before the annual review date, (c) when considering a change to the IEP, (d) when requested by an IEP team member including the parents, and (e) to review or develop a behavior intervention plan. An IEP is written and serves the student for one year and several steps must be taken before a student is considered for SPED services and related services and before planning a multidisciplinary team meeting. Pierangelo and Giuliani (2007) offered the following suggestions:

- Work with families to try to evaluate intervention methods focused on the concerns that led to the referral.
- Decide if the student should be formally evaluated (written consent from the parents is required).
- Using a variety of assessments (see Chapter 3) including observation and information gathering, to evaluate the student targeting all areas related to the suspected exceptionality.
- Examine the data and determine if the student meets the criteria to be considered eligible for SPED and, if appropriate, related services (document determination results).
- Inform the school and other personnel of the need for a meeting.
- Schedule a time when all of the participants are available to meet (arrangements may need to be made to cover a class or relieve someone from other responsibilities so that they are able to attend).
- Schedule the meeting to review the evaluation and determine the student's eligibility for services.
- Send a written notice to the parents informing and inviting them to the meeting.
- Allow sufficient time for the participants to respond and have an opportunity to request another time if needed.

Once the logistics have been addressed of the multidisciplinary team has determined that an IEP meeting is the next step for the student, it is important to ensure that all of the people who will make up the multidisciplinary team are notified and have plenty of notice to make arrangements to attend. Parents must be notified in writing of an IEP meeting—phone conversations and verbal invitations do not meet the requirements outlined by IDEIA (2004). The written notice should include the contact person's name and telephone number if the parents should have questions, along with the purpose, time and date, and location of the meeting. It should also include who will be attending and let them know that they may invite people to the meeting who may have knowledge or information regarding their child.

The parents must also be given the opportunity to reschedule the meeting. When a student is 16 years old or when transition services will be discussed, the student may participate in the IEP and they should receive an invitation to participate in the meeting. A copy of parental rights should be included with the meeting notice (this is mandatory). If it is known, that a parent will not be able to read and understand the documents, other ways to provide the parents with the information should be considered (i.e., a home visit) (Pierangelo & Giuliani, 2007).

It is equally important to ensure, homes where English is not the primary language, have access to the information in the meeting notice (Pierangelo & Giuliani, 2007). Documents written in the family's primary language or an interpreter may need to be considered to ensure the family has access to the information. Educators should not assume that parents understand the information, often the documents are written at a level above the parent's understanding (Diliberto & Brewer, 2012; Fitzgerald & Watkins, 2006). In such cases, school districts may consider providing workshops for parents.

TIPS FOR A SUCCESSFUL IEP MEETING

Educational professionals and family members need to understand federal requirements for IEP meetings, both to ensure compliance and to guarantee that they will be able to recognize potential violations (Cheatham, Hart, Malian, & McDonald, 2012). This understanding needs to also include knowledge of the core principles of IDEIA (2004): (a) zero reject, (b) nondiscriminatory evaluation, (c) individualized and appropriate education, (d) least restrictive environment, (e) procedural due process, and (f) parent participation (Turnbull, Stowe, & Huerta, 2007). Since the implementation of the SPED law in 1975, schools have made significant strides in providing SPED services to students with disabilities. However, recent studies indicate children with disabilities and their families still experience challenges that pose as barriers to the full implementation of IDEIA. For example, some general and SPED teacher along with administrators do not fully support inclusive services (Wolery & Odom, 2000) due to lack of resources, class size, and inadequate preparation for teachers (Carlson, Bruen, Klein, Shroll, & Willig, 2000). In addition, families reported schools do not provide them with helpful and understandable information regarding IDEIA (Lake & Billingsley, 2000; Fitzgerald & Watkins, 2006).

Recent research of family experiences during the IEP process suggests that favorable practices are the exception rather than the norm (Cheatham et al., 2012). Families reported being intimidated by educators and blamed for their children's academic and behavioral challenges (Fish, 2006) and their participation during IEP meetings was limited to listening to information answering questions, and signing forms (Childre & Chambers, 2005). When educators and families collaborate to through the IEP process and work to resolve disputes, family satisfaction with SPED services increases (Mueller, Singer, & Draper, 2008).

While communication through the process often becomes a challenge for team members, a critical component of a successful IEP meeting and IEP development is open communication (Diliberto & Brewer, 2012). The Council for Exceptional Children's (2009) best practice recommendations for collaboration includes guidance for parents and educators to work together in the best interest of the child with a disability. Some first steps towards effectively working through conflicts that arise in the IEP process include the members of the team understanding the IDEIA (2004) requirements and core principles

(Turnbull et al., 2007). This means that when team members see that mandates are not being followed, they must have the confidence to speak up (Cheatham et al., 2012).

Communication and planning are essentially the driving forces behind successful IEP meetings. To foster positive communication with families, they should be included from the start. To comply with the spirit and intent of IDEIA (2004) regulations, educators need to refrain from predetermining IEP decisions, completing IEP documents without family input, and discounting families when writing goals and objectives (Fish, 2008). Understanding parent and student needs is part of building a positive rapport that is necessary for open communication to take place which is needed for home-school communication throughout the school year (Staples & Diliberto, 2010). Ensuring open communication fosters successful teaming that is needed during IEP meetings for developing the most accurate IEP, that become a useful tool for guiding instruction and monitoring progress (Diliberto & Brewer, 2012).

Family participation at an IEP meeting is critical. Federal and state regulations require that efforts be made to ensure family members have the opportunity to participate. Many parents work and it is difficult to make arrangements to leave work for meetings. It is important to check with the parent whenever possible before scheduling an IEP meeting. Being sensitive to family needs and time limitations can foster a relationship between home and school and help increase parental participation during IEP meetings. It is also important to provide parents with at least 10 days' notice of a meeting. The school is often the best and most convenient place to host the IEP meeting. However, the school should be prepared to offer alternatives if the school is not the most appropriate place. For example, in rural areas where families live long distances from the school, it might be necessary to consider other alternatives such as a conference call (Pierangelo & Giuliani, 2007). In cases where an alternative is selected as the most appropriate solution, it is important to ensure all participants have access to the required materials that will be referred to during the meeting (Pierangelo & Giuliani, 2007).

The field of education is filled with jargon and acronyms. This can be overwhelming and intimidating to parents. While it is familiar to teachers and related service providers, it should be recognized, it is not to all team members (parents) and should be left out or explained. The use of jargon often negates clarity to the IEP process and meeting and does not promote a collaborative team environment (Diliberto & Brewer, 2012). One suggestion would be for schools to provide parents with a document explaining the meanings of various acronyms and terminology (Diliberto & Brewer, 2012).

Pierangelo and Giuliani (2007) described the characteristics of an effective IEP multidisciplinary team meeting as having (a) clear goals, (b) members feeling involved, (c) voices heard, (d) opinions respected, (d) solutions sought, and (e) sense of accomplishment. Effective meetings allow all group members the opportunity to offer input and express opinions, while remaining positive and on task focused on the intended purpose and outcomes. One member should take on the responsibilities of the facilitator guiding the members through the process. It should not be the expectation of the members of the group to finish developing an IEP in a specified allotted amount of time (i.e., an hour), some meetings may take more time and may require multiple meeting dates.

Ideally, an agenda helps all multidisciplinary team members know the items that will be covered during the meeting and the opportunity to provide input (Diliberto & Brewer, 2012). The agenda should serve as a guide to the meeting but be flexible to help meet the needs of the team. An effective meeting agenda should include the following (a) welcome and introductions, (b) ground rules, (c) summary of assessment data, (d) review of student strengths and needs, (e) IEP development, (f) next steps, and (g) closure.

Student Involvement. Student involvement in the IEP process promotes self-advocacy and self-determination. In addition, it enhances student motivation (Deci & Ryan, 2000), improves academic achievement (Test, Mason, Hughes, Konrad, Neale, & Wood, 2004), and increases the IEP team's knowledge of the student (Martin, Van Dycke, Greene, Gardner, Christensen, & Woods, et al., 2006). In order for students to have meaningful involvement, members of the IEP team must take the time to teach students about the purpose of an IEP, self-awareness, and the IEP process. When the IEP is viewed as a process rather than a once a year meeting, it is easier to find ways for students to participate in meaningful ways (Thoma & Wehman, 2010).

DEVELOPING AN IEP

There are many considerations to think about when developing an IEP for a student. This legal document contains goals and objectives and the supports needed to attain the goals successfully while participating in the general education curriculum. Janzen (2003) described the IEP as a travel plan. It states the starting point (**present level of performance**) and a final destination (goals). The lodging, restaurants, gas stations, and attractions along the way (e.g., related services, teaching strategies, evaluations, and accommodations). The travel plans (starting point to destination) vary from individual-to-individual. A skilled travel agent (the multidisciplinary team) carefully assesses the student's needs be for developing the travel itinerary (IEP document).

IDEIA (2004) requires that the IEP include eight components and five special factors. It is important for school districts to comply with IDEIA and to ensure that the each student will benefit from SPED and related services, in order to do both the multidisciplinary team must include every component in each IEP (Turnbull et al., 2010). The eight required components to every IEP include:

- The student's present level of academic achievement and functional performance.
- Measureable annual goals, including both academic and functional.
- How the student's progress toward the goals will be measured and when the progress will be reported
- SPED, related services, and supplementary aids and services that will be provided to the student or on the student's behalf.
- An explanation of the extent (if any) the student will not participate with their nondisabled peers in the general education classroom.
- Any appropriate accommodations that is necessary to support academic and functional performance on state and district assessments.
- An anticipated date for beginning the SPED, related services, supplemental aids and services, and modifications as well as duration, location, and frequency.
- On the student's 16th birthday or before a transition plan must be included.

According to Arnett et al.(2013) an addition to the eight components multidisciplinary team should consider the following:

- Does the student's behavior impede his or her learning or the learning of others? If so, the IEP team must consider if positive behavioral interventions, supports, or strategies to use to address the student's behavior.
- Does the student have limited English proficiency? If so, the multidisciplinary team must consider language needs as part of the IEP.
- Is the student blind or visually impaired? If so, the multidisciplinary team must provide instruction in Braille or the use of Braille. After an evaluation, the multidisciplinary team can determine if this is appropriate to continue.
- Does the student have communication needs? If the child is deaf or hard of hearing, the team must consider his language and communication needs, as well as opportunities for direct communication.
- Does the child need assistive technology to support their goals and services?

Below is information that will assist with writing a present level of performance and IEP goals. Additional information will be addressed that the multidisciplinary team members need to include in an IEP.

Present Level of Performance. The multidisciplinary team reviews the evaluation data on the student, this includes observations and information from parents. This information is summarized and included in the student's present level of performance. The statements of present level of academic and functional performance should include how the student's disability impacts involvement and progress in the general education curriculum. The statement should accurately depict the effect of the disability on student performance (Pierangelo & Giuliani, 2007). Pierangelo and Giuliani (2007) offered the following guidelines for developing the statement of the present level of academic achievement of functional performance:

- Should be written in easy to understand language, be concise, free from acronyms and educational jargon.
- Information should be current and accurate.
- Should reflect the results of assessment data.
- Have a direct relationship to other parts of the IEP and should be related to an area of need.
- Describe performance in the general education curriculum.
- Share student's strengths and what they need to be able to do.

Writing Goals. Annual goals state the anticipated achievement expected within a one-year period, though they could be written for a shorter time period. Well-written annual IEP goals should be both clear and concise. They should be expressed in measurable and observable terms and include the conditions for the behavior to occur. They should also align with one or more of the student's present level of performance (Knowlton, 2007). While, the goals do not need to restate the present level of performance, there should be a clear alignment and direct relationship between the two. Finally, areas of the general education curriculum that are not impacted by the student's disability do not need to be addressed in the IEP or reflected in the annual goals (Pierangelo & Giuliani, 2007). Heinich, Molenda, Russel, and Smaldino (1999) recommended that well-written goals address the ABCEs of goal writing:

- **A**udience: Who is the goal written for?
- **B**ehavior: What do you expect the target for the goal to be able to do? This should be observable and measurable.
- **C**ondition: Under what condition is the student expected to perform the task or behavior?
- **D**egree: What will be the criteria established to determine if the goal has been met?

Transition. It is important for multidisciplinary teams to begin planning for the student's future while the student is still in school. IDEIA (2004) mandates the time to begin is at age 16 or earlier. A statement of the transition serves need to be included in the IEP. This should include courses needed to help the student reach their postsecondary goals. Age appropriate goals should be based on transition assessments related to training, education employment, and independent living (Pierangelo & Giuliani, 2007). More detailed information is provided related to transition services in Chapter 5.

Assistive Technology. Some students may need assistive technology devices and services to benefit from FAPE and make progress towards their annual goals. (Assistive Technology will only be mentioned briefly as it relates to the IEP. Assistive Technology is discussed in more detail in Chapter 10). In addition to deciding if assistive technology is necessary to make progress, the multidisciplinary team must also consider if the use of assistive technology purchased by the school must be used in the home or other environments in order for to meet FAPE requirements. Parental input and support during this discussion is extremely important. Pierangelo and Giuliani (2007) suggest that an IEP team ask the following questions when considering assistive technology for a student:

- What is the student able to do currently with and without assistive technology?
- Will assistive technology facilitate student success in a less restrictive environment?

- Which assistive technology would help the student participate in the general education curriculum?
- How can assistive technology devices and services be integrated in to the student's program across environments such as home, school, community, and work?

In addition to these questions, more specific queries can be asked related to specific supports, such as to access auditory information or for written communication. After it is determined if the student would receive benefit from assistive technology, which technology would be the most beneficial, how to teach the student to use the technology, and determine how it will be used in the classroom, the multidisciplinary team will decide if the student requires the assistive technology device to participate in district and state assessments.

Related Services. Like assistive technology, related services is discussed in more detail in Chapter 8 and is only discussed here as it relates to the student's IEP. Related services support students with disabilities and assist them with reaching their goals and progressing in the general education curriculum. When an IEP is developed, it should state the services needed to meet the student's goals. Each IEP is individualized, so some students will require more support from related services than others. The IEP should state how services will be delivered and how often in order to best meet the student's educational needs. When an multidisciplinary team has determined related services are necessary, it is the responsibility of the school district to pay for these services. Parents cannot be charged for cost associated with the provided related services.

Modifications & Accommodations. Part of the student's IEP must also include program modifications or accommodations that will be provided so that the student can make progress toward their annual goals, participate and make progress in the general education curriculum, participate in extracurricular and other nonacademic activities, and participate in the least restrictive environment with their nondisabled peers.

The term modification means a substantial change in what a student is expected to learn or how they will demonstrate their knowledge. These changes may be made to the instruction, the content, or assessment. Modifications help ensure the student has a meaningful learning experience that is based on their individual needs (Pierangelo & Giuliani, 2007). These changes could include a change in the amount of work, extra time to complete an assignment, or material provided using larger font.

Accommodations are provisions made to allow a student access to the content and to demonstrate their learning. These are not substantial changes to the instruction, content, or the assessments. Accommodations change how students learn and they demonstrate their knowledge of the content (Pierangelo & Giuliani, 2007).

Evaluating and Reporting Progress Toward the Goals. Goals and objectives need to be written in measurable terms. Writing measurable goals allows the multidisciplinary team to identify the extent and duration the student must perform the task or behavior in order for the goal to be met. Evaluation procedures identify the method that should be used to measure the student's progress and determine if goals have been met. It is important to determine a data collection system. This helps to ensure all multidisciplinary team members are on the same page when assessing and gathering data. It also helps safeguard that the student's progress is objectively assessed. This is important to as it will be helpful when assessing how and what information to report to the multidisciplinary team including the parents.

The IEP must include a statement describing the process parents will be informed of their child's progress towards their IEP goals. This statement should also include if the progress is on target for the student to meet the annual goal by the end of the year. Parents must be informed as often as parents of their nondisabled peers. This typically means when report cards go home every 9 weeks or once a quarter. These progress reports provide parents with a way to monitor how their child is progressing towards meeting their annual goal and serves as a way to evaluate the effectiveness of the SPED services the student is receiving (Pierangelo & Giuliani, 2007).

Where to go from here? The process of evaluating and reporting student's progress allows the multidisciplinary team to monitor student learning and note when action is needed and determine what steps to take. For example, if a student is not making the expected progress, the multidisciplinary team needs to review the current IEP and if needed make revisions.

PROFESSIONAL ANALYSIS

The IEP Process: Adhering to Both the Letter & the Spirit of the Law

By

Dr. Catherine Krammer, Lake Erie College

When the 94th congress wrote their 142nd law in 1975, The Education for all Handicapped Children Act now known as IDEIA (2004), they did so due to the efforts of many parents and professionals who fought hard in order to have the rights of those with disabilities be recognized and respected. This was a long and hard battle (U.S. Department of Education).

The title of this professional analysis is one borrowed from a phrase that a former professor of mine, Rud Turnbull, who I admire greatly, often used in his talks regarding IDEIA. Dr. Turnbull is now a professor emeritus at the University of Kansas, and someone who I and many others hold in the highest regard. The saying alludes to the fact that while yes, this law does set out rules and regulations pertaining to the education of children with disabilities, if we simply look at IDEIA as a legal document, or *letters* to abide by, we are missing out on the true intentions behind the law. In other words, *the spirit of the law*.

The *spirit of the law* takes into account the individuals themselves and the concepts of self-determination and self-advocacy. It takes into account the pioneering parents who would not back down when told their child could not attend their neighborhood school. It accounts for the professionals who made it their mission in life to see to it that all children, regardless of the nature and severity of their disability are provided the same rights as their non-disabled peers.

The law itself is lengthy, however the majority of the many rules and regulations defining how IDEIA (2004) operates can be narrowed down to six major principles that have remained basically unchanged despite several reauthorizations since 1975 (Turnbull et al., 2007). As noted briefly above, the six major principles are:

- **Zero Reject**. Schools or required to educate all children regardless of the nature or severity of a disability.
- **Nondiscriminatory Identification & Evaluation**. Schools must use non-biased, multi-factored evaluations administered by a team of trained professionals in order to determine if a child has a disability.
- **FAPE**. Regardless of the nature or severity of the disability, all children must receive FAPE. Each child who has been determined to have a disability will receive an Individualized Education Program to meet their unique needs.
- **Least Restrictive Environment**. Students with disabilities should be educated in the general education classroom with their non-disabled peers to the maximum extent possible unless the nature or severity of their disability would necessitate that they be removed to another setting on the continuum of placements that would better suit their needs.
- **Due Process Safeguards**. Schools must provide due process safeguards to protect children with disabilities and their families. They must obtain consent prior to evaluating, identifying and placing students in SPED, and they must provide for mediation and due process should there be disagreement concerning any of these decisions.

- **Parent & Student Participation and Shared Decision Making.** Parents and students are both part of the multidisciplinary team and thus schools must collaborate with them in order to make educational decisions.

This chapter has very effectively addressed the IEP process which is included in the third principle of IDEIA (2004) of FAPE. The principle includes the provision that in addition to providing a free and appropriate education, the school must develop an IEP. In this professional analysis I hope to build upon what has been outlined regarding the IEP process and provide some recommendations from the field as to how professionals can still adhere to the letter, while preserving the spirit of the law.

One of the most important ways to do this is to not see IEP meetings as an event to schedule and then check off one's calendar. That said, I recommend that special education teachers make a spreadsheet at the beginning of the year with every student's name, IEP due date, and reevaluation due date if applicable, along with other pertinent information such as grade level, contact information, etc. However, once you are aware of the due date it is then important to put the process in perspective and see it as just that; a process or cycle that is continuous.

This process includes: (a) collaborating with all members of the team in order to gather information pertinent to the child, (b) jointly developing the IEP, (c) implementing the IEP, (d) continuing to gather data, (e) sharing the child's progress, and (f) reviewing the IEP. Thus, when the meeting takes place that is not the end of the IEP, rather the beginning. It should be a living, breathing, working document that is carried out, not filed in a locked cabinet and never seen again. However, it is still important to protect confidentiality so yes, in a sense it should be locked up but just the document; not the practices contained within.

Once you know the date the meeting must be held, then you start planning. Because this is a collaborative process it is the SPED teacher, or case manager's job, to ensure that everyone has ample input into the planning. One of the most important ways to do this is to involve the parents. This can be done by sending home a questionnaire or survey ahead of time perhaps asking questions such as (a) what do you see as your child's strengths, (b) what are areas you feel they need to work on, and (c) what do you see as some long term goals for your child? This gives the parents or caregivers time in a non-stressful environment (because we know IEP meetings can be stressful) to think over their responses.

Once the parents have sent back their thoughts you can begin a draft copy of the IEP so that this too can be sent home ahead of time. Again, in the midst of a meeting where sensitive information is being shared by multiple professionals, parents are not always able to digest everything that is being thrown their way. Thus, sending home a draft copy of the IEP is a respectful way to allow them time to process the information, formulate questions, and then come prepared to fully participate in the meeting.

There are also many considerations to take into account during the meeting. I think one of the biggest mistakes I have seen made is to assume that everyone knows each other. Consequently, introductions should never be skipped. Additionally, the team should strive to create a comfortable atmosphere which means considering chair size (i.e., *do not* make parents sit on kindergarten size chairs), temperature, lighting, table size, etc. All of these aspects go a long way towards making parents feel more at ease. It is also not a bad idea to have tissues at hand because IEP meetings can certainly be emotional, and of course snacks and coffee never hurt. I personally always bring chocolates to my IEP meetings.

I would recommend building in time for questions, not rushing through and just reading the IEP, and making the meeting more of a conversation concerning strengths as well as goals versus a formal meeting that feels more procedural rather than about someone's child. As mentioned earlier, once the IEP meeting is completed, this is really where things begin.

The multidisciplinary team will set the wheels in motion and should regularly update the parents in regards to their child's progress. Finally, always remember that the IEP is a living, working document that should drive the child's programming and be regularly considered in terms of the child's progress. While the *letters* of this document may be written for now, the *spirit* is in fact just beginning.

FIRST PERSON TESTIMONIAL

Socialization Integration

By

Heather Fitzpatrick, West Monona Community School District

One day Fred walked down the hall on his way to class and saw a teacher that he knew he yelled, *boo*, and expected the teacher to be scared and jump. Fred often forgets the first thing you say to someone is usually *hello*. He then walked into my classroom and yelled, *Heather, I am here*, from the door. No matter how many times I tell him that I know he is *here* because I can see him, he still has to yell across the room almost every morning.

Fred is an 8th grade student with Autism. He loves to talk to people that he knows. He loves to talk so much that he interrupts conversations to tell a joke or discuss his favorite zombie game. He has three jokes that he tells me on a daily basis. They are about zombies, ghosts, and bananas. What makes the jokes so funny is that he usually forgets the punch lines. He makes me laugh because no matter how many times we work on different jokes, he always goes back to the original three.

Fred is social; however as an 8th grader, he still struggles with how to appropriately interact with adults and peers in different social settings. This is an area that has always been a great concern for his parents. At the start of the school year, Fred's parents called an IEP meeting to address some of these social communication issues. As a team (i.e., parents, teacher, principal, strategist, and case worker), we worked together to brainstorms ways to help Fred learn appropriate social communication with his peers and teachers in the school. Prior to the IEP meeting, Fred spent about 40% of his day in the general education classroom.

One solution that the team came up with was to increase his time in the general education classroom thus giving him more time with his same age, general education peers. In addition, a social group was created were peers came into the SPED classroom to play games with Fred. Finally, a rubric was created that focused on several areas of conversation including: (a) eye contact, (b) appropriate proximity, (c) age appropriate comments, (d) appropriately greeting peers and adults, (e) listening to conversations in a group without interrupting others, and (f) waiting to talk to a teacher.

Similar to Max, Fred has come a long way in the past two months in the area of social communication. His progress is due to the multidisciplinary team working together to amend his IEP in order to create meaningful opportunities for him to interact and communicate with his peers in a variety of different social settings.

SUMMARY & CONCLUSION

IDEIA (2004) requires each student with a disability to have an IEP. Students with autism are entitled to FAPE and an IEP which should include the eight components and the five factors. The IEP must be based on the student's strengths, parental concerns, nondiscriminatory evaluation, student's needs, etc.

One of the key outcomes for IDEIA (2004) is to ensure that students with disabilities have equal opportunities in education and that these opportunities lead to self-sufficiency, independent living, and full participation. To ensure these outcomes are possible, multidisciplinary teams must develop and deliver a well-developed IEP that meets the individual needs of the student that considers the modifications and accommodations, supplementary aids and services, related services, assistive technology, and transition services.

References

Arnett, S., Fitzpatrick, M., & Theoharis, R. (2013). *Foundations of SPED: Understanding students with exceptionalities.* Dubuque, IA: Kendall Hunt.

Attwood, T. (1998). *Asperger's syndrome: A guide for parents and professionals.* London: Jessica Kingsley Publishers.

Bate, C. (2004). Enhancing relationships through speech and language intervention. In L. C. Levental-Belfer (Ed.), *Asperger's syndrome in young children* (pp. 190–210). London: Jessica Kingsley Publishers.

Buron, K. D., & Wolfberg, P. (2008). *Learners on the autism spectrum: Preparing highly qualified educators.* Shawnee Mission, KS: Autism Asperger Publishing Co.

Carlson, E., Brauen, M., Klein, S., Shroll, K., & Willig, S. (2002). *SPeNSE: Study of personnel needs in SPED. Key findings.* Washington, DC: U.S. Department of Education Office of SPED Programs. Retrieved August 1, 2014, from http://spense.education.ufl.edu/keyfindings.pdf

Cheatham, G. A., Hart, J. E., Malian, I., & McDonald, J. (2012). Six things to never say or hear during an IEP meeting: Educators as advocates for families. *Teaching Exceptional Children, 44*(3), 50–57.

Childre, A., & Chambers, C. R. (2005). Family perceptions of student-centered planning and IEP meetings. *Education and Training Developmental Disabilities, 40*, 217–233.

Deci, E. L., & Ryan, R. M. (2000). The "what" and "why" of goal pursuits: Human needs and the self-determination of behavior. *Psychological Inquiry, 11*(4), 227–268.

Diliberto, J. A., & Brewer, D. (2012). Six tips for successful IEP meetings. *Teaching Exceptional Children, 44*(4), 30–37.

Fish, W. W. (2008). The IEP meeting: Perceptions of parents of students who receive special education services. *Preventing School Failure, 53*(1), 8–14.

Fitzgerald, J. L., & Watkins, M. W. (2006). Parents' rights in special education: The readability of procedural safeguards. *Exceptional Children, 72*(4), 497–510.

Fitzpatrick, M. (2010). Operation mind crime: An era of globalized media consumers. Educating Youth for Citizenship*: East and West.*

Heinich, R., Molenda, M., Russel, J. D.,& Smaldino, S. E. (1999). *Instructional media and technologies for learning.* Upper Saddle River, NJ: Prentice Hall.

Individuals With Disabilities Education Act, 20 U.S.C. 4301 *et seq.* (2006).

Janzen, J. E. (2003). *Understanding the nature of autism: A Guide to autism spectrum disorders.* (2nd ed.). San Antonio, TX: PsychCorp.

Klin, A., Volkmar, F. R., & Sparrow, S. S. (2000). *Asperger syndrome.* New York: Guilford Press.

Knowlton, E. (2007). *Developing effective Individualized Education Programs: A case-based tutorial* (2nd ed.). Upper Saddle River, NJ: Pearson Education.

Lake, J. F., & Billingsley, B. (2000). An analysis of factors that contribute to parent-school conflict in SPED. *Remedial and SPED, 21*, 240–251.

Martin, J. E., Van Dycke, J. L., Greene, B. A., Gardner, J. E., Christensen, W. R., Woods, I. L., et al. (2006). Direct observation of teacher-directed IEP meetings: Establishing the need for student IEP meeting instruction. *Exceptional Children, 72*, 182–200.

Mueller, T. G., Singer, G. H., & Draper, L. M. (2008). Reducing parental dissatisfaction with special education in two school districts: Implementing conflict prevention alternative dispute resolution. *Journal of Educational and Psychological Consultation, 18*(3), 191–233.

Pierangelo, R., & Guiliani, G. (2007). *A step-by-step guide for educators: Understanding, developing and writing effective IEPs.* Thousand Oaks, CA: Corwin Press.

Staples, K., & Diliberto, J. A. (2010). Guidelines for successful parent involvement: Working with parent of students with disabilities. *Teaching Exceptional Children, 42*(6), 58–63.

Test, D. W., Mason, C., Hughes, C., Konrad, M., Neale, M., & Wood, W. (2004). Student involvement in individualized educational program meetings. *Exceptional Children, 70*, 391–412.

Thoma, C. A., & Wehman, P. (2008). *Getting the most out of IEPs: An Educator's guide to the student-directed approach.* Baltimore, MD: Paul H. Brooks.

Turnbull, A., Turnbull, R., & Wehmeyer, M. L. (2010). *Exceptional lives: SPED in today's schools.* Upper Saddle River, NJ: Pearson.

Turnbull, H. R., Stowe, M. J., & Huerta, N. E. (2007). *Free appropriate public education: The law and children with disabilities* (7th ed.). Denver, CO: Love.

U.S Department of Education. Archived: A 25 year history of IDEA.

Wiss, T. (2004). Building connections through sensory and motor pathways: Occupational therapy. In L. C. Levental-Belfer (Ed.), *Asperger's syndrome in young children* (pp. 211–237). London: Jessica Kingsley Publishers.

Wolery, R. A., & Odom, S. L. (2000). *An administrator's guide to pre-school inclusion.* Chapel Hill, NC: University of NC, FPG Child Development Center, Early Childhood Research Institute on Inclusion.

5 Transition

Chapter Objectives

After studying this chapter readers should be able to:

- Compare and contrast the similarities and differences between the various definitions of transition.
- Discuss how transition assessment, planning, and services relate to a free appropriate public education.
- Explain how transition assessment, planning, and servicing enhance post-high school options.
- Identify personal experiences with transition(s) and determine if—and how—they relate to Max's scenario.

Chapter 5 Subject Index:

1. Americans with Disabilities Act
2. Autism Spectrum Disorders
3. Customized Employment
4. Education for All Handicapped Children Act
5. Employment Specialists
6. Federal Register
7. Free and Appropriate Public Education
8. Individualized Education Program (IEP)
9. Individuals with Disabilities Education Act
10. Individuals with Disabilities Education Improvement Act
11. Job Coaches
12. Multidisciplinary Team
13. Office of Disability Employment Policy
14. Person-Centered Transition Planning
15. Postsecondary Education
16. Section 504 of the Rehabilitation Act
17. Supported Employment
18. Transition Assessment
19. Transition Planning
20. Transition Services

INTRODUCTION

Reflect upon your average day, starting from the moment you wake up until you returned to bed for the evening. Ask yourself, did I independently: (a) consume nourishment (e.g., breakfast, lunch, etc.), (b) care for my personal hygiene (e.g., shower, brush teeth, etc.), (c) arrive to destinations in a timely fashion (e.g., school, work, etc.), (d) engage in face-to-face or digital conversations (e.g., texts, calls, etc.), and (e) complete responsibilities (e.g., homework, errands, etc.). Although many of the functional routines; personal, social, and professional interactions; and tasks, activities, and duties may appear to be repetitive, when viewed with a different lens these sequences of events can be much more difficult than meets the eye.

Now consider the thought processes involved in making many of your major life decisions. Ask yourself, how did I: (a) select which college to attend, (b) accept my first teaching position, and (c) decide which graduate school to apply to. Theoretically, unlike the daily routines outlined above, the vast majority of readers put ample thought into each major life decision prior to pursuing their personal and professional aspirations.

Obviously these two summaries do not represent an exhaustive list of daily activities or major life decisions. However, ponder if you have encountered, or continue to encounter, any difficulties with one-or-more of the routines or choices noted above. For example, some individuals are self-proclaimed *morning people* and absolutely cannot stand staying in bed once they are awake. Conversely self-proclaimed *night owls* tend to experience tremendous challenges negotiating early morning hours and try sleeping as long as possible. Essentially, the daily structure for these two divergent groups, typically, can be vastly different with regard to day-to-day functioning. Similarly, the decision-making process for individuals with Type A and Type B personalities are likely in sharp contrast.

If you, the reader, are asking "What do these self-reflection exercises have to do with special education (SPED) or more importantly students with **autism spectrum disorder** (ASD)?" the answer is simple; virtually everything throughout a day and major life decisions are based on transitions. Whether they are seamless (i.e., routine) or extremely complex, transitions occur to most people without disabilities effortlessly, whereas students with disabilities, especially those with ASD, struggle with this process regardless of the level of *involvedness.*

Given the reality that *all* students entering adolescence and young adulthood encounter many challenges (Wehman, Smith, & Schall, 2009) the focus of this chapter is on transition which is an area that continues to receive ample attention (see Miller, Lombard, & Corbey, 2007; Rusch, Hughes, Agran, Martin, & Johnson, 2009; Test, Mazzotti, Mustian, Fowler, Kortering, & Kohler, 2009; Wehman, et al., 2009).

DEFINITIONS OF TRANSITION

There have been multiple attempts to define transition since its inception in the early 80s. The **Individuals with Disabilities Education Act** (IDEA, 1990) defined **transition services** as:

> A coordinated set of activities for a student, designed within an outcome oriented process, which promotes movement from school to post school activities, including post-secondary education, vocational training, integrated employment (including supported employment), continuing and adult education, adult services, independent living, or community participation (20 U.S.C. 1401(19)).

More recently, the reauthorization and renaming of IDEA (1990) now known as the, **Individuals with Disabilities Education Improvement Act** (IDEIA, 2004), updated the definition of transition services for students with disabilities and included the following three prongs:

- Is designed to be within a results-oriented process, that is focused on improving the academic and functional achievement of the child with a disability to facilitate the child's movement from school to post-school activities, including postsecondary education, vocational education, integrated employment (including supported employment); continuing and adult education, adult services, independent living, or community participation;

- is based on the individual child's needs, taking into account the child's strengths, preferences, and interests; and
- includes instruction, related services, community experiences, the development of employment and other post-school adult living objectives, and, if appropriate, acquisition of daily living skills and functional vocational evaluation [34 CFR 300.43 (a)] [20 U.S.C. 1401(34)].

According to Miller et al. (2007) these definitions represent an attempt for making education relevant to students with disabilities and their families. However, the Division of Career Development and Transition adopted Halpern's (1994) definition which, according to Wehmeyer and Webb (2012) is considered the most comprehensive:

> Transition refers to a change in status from behaving primarily as a student to assuming emergent adult roles in the community. These roles include employment, participating in post-secondary education, maintaining a home, becoming appropriately involved in the community, and experiencing satisfactory personal and social relationships. The process of enhancing transition involves the participation in coordination of school programs, adult agency services, and natural supports within the community. The foundations for transition should be laid during the elementary and middle school years, guided by the broad concept of career development. Transition planning should begin no later than age 14, and students should be encouraged, to the full extent of their capabilities, to assume a maximum amount of responsibility for such planning (p. 117).

TRANSITION & FAPE

Arguably one of the primary roles and responsibilities of K-12 educational institutions is to prepare *all* students for the *real world* (Fitzpatrick, 2010). As discussed in Chapter 2, students with disabilities receiving SPED services are entitled to a **free and appropriate public education** (FAPE).

To help ensure FAPE, the **Education for All Handicapped Children Act** (1975) was reauthorized and renamed in 1990 and included two notable amendments (Arnett, Fitzpatrick, & Theoharis, 2013). First, IDEA (1990) expanded services to include students 18-21 and second, as alluded to above, mandated local education agencies to focus on services and instructional needs to enable students to transition from high school to either postsecondary education or adult life (Wehmeyer & Webb, 2012). Moreover IDEIA (2004) enhanced these precepts by stating "as the graduation rates for children with disabilities continue to climb, providing effective transition services to promote successful post school employment or education is an important measure of accountability for children with disabilities" (20 U.S.C. Sec. 1400(c)(14)).

TRANSITION ASSESSMENT

The notion of transition is not a new concept; however, according to Fragoso, Gonçalves, Ribeiro, Monteiro, Quintas, Bago, Fonseca, and Santos (2013) the process has evolved in complexity within the last two decades. Currently, students encounter a copious number of transitions throughout their K-12 educational career. From subject-to-subject, class-to-class, grade-to-grade, building-to-building, and school-to-*life*, transitions have become a function of necessity. As noted above, students without disabilities usually can handle changes with minimal assistance, whereas students with ASD often experience great difficulties across the majority of these disruptions in schedule. Thus, assessment and planning have become a critical component to help ensure students with ASD are prepared for the various transitions they will encounter throughout their day and lifetime.

Although students with ASD share common characteristics including but not limited to (a) communication and language impairments (see Koegel, 2000; National Research Council, 2001), (b) socialization deficits (see Baron-Cohen & Wheelwright, 2004), (c) aggressive and self-injurious behaviors (see Hyman & Towbin, 2007), (d) repetitive and unusual behavior patterns (see Loftin, Odom, & Lantz, 2007), and (e) sensory stimulations (see Harrison & Hare, 2004) it is important for the **multidisciplinary team** to focus on the individual and avoid overgeneralizations. Moreover, given that the majority of students with ASD experience extreme difficulties with changes in their daily routines—which is in direct contrast to the day-to-day fluctuations that occur within the classroom and school setting—it is important to assess and develop an appropriate transition plan for each student based on his or her unique individual needs.

Transition assessment has been defined as "an ongoing process of collecting information on a student's strengths, needs, preferences, interests as they relate to the demands of current and future living, learning, and working environments" (Sitlington, Neubert, Begun, Lombard, & Leconte, 2007, p. 2). Comparably, Miller et al. (2007) expanded on this definition and defined the process as ascertaining "a student's abilities, attitudes, aptitudes, interests, work behaviors, levels of self-determination and self-advocacy skills, interpersonal skills, academic skill level, and independent living skills over an extended period of time for the purpose of planning and appropriate individual education program" (p. 5).

From these viewpoints, prior to formulating or updating a transition plan, for students with ASD, it is important for the multidisciplinary team to use age/grade appropriate assessment protocols. According to Mazzotti, Rowe, Kelley, Test, Fowler, Kohler, and Kortering (2009) this is a critical first step and should include both formal and informal assessments. Table 1 provides a summary of various formal standardized assessments.

Unlike formal standardized assessments, informal assessments are nonstandardized and tend to be subjective (Mazzotti et al., 2009). Below is a truncated list of examples of informal evaluations:

- **Curriculum-Based Assessments**: Classroom work samples (e.g., homework, tests, etc.)
- **Direct Observations**: Observations in multiple settings and environments (e.g., classroom, lunchroom, etc.)

Table 1: Formal Assessment

Type of Assessment	Assessment Protocols
• Intelligence Test	• Stanford-Binet Intelligence Test • Wechsler Intelligence Scale for Children IV
• Achievement Test	• Brigance • Woodcock-Johnson III
• Adaptive Behavior Rating Scale	• Scales of Independent Behavior-Revised • Vineland Adaptive Behavior Scales
• Aptitude Test	• Differential Aptitude Test • Bennett's Mechanical Comprehension Test
• Personality & Performance	• Personal Career Development Profile • Student Styles Questionnaire
• Employability Assessment	• Career Decision Scale • Career Thought Inventory
• Self-Determination	• ARC Self-Determination Scale • Self-Determination Assessment Battery
• Work-Related Temperament Scales	• Becker Work Adjustment Inventory
• Postsecondary Support Needs Assessment	• AAIDD Supports Intensity Scale

- **Ecological Assessments**: Analysis of various settings and environments (e.g., classroom, bedroom, etc.)
- **Interviews**: Structured and unstructured conversations with the student and various stakeholders in his or her life (e.g., parents, siblings, etc.)
- **Questionnaires**: Surveying the student and individuals involved in his or her life (e.g., interest inventories, etc.)

Ultimately, **transition assessment** for students with ASD should begin as early as possible (see Schall, 2009) and Test, Aspel, and Everson (2005) suggested the various procedures should consist of the following six prongs:

- Ongoing & Continuous Process
- Student Centered
- Occur Across a Variety of Environments
- Involve Multiple Stakeholders
- Understandable Data
- Cultural Sensitivity

Finally, transition assessment should encompass all areas which (a) assist multidisciplinary teams when developing effective transition components and (b) better serve the needs of students (Test & Mazzotti, 2011).

TRANSITION & FAMILIAL INVOLVEMENT

Although Chapter 6 was dedicated to collaborating with families, it would be negligent not to provide a mere snapshot of the vital role families play during the various transitional phases. Without delving into the intricacies, the literature reports that family involvement has been identified as one of the primary components of best practices in transition planning, without their input, multidisciplinary teams are often left floundering. For additional information for working with families see deFur, Todd-Allen, and Getzel (2001); Grigal and Neubert (2004); Kohler and Field (2003); Mundschenk and Foley (1994); Test, et al. (2006); Wandry and Pleet (2012); Walraven, Fitzpatrick, Velarde, Allen, and Rodriguez (2010).

TRANSITION PLANNING

It should be fairly evident multidisciplinary teams serve numerous functions including identifying and ensuring appropriate supports (e.g., accommodations and modifications, transportation, etc.) are being provided to students with disabilities in accordance with their **individualized education program** (IEP).

Transition planning is a vital section of the IEP. The team, in conjunction with several internal and external stakeholders, including but not limited to the (a) student (as appropriate), (b) parents or guardians (see Chapter 6 for the value & importance of family involvement), (c) siblings (as appropriate), (d) educational constituents (e.g., teachers, administrators, etc.), (e) outside service providers (e.g., Vocational Rehabilitation), and (f) medical personnel (e.g., doctor, nurse, etc.) is responsible for developing a transition plan.

IDEIA (2004) mandated that transition planning must begin prior to the students sixteenth birthday and be updated annually. Additionally IDEIA included the following provisions: (a) appropriate measurable postsecondary goals based upon age appropriate transition assessments (Section 614(d)(1)(A)(VII)(aa)), (b) development of transition services to help students achieve the goals (Section 614(d)(1)(A)(VII)(bb)), and (c), no later than one year before reaching the age of majority under State law, document that the student was informed of his or her rights (Section 614(d)(1)(A)(VII)(cc)).

Transition planning is typically associated with students in high school, however, Hallahan and Kauffman (2006) advocated that such preparation for students with ASD should begin in elementary school, if not sooner. Similarly, the mission of a middle school education is to prepare students for their future (Repetto, 2012) and as students with ASD enter this phase of their educational careers, multidisciplinary teams should begin shifting their focus away from academic deficits towards the skills they require to be successful in life.

PERSON-CENTERED TRANSITION PLANNING

Within the last decade **person-centered transition planning** has emerged as an approach to serving students with disabilities (Hagner, May, Kurtz, & Cloutier, 2014). The goal of this multipronged method is to assist the student and the family to cultivate a vision for the future (Schall 2009; Weham & Targett, 2012). Similar to most SPED processes, person-centered transition planning requires a multidisciplinary team approach and allows students with disabilities to be active participants when developing their transition plan.

As discussed in Chapter 2, full participation—by the student—is one of the four stated outcomes of IDEIA (see Turnbull, Turnbull, Wehmeyer, & Shogren, 2010), however, it poses several significant challenges when engaging students with ASD (see Hagner et al., 2014). Nevertheless researchers have reported notable positive outcomes for students with ASD when they have been involved in the development of their transition plan (see Held, Thoma, & Thomas, 2004; Smith, McDougall, & Edelen-Smith, 2006).

Multidisciplinary teams can select from numerous person centered models including but not limited to (a) Essential Lifestyle Planning (see Smull & Harrison, 1992), (b) Making Action Plans (see Falvey, Froest, Pearpoint, & Rosenbuerg, 1997), (c) McGill Action Planning System (see Vandercook, York, & Forest, 1989), (d) Personal Futures Planning (see Mount, Ducharme, & Beeman, 1991), (e) Planning Alternative Tomorrows with Hope (see Falvey, Pearpoint, & Rosenbuerg, 1994), and (f) Whole Life Planning (see Butterworth, Hagner, Heikkinen, Faris, Demello, & McDonough, 1993).

Each of the aforementioned models encapsulates common characteristics (Whitney-Thomas, Shaw, & Honey, 1998) including personal empowerment; involvement of family and friends; and focus on preferences, talents, and dreams (Butterworth, Whitney-Thomas, & Steer, 1997). Despite which model the multidisciplinary team chooses to adopt and/or employ, there are five basic steps they must follow when developing a person-centered transition plan. The team must:

- Identify leadership roles.
- Review assessment data and conduct additional assessments (as necessary).
- Develop service and support plans.
- Update the IEP or transition plan IEP.
- Hold an exit meeting (see Wehman et al., 2009; p. 28).

TRANSITION SERVICES

IDEIA (2004) outlined the provisions for transition services as (a) a coordinated set of activities for a child with a disability that (1) is designed to be within a results-oriented process that is focused on improving the academic and functional achievement of the child with a disability to facilitate the child's movement from school to post-school activities, including postsecondary education, vocational education, integrated employment (including supported employment), continuing an adult education, adult services, independent living, and community participation; (2) is based on the individual child's needs while taking into account the child's strengths preferences, and interests; and (3) includes:

- Instruction;
- Related services;

- Community experiences;
- The development of employment and other post school adult living objectives; and
- If appropriate, acquisition of daily living skills and functional vocational evaluation.

(b) Transition services for children with disabilities may be special education, it provided as specially designed instruction, or related services, if required…The challenge the disability benefit from special education (see 20 U.S.C. 1401(34); 34 CFR § 300.43(a)).

TRANSITION & POST-HIGH SCHOOL OPTIONS

Developing and implementing a transition plan is often time consuming and can be extremely tedious. However, despite the intensive efforts, the ultimate aim is to develop appropriate goals, benchmarks, services, etc. to help each student meet his or her post-high school aspirations, this is especially true for students with ASD. Therefore it is vital for team members to provide transition services that empower the student in order to help him or her achieve optimal success upon graduation.

Over the last few decades community support services for individuals with disabilities have greatly increased. This is especially evident when considering the monumental progress the disability community has made since Blatt and Kaplan (1974) published *Christmas in Purgatory: A Photographic Essay on Mental Retardation* which provided readers with shocking images resulting from The Eugenics Movement. Keeping this in mind, there are abundant available resources for individuals with ASD after graduating from high school, however, this section will focus on (a) **postsecondary education**, (b) **supported employment**, and (c) **customized employment** options.

Postsecondary Education. Within the last two-to-three decades the number of individuals with disabilities attending colleges and universities has greatly increased. Unlike students with high incidence disabilities (i.e., learning disability), for students with ASD selecting the appropriate postsecondary institution is vital to helping ensure they are successful academically, socially, and emotionally.

While the student is still in high school, the multidisciplinary team can assist the transition process by identifying vocational technical schools and/or 2-and-4 year institutions which have (a) the training certificate or degree program the student is seeking and (b) an outstanding disability support service office. However, it is important to note, in accordance with **Section 504 of the Rehabilitation Act** and **Americans with Disabilities Act,** postsecondary institutions are only required to offer reasonable supports, thus FAPE no longer applies.

Supported Employment. Traditionally, individuals with ASD were either (a) institutionalized or continued to receive home care (see Howlin & Chalmers, 2002; Howlin, Goode, Hutton, & Rutter, 2004) or (b) minimally employed at vocational workshops or activities centers (see García-Villamisar, Wehman, & Diaz Navarro, 2002; Howlin, 2000). Although it is beyond the scope of this chapter to delve into the various reasons for unemployment and underemployment for individuals with ASD, the literature suggested factors range from a dearth of sophisticated support networks (e.g., family, friends, etc.) to negative perceptions and public opinion (e.g., employer, customer, etc.).

Supported employment has become an effective method to help alleviate the unemployment gap, thus increasing the employability of individuals with disabilities (see Dowler & Walls, 2014). The **Federal Register** (2001) defined supported employment as:

(i) Competitive employment in an integrated setting with ongoing support services for individuals with the most severe disabilities—

  (A) For whom competitive employment has not traditionally occurred or for whom competitive employment has been interrupted or intermittent as a result of a severe disability; and

  (B) Who, because of the nature and severity of their disabilities, need intensive supported employment services for the designated State unit and extended services after transition in order to perform this work; or

(ii) Transitional employment for individuals with the most severe disabilities due to mental illness (34 CFR 361.5[b] [53]).

There are several supported employment models including but not limited to (a) Diversified Placement Approach, (b) Enclave, (c) Individual Placement and Support, (d) Mobile Work Crew, (e) Small Business, and (f) Vocational Rehabilitation (see Dowler & Walls, 2014; Kellerman, 2001; Test et. al., 2005; Test & Mazzotti, 2011). Each of these approaches often has either **job coaches** or **employment specialists** who work with individuals to help them achieve their employment goals while simultaneously maintaining competitive employment in the community (Targett & Wehman, 2011; Wehman, Targett, & Young, 2007).

Customized Employment. Individuals with severe disabilities have abysmal employment rates (Griffin, Hammis, Geary, & Sullivan, 2008). Therefore, in 1988 Congress made a concerted effort to support the employment needs of individuals with severe disabilities by passing the Workforce Investment Act which consolidated over 60 federal training programs into three block grants to states (a) adult employment and training, (b) disadvantaged youth employment and training, and (c) adult education and family literacy programs (Targett, Young, Revell, Williams, & Wehman, 2007)). Unlike traditional employment methods, customized employment offers alternative approaches which have helped improve the career outcomes of individuals with disabilities (Silverman (2013)). The **Office of Disability Employment Policy** (2014) defined customized employment as:

> Customized employment is a flexible process designed to personalize the employment relationship between a job candidate and an employer in a way that meets the needs of both. It is based on an individualized match between the strengths, conditions, and interests of a job candidate and the identified business needs of an employer. Customized Employment utilizes an individualized approach to employment planning and job development—one person at a time…one employer at a time. Customized employment will often take the form of:
>
> - **Task Reassignment**: Some of the job tasks of incumbent workers are reassigned to a new employee. This reassignment allows the incumbent worker to focus on the critical functions of his/her job (i.e., primary job responsibilities) and complete more of the central work of the job. Task reassignment typically takes the form of job creation, whereby a new job description is negotiated based on current, unmet workplace needs.
> - **Job Carving**: An existing job description is modified—containing one or more, but not all, of the tasks from the original job description.
> - **Job Sharing**: Two or more people share the tasks and responsibilities of a job based on each other's strengths.
>
> Less common—though becoming more established throughout the country—is Self-Employment as a form of Customized Employment. Self-Employment allows for an individual to receive assistance in the creation of an independently owned small business (typically a micro enterprise, under five employees) based on the strengths and dreams of an individual and the unmet needs of a local market while incorporating the individualized planning and support strategies needed for success.

Similar to supported employment, customized employment increases competitive employment, career advancement, competitive pay, job satisfaction, and integration for individuals with severe disabilities (Fesko, Varney, DiBiase, & Hippenstiel, 2008) including those with ASD.

MAX'S SCENARIO

Max and I have been through many life transitions, several of which have been directly related to his education and academic outcomes. For example, on a macro level, he has transitioned from being at home—with mom—to pre-school, pre-school to elementary school, elementary school to middle school, and is now preparing to make the major leap from middle school to high school. Additionally, on a micro level, Max has daily transitional routines such as going from home-to-school, class-to-class, and school-to-home. Regardless of the level, these experiences have been different and brought up many feelings and emotions.

Unlike families who do not have kids with disabilities, those with children with disabilities encounter additional challenges during new developmental phases. Our family faced these additional challenges as we transitioned Max from a SPED early childhood program (our safe and familiar place) into kindergarten (the great unknown).

When Max transitioned from pre-school to kindergarten, it was a milestone that brought about the realization a phase in our life was ending and a new era was about to begin.

Similar to most parents of children entering into new developmental phases, this transition was accompanied with a myriad of feelings including apprehension, excitement, nervousness, anticipation, and fear of the unknown. Knowing how difficult it was for Max to adapt to change, we began early by preparing for this transition the previous spring.

As a former teacher and a current teacher educator, I knew early school success would build a solid foundation for Max's long-term academic career while simultaneously positively impacting his overall achievement, so we engaged in many typical preparatory events. To prepare for his entry into kindergarten, we attended Kindergarten Round Up, completed the required forms, scheduled doctor's appointments to ensure immunizations were up to date, and headed to the store for new clothes and school supplies. As a mother, I knew participating in these activities would help facilitate his success, not just for the transition into kindergarten, but the duration of the school year.

Looking back, Max's transition into kindergarten was far from smooth, but the extensive time and effort on the part of all of the adults who helped make his first year was successful. As discussed throughout this chapter, transitioning is often extremely difficult for students with ASD, and this was especially true for Max during the early grades. Despite the tumultuous start, somewhere between third and fourth grade, elementary school became our new safe haven. The thought of leaving this place was scary—one teacher who knew Max well, responded to his needs, accommodated for his disability (i.e., academically, behaviorally, & socially), ensured we were notified about the information they needed in a timely manner (i.e., notes, emails, phone calls, etc.). Further, this teacher helped create a safe haven where Max began establishing friendships.

At the beginning of his fifth grade year, we suddenly realized Max would be leaving his familiar refuge and transition to a new environment—a middle school which would be—double in size of the elementary school—where he would experience complete anonymity. He would be shuffled between more than six teachers a day with 25-35 students per class. Doing the math, I concluded most teachers would encounter more than 100 students a day which meant there would be no more notes, emails, or phone calls informing us about his successes or concerns. I was also worried how they would ever have time to get to know Max, let alone provide him with the appropriate accommodations and modifications he required to be successful. A compounding issue was he would be intermingling with students from all over the district and basically starting over socially. My fears of Max wondering around lost and never making it home, set in. Were they exaggerated? Perhaps or perhaps not, regardless, the feelings and scenarios that ran through my mind were very real and extremely overwhelming.

The transition meeting from elementary to middle school was much different than what I had experienced from pre-school to elementary school. Only the guidance counselor was in attendance which did not help quiet my qualms about how the teachers would get to know Max and learn what he needed. I began thinking the teachers are already too busy for him.

I was hoping at least a sixth grade teacher would have attended the meeting, so the team would hear how well he was doing, but more importantly to discuss the strategies, accommodations, and modifications that were in place to help Max be successful.

Several strategies were mentioned, some were accepted, some maybe's, some no's, and some, "we don't do that in middle school." I felt myself growing frustrated and was about to cry as I tried expressing my concerns:

> These (elementary) teachers don't do all of these things (one being Lunch Bunch--where several teachers joined the group just because they wanted to, even though it wasn't on Max's IEP), because they have to; they do it because they care about Max and because they know it makes a difference.

At the conclusion of the meeting, the counselor and I were left at the table. He leaned over and said, "It will be okay. Max really is going to be ok. We will take good care of him." I was skeptical and spent the summer doubting and worrying. Who was this guy kidding? No one enjoys middle school!

At the time of writing this book, Max is getting ready to transition to high school. I am not sure if I am ready—in fact, I know I am not. But, Max is more than ready. His teachers in middle school, at each grade level and at two different schools (we moved in the middle of his 7th grade year) have gone *above and beyond* by working to meet Max's needs and by making sure I have the information I needed. In addition, his teachers made sure he was not only successful with his academic goals, but also his social goals.

While I recognize Max had three wonderful and successful middle school years, I know this is not the case for all students with disabilities. Middle school often provides less inclusion opportunities and is a time when the gap grows wider between students with disabilities and their nondisabled peers.

While we have endured several life and school transitions, some have gone smoother than others, and new transitions are still accompanied with the anxiousness, apprehension, nervousness, excitement, and fear. Some less than others, and preparation helps, but leaving the safe place to step into the unknown is always tough. However, with the support of understanding teachers and loving parents and caregivers, transitions do not always have to be negative.

PROFESSIONAL ANALYSIS

Transition: The Historical Evolution from Voluntary to Mandated Supports and Services

By

Dr. Jerald M. Liss, Emporia State University

The area of transition has evolved from a one dimensional focus on employment used in the work-study movement of the 1960s and the career education movement of the 1970s to a multi-dimensional perspective that now includes independent living, community participation, social and interpersonal relationships and postsecondary education or training (Sitlington & Clark, 2006). But this evolution has taken time to become mandated in legislation. The original Education for All Handicapped Children Act of 1975 did not mandate transition services (Sitlington & Clark, 2006). The Education for All Handicapped Children Act Amendments of 1983 *encouraged* states and local school districts to voluntarily provide transition services and supports for students with disabilities (Kochar, Shaw, & Izzo, 2007).

In 1990, Congress made the decision to mandate transition services for students with disabilities when the Education for All Handicapped Children Act was reauthorized as IDEA (Repetto & Correa, 1996). IDEA (1990) included a section where "a requirement is stipulated that transition planning as part of the Individualized Education Program must occur for all students with disabilities no later than age 16" (Halpern, 1994, p. 117).

Another critical advance that emerged from the 1990 reauthorization was how the federal definition of transition services moved beyond a sole focus of employment. The new definition for transition services was:

> A coordinated set of activities for a student, designed within an outcome-oriented process, which promotes movement from school to post-school activities, including postsecondary education, vocational

> training, integrated employment (including supported employment), continuing and adult education, adult services, independent living, or community participation. The coordinated set of activities shall be based upon the individual student's needs, taking into account the student's preferences and interests, and shall include instruction, community experiences, the development of employment and other post-school adult living objectives, and when appropriate, acquisition of daily living skills and functional vocational evaluation.(IDEIA 2004, 20 U.S.C. § 1401 et seq.)

Importantly, this legislative definition had moved much closer to the broad professional position that had been put forward by the field (Halpern, 1994). When IDEA was reauthorized in 1997, it maintained the definition of transition services from IDEA 1990, but added a provision that the "coordinated set of activities" could include related services such as counseling services or orientation and mobility (Neubert, 2006).

In addition, IDEA 1997 introduced several critical changes. First, it required transition services to begin at age 14 instead of age 16, a change which was widely praised by the field (Clark, 2007), though, inexplicably, it was changed back to 16 in IDEIA 2004. Second, IDEA 1997 mandated interagency collaboration to coordinate and plan transition services (Kochhar-Bryant, 2003). IDEA 1997 also required students with disabilities be included in state and district assessments along with their peers in the general population (Neubert, 2006). While this was not a mandate for additional transition services, it served as a precursor for later legislative evolutions in transition.

Indeed, the next evolution occurred when IDEA was reauthorized in 2004 and the policy language became far more results-oriented (Turnbull, Stowe, & Huerta, 2007). The earlier transition provisions in IDEA 1990 and 1997 focused on transition processes that used an outcome-oriented approach. But the IDEIA 2004 transition provisions shifted the language from outcome-oriented to results-oriented.

To attain a results-oriented approach, the transition provisions in IDEIA (2004) called for measurable postsecondary goals based upon age-appropriate transition assessments (Morningstar & Liss, 2008). The transition definition in IDEIA (2004) also stated that transition services were to be within a results-oriented process that is focused on improving the academic and functional achievement of the student with a disability to facilitate the student's movement from school to post-school activities (Sec. 614). The key term was *academic and functional achievement.* Clearly, the legislative definition and the ensuring transition mandates had evolved significantly from a sole focus on employment to a far broader perspective.

The field of transition has made many progressive steps. This is good news for students such as Max, whose life story is shared throughout this book. The field of transition now can provide students with ASD with assistance to prepare for many areas of life. The evolution described in the section above focuses on the legislative history of transition. As was described, transition supports and services are now mandated by IDEIA (2004) for students with disabilities, and this includes students with ASD. Transition supports and services have evolved to where they now require results-oriented processes that use transition assessments and measurable goals for life after high school. These strides forward mean students such as Max will receive a written IEP which now includes measurable postsecondary goals based upon transition assessment data (Neubert & Leconte, 2013). This represents a significant evolution in the field.

Thus the field of transition has come a long way from the time when states and local school districts were *encouraged* to voluntarily provide transition supports and services to a student such as Max. Though many challenges remain, it is clearly evident how much Max and other students with ASD will benefit from mandated transition services.

SUMMARY & CONCLUSION

In the introduction of this chapter, readers were asked to reflect on their daily routines and the thought processes they employed while making major life decisions. While the structure of these exercises was fairly broad, the goal was to help readers contextualize the various transitional phases that take place during the day and throughout a lifetime.

From these perspectives, it should be evident the multidisciplinary team—including the family and outside service providers (as appropriate)—have a tremendous responsibility for mapping out and developing age, grade, and developmentally appropriate transition plans and services to help students with ASD be successful academically, socially, emotionally, and ultimately in life after high school.

References

[34 CFR 300.43 (a)] [20 U.S.C. 1401(34)], (2004). Retrieved April 26, 2014, from http://www.law.cornell.edu/uscode/text/20/1401

20 U.S.C. § 1400 et seq. (1990). Individuals with disabilities education act.

20 U.S.C. § 1400 et seq. (2004). Individuals with disabilities education improvement act.

Arnett, S., Fitzpatrick, M., & Theoharis, R. (2013). *Foundations of special education: Understanding students with exceptionalities.* Dubuque, IA: Kendall Hunt.

Baron-Cohen, S., & Wheelwright, S. (2004). The empathy quotient: An investigation of adults with Asperger syndrome or high functioning autism, and normal sex differences. *Journal of Autism and Developmental Disorders, 34*(2), 163–175.

Blatt, B., & Kaplan, F. (1974). *Christmas in purgatory: A photographic essay on mental retardation.* Syracuse, NY: Human Policy Press.

Butterworth, J., Hagner, D., Heikkinen, B., Faris, S., Demello, S., & McDonough, K. (1993). Whole life planning: A guide for organizers and facilitators. Boston, Morningside College Graduate Studies Program: Institute for Community Inclusion, Children's Hospital. Retrieved May 13, 2014 from http://www.google.com/url?sa=t&rct=j&q=&esrc=s&source=web&cd=8&ved=0CF4QFjAH&url=http%3A%2F%2Ffiles.eric.ed.gov%2Ffulltext%2FED411616.pdf&ei=Gz1-U-mQLoqPqgac7YCoAw&usg=AFQjCNEeHGStwCcocw8XbtttsAwBOXomEA&sig2=ULFfol5oOYQHYSSLkpXLyQ&bvm=bv.67229260,bs.1,d.b2U&cad=rja

Butterworth, J., Whitney-Thomas, J., & Steere, D. (1997). Using person-centered planning to address personal quality of life. In R. Schalock (Ed.), Quality of life: its application to persons with disabilities. Washington, DC: American Association on Mental Retardation.

Clark, G. M. (2007). *Assessment for transitions planning* (2nd Ed.). Austin, TX: Pro-Ed.

deFur, S. H., Todd-Allen, M., & Getzel, E. E. (2001). Participation in the transition planning process [Electronic version]. *Career Development for Exceptional Individuals, 24*(1), 19–36.

Dowler, D. L., & Walls, R. T., (2014). A review of supported employment services for people with disabilities: Competitive employment, earnings, and service costs [Electronic version]. *Journal of Rehabilitation, 80*(1), 11–21.

Education of All Handicapped Children Act of 1975. PL 94--142.

Falvey, M. A., Froest, M., Pearpoint, J., & Rosenbuerg, R. L. (1997). All my life's a circle. Toronto, Ontario: Inclusion Press.

Falvey, M. A., Pearpoint, J., & Rosenbuerg, R. L. (1994). Building connections. In J. S. Thousand, R. A. Villa, & A. I. Nevin (EDs.). Creativity and collaborative learning: A practical guide to empowering students and teachers. Baltimore, MD: Paul H Brookes.

Federal Register, (2001). Rules and regulations 34 CFR 361.5[b] [53].*66*(11) p. 4389. Retrieved April 26, 2014, from http://www.ors.ri.gov/SE.html

Fesko, S., Varney, E., DiBiase, C., & Hippenstiel, M. (2008). Effective partnerships: Collaborative efforts that support customized employment [Electronic version]. *Journal of Vocational Rehabilitation, 28,* 159–169.

Fitzpatrick, M. (2010). Operation mindcrime: An era of globalized media consumers. Educating Youth for Citizenship*: East and West.*

Fragoso, A., Gonçalves, T., Ribeiro, C. M., Monteiro, R., Quintas, H., Bago, J., Fonseca, H., & Santos, L. (2013). The transition of mature students in higher education: Challenging traditional concepts? [Electronic version]. *Studies in the Education of Adults, 45*(1), 67–81.

García-Villamisar, D., Wehman, P., & Diaz Navarro, M. (2002). Changes in the quality of autistic people's life that work and supported and sheltered employment: A 5-year follow-up study [Electronic version]. *Journal of Vocational Rehabilitation, 17*(4), 309–312.

Griffin, C., Hammis, D., Geary, T., & Sullivan, M. (2008). Customized employment: Where we are; where we're heading [Electronic version]. *Journal of Vocational Rehabilitation, 28*, 135–139.

Grigal, M., & Neubert, D. A. (2004). Parents' in-school values and post-school expectations for transition aged youth with disabilities [Electronic version]. *Career Development for Exceptional Individuals, 27*(1), 65–85.

Hagner, D., May, J., Kurtz, A., & Cloutier, H. (2014). Person-centered planning for transition-aged youth with autism spectrum disorders [Electronic version]. *Journal of Rehabilitation, 80*(1) 4–10.

Hallahan, D. P., & Kauffman, J. M. (2006). *Exceptional learners: An introduction to special education* (10th ed.). Upper Saddle River, NJ: Pearson.

Halpern, A. S. (1994). The transition of youth with disabilities to adult life: A position statement of the Division on Career Development and Transition [Electronic version]. *Career Development for Exceptional Individuals, 17*(2), 115–124.

Halpern, A. S. (1994). The transition of youth with disabilities to adult life: A position statement of the Division on Career Development and Transition. *Career Development for Exceptional Individuals, 17*(2), 115–124.

Harrison, J., & Hare, D.J. (2004). Brief report: Assessment of sensory abnormalities in people with autistic spectrum disorders. *Journal of Autism and Developmental Disorders, 34*, 727–730.

Held, M. F., Thoma, C. A., & Thomas, K. (2004). The John Jones show: How one teacher facilitated self-determination planning for a young man with autism [Electronic version]. *Focus on Autism and Other Developmental Disabilities, 19*, 177–188.

Howlin, P. (2000). Outcome in adult life were more able individuals with ASD or Asperger syndrome [Electronic version]. *ASD, 4*(1), 63–83.

Howlin, P., & Chalmers, L. (2002). Adults with ASD speak out: Perceptions of their life experiences [Electronic version]. *Focus on ASD and Other Developmental Disabilities, 17*(2), 103–111.

Howlin, P., Goode, S., Hutton, J., & Rutter, M. (2004). Adult outcomes for children with autism [Electronic version]. *Journal of Child Psychology and Psychiatry, 45*, 212–249.

Hyman, S. L., & Towbin, K. E. (2017). Autism spectrum disorders. In M. L. Batshaw, L. Pellegrino, & N. J. Roizen (Ed). Children with disabilities (6th ed. p. 325–343). Baltimore, MD: Brookes.

Kellerman, K. (2001). What's a job coach? Retrieved April 26, 2014, from http://www.come-over.to/FAS/Job Coach.htm

Kochhar-Bryant, C. A. (2003). Federal legislation and state initiatives supporting transition services. In G. Greene & C. A. Kochhar-Bryant (Eds.). *Pathways to successful transition for youth with disabilities* (pp. 64–106). Upper Saddle River, NJ: Pearson Education, Inc.

Koegel, L. (2000). Interventions to facilitate communication in autism. *Journal of Autism and Developmental Disorders, 30*(5), 383–391.

Kohler, P. D., & Field, S. (2003). Transition-focused education: Foundation for the future [Electronic version]. *The Journal of Special Education, 37*, 174–183.

Loftin, R. L., Odom, S. L., & Lantz, J. F. (2007). Social interaction and repetitive motor behaviors. *Journal of Autism and Developmental Disorders, 38*, 1124–1135.

Mazzotti, V. L., Rowe, D. A., Kelley, K. R., Test, D. W., Fowler, C. H., Kohler, P. D., & Kortering, L. J. (2009). Linking transition assessment and postsecondary goals: Key elements in the secondary transition planning process [Electronic version]. *Teaching Exceptional Children, 42*(2), 44–51.

Miller, R. J., Lombard, R. C., & Corbey, S. A. (2007). Transition assessment: Planning transition and IEP development for youth with mild to moderate disabilities. Boston, MA: Pearson.

Morningstar, M. E., & Liss, J. M. (2008). A preliminary investigation of how states are responding to the transition assessment requirements under IDEIA 2004. *Career Development for Exceptional Individuals, 31*(1), 48–55.

Mount, B., Ducharme, G., & Beeman, P. (1991). Person-centered development: A journey in learning to listen to people with disabilities. Manchester, CANNOT: Communitas, Inc.

Mundschenk, N. A., & Foley, R. M. (1994). Collaborative relationships between school and home: Implications for service delivery [Electronic version]. *Preventing School Failure, 39*(1), 16–21.

National Research Council. (2001). *Educating children with autism.* Washington, DC: National Academy Press.

Neubert, D. A. (2006). Legislation and guidelines for secondary special education and transition services. In P. L. Sitlington & G. M. Clark (Eds.). *Transition education and services for students with disabilities (*4th ed.*)* (pp. 35–71). Boston: Pearson Education, Inc.

Neubert, D. A., & Leconte, P. J. (2013). Age-Appropriate transition assessment: The position of the Division on Career Development and Transition. *Career Development and Transition for Exceptional Individuals, 36*(2), 72–83.

Office of Disability Employment Policy (2014). What is customized employment? Retrieved May 13, 2014, from http://www.dol.gov/odep/categories/workforce/CustomizedEmployment/what/index.htm

Repetto, J. B. (2012). Middle school transition education planning and services. In M. Wehmeyer & K. Webb (Ed). Handbook of Adolescent Transition: Education for Youth with Disabilities. NY, NY: Routledge.

Repetto, J. B., & Correa, V. I. (1996). Expanding views on transition. *Exceptional Children, 62*(6), 551–563.

Rusch, F. R., Hughes, C., Agran, M., Martin, J. E., & Johnson, J. R. (2009). Toward self-directed learning, post-high school placement, and coordinated support: Constructing new transition bridges to adult life [Electronic version]. *Career Development for Exceptional Individuals*, *32*, 1–7.

Schall, C. (2009). Educational and transition planning. In P. Wehman, M.D. Smith, & C. Schall (Ed.). Autism & the Transition to Adulthood: Success Beyond the Classroom. Baltimore, MD: Paul Brooks.

Schall, C., & Wehman, P. (2009). Understanding the transition from school to adulthood for students with autism. In P. Wehman, M.D. Smith, & C. Schall (Ed.). Autism & the Transition to Adulthood: Success Beyond the Classroom. Baltimore, MD: Paul Brooks.

Silverman, R. (2013). How customized employment can improve outcomes for adults with intellectual disabilities [Electronic version]. *Exceptional Parent*, *43*(10), 32–34.

Sitlington, P. L., & Clark, G. M. (2006). *Transition education and services for students with disabilities* (4th ed.). Boston: Pearson Education, Inc.

Sitlington, P. L., Neubert, D. A., Begun, W., Lombard, R., & Leconte, L. P. (2007). Assess for success: A practitioner's handbook on transition assessment (2nd ed.). Thousand Oaks, CA: Corwin Press.

Smith, G. J., McDougall, D., & Edelen-Smith, P. (2006). Behavioral cusps: A person-centered concept for establishing pivotal individual, family, and community behaviors and repertories [Electronic version]. *Focus on Autism and Other Developmental Disabilities*, *21*, 223– 229.

Smull, M., & Harriosn, S. B. (1992). Supporting people with severe reputations in the community. Alexandria, VA: NASMRPD.

Targett, P. S., & Wehman, P. (2011). Employment: Community-based choices. In P. Wehman (Ed). Essentials of Transition Planning. Baltimore, MD: Paul H Brookes.

Targett, P., Young, C., Revell, R., Williams, S., & Wehman, P. (2007). Customized employment in the one-stop career centers [Electronic version]. *Teaching Exceptional Children*, *40*(2), 6–11.

Test D. W., & Mazzotti, V. L. (2011). Transitioning from school to employment. In M. Snell & F. Brown (Ed). Instruction of Students with Severe Disabilities (7th ed.). Boston, MA: Pearson.

Test, D. W., Aspel, N., & Everson, J. (2005). Transition methods for youth with disabilities. Columbus, OH: Merrill/Prentice Hall.

Test, D. W., Mazzotti, V. L., Mustian, A. L., Fowler, C. H., Kortering, L., & Kohler, P. (2009). Evidence-based secondary transition predictors for improving postschool outcomes for students with disabilities [Eectronic version]. *Career Development for Exceptional Individuals*, *32*(3), 160–118.

Turnbull, A. P., Turnbull, H. R., Wehmeyer, M. L., & Shogren, K. (2010). Exceptional lives: Special education in today's schools (6th ed.). Upper Saddle River, NJ: Merrill/Prentice Hall.

Turnbull, H. R., Stowe, M. J., & Huerta, N. E. (2007). *Free appropriate public education: The law and children with disabilities* (7th ed.). Denver: Love Publishing.

Vandercook, T., York, J., & Forest, M. (1989). The McGill action planning system (MAPS): A strategy for building the future [Electronic version]. *The Journal of the Association for Persons with severe Handicaps*, *14*(3), 205–215.

Walraven, R., Fitzpatrick, M., Velarde, A., Allen, C., & Rodriguez, J. B., (2010). Analyzing systems for students with emotional and behavior disorders: Bridging the gap via a home visit model. *Border Walking Journal*, *8*(1), 33–43.

Wandry, D. L., & Pleet, A. M. (2012). Family involvement in transition planning. In M. Wehmeyer & K. Webb (Ed). Handbook of Adolescent Transition: Education for Youth with Disabilities. NY, NY: Routledge.

Weham, P., & Targett, K. S. (2012). IEP development in adolescent transition education. In M. Wehmeyer & K. Webb (Ed). Handbook of Adolescent Transition: Education for Youth with Disabilities. NY, NY: Routledge.

Wehman, P., Smith, M. D., & Schall, C. (2009). *Autism & the transition to adulthood: Success beyond the classroom.* Baltimore, MD: Paul Brooks.

Wehman, P., Targett, P., & Young C. (2007). To work for individuals with autism: A supported employment approach [Electronic version]. *Autism Advocate*, *46*(1), 54–58.

Wehmeyer, M., & Webb, K. W. (2012). An introduction to adolescent transition education. In M. Wehmeyer & K. Webb (Ed). Handbook of Adolescent Transition: Education for Youth with Disabilities. NY, NY: Routledge.

Whitney-Thomas, J., Shaw, D. M., & Honey, K. (1998). Building a future: A study of student participation in person-centered planning [Electronic version]. *Persons with Severe Handicaps*, *23*(2), 119–133.

Winn S., & Hay, I. (2009). Transition from school for use with a disability: Issues and challenges [Electronic version]. *Disability & Society*, *24*, 103–115.

6

Working with Families

Chapter Objectives

After studying this chapter readers should be able to:

- Develop an operational definition of family.
- Explain the importance of collaboration between educators and families.
- Summarize 2-to-3 challenges families (i.e. parents, siblings, grandparents, etc.) of children with disabilities often encounter.
- Evaluate the value of familial support networks.

Chapter 6 Subject Index:

1. Autism
2. Collaborating with families.
3. Communication
4. Culture/Diversity
5. Employment Proximity
6. Extended Family Members
7. Families
8. Family Experiences
9. Family Quality of Life
10. Family Size
11. Family Stress
12. Family Systems Theory
13. Fatigue
14. Geographical Location
15. Individuals with Disabilities Education Improvement Act
16. Job Lock
17. Multidisciplinary Teams
18. Quality of Life
19. Siblings
20. Socioeconomic Status
21. Special Education
22. Time Stress

INTRODUCTION

Families have a direct influence on their child's long term academic and social success, as well as their ability to productively participate in society including but not limited to (a) physical and economic resources, (b) emotional support, (c) developing positive environments (i.e., school and career), (d) life expectations, and (e) values and beliefs (Kluwin & Gaustand, 1992). Therefore, working with families is an integral and significant part of the education of any child, especially those with disabilities receiving **special education** (SPED) services (Walraven, Fitzpatrick, Valverde, Allen, & Rodriguez, 2010). This is true across families of all ethnic, racial, economic, and educational backgrounds and for children of all ages and at all grade levels.

Regardless when parents learn about their child's disability (i.e., at birth or during their academic career) tends to have a direct impact on family life (Jackson & Turnbull, 2004). Thus, the family's well-being is critical because the importance of their influence in the lives and development of young children and children with disabilities is widely recognized (Allen & Petr, 1996; Bodner-Johnson, 1986; Karpowitz, 1991; Turnbull & Turnbull, 2001).

Given the abundance of research regarding the importance of supporting familial involvement in relation to improving academic outcomes, social achievements, and ultimately success in life—it is not surprising—that the **Individuals with Disabilities Education Improvement Act** (IDEIA, 2004), strongly supports parental rights through active involvement in their child's education.

From these perspectives this chapter will explore the following vital topics (a) who makes up today's **families** of children with disabilities, (b) the challenges these families often face, (c) issues of **quality of life**, (d) relationships with **extended family members**, (e) thoughts and feelings of **siblings**, and (f) **collaborating with families**.

TODAY'S FAMILIES

While families may be considered the building blocks of the world, each of these blocks has their own unique characteristics. Moreover, the word family is often associated with memories and mental images—and for each of us these are different. For example, do the images conjure up only the people you live with? Or can they include extended family members, close friends, or even outside caregivers (i.e., nanny or butler)? For many, these mental images can be redefined over time as the status of parents, partners, and siblings change as a result of divorce, separation, death, or remarriage.

Historically, little agreement exists among researchers and theorists regarding the definition of family. Burgess's (1926) defined family as a "unity of interacting personalities with its own history" (p. 3). In 1964 Christensen defined family as married couples with children. The U.S. Census Bureau defined family as a group of two or more people related by birth, marriage, or adoption who live together (Iceland, 2000). Each of these definitions creates a lens through which to view families, and these images that appear shape both policy and practice (Lynch & Hanson, 2011). Consider Boyden's (1993) explanation:

> Families bear the brunt of humanity's troubles. At their best, they make a profound contribution to the health of society and its individuals: preserving culture, values, ethics, and wealth; defending the weak; carrying out the great unpaid work of the world. At their worst, they resist change, restrict individual freedom, and indulge in prejudices that can lead to conflict. Their power to form and reshape human minds is forever being rediscovered. Good or ill, we cannot do without them—they are the building blocks of our world (p. 20).

As you, the reader, reflect on these definitions, do they align with the images that come to mind when you think of the word family? Regardless of your stance, it is important to note, as a current or future educator, the students in your classroom will likely be a part of families different than your own. Similarly their families may significantly vary from how you define the term. In alignment with Poston, Turnbull,

Mannan, Marquis, and Wang's (2003) summary, this textbook will refer to family as two-or-more individuals who carry out the functions, roles, and responsibilities a family generally performs.

Schools rely strongly on family involvement in order for students to achieve academically, behaviorally, socially, and emotionally (Decker, 2001; Walraven et al., 2010). In order to attain any level of success, educators need to recognize the family unit is still a significant source of influence (Wedig & Nock, 2007) and become familiar with the characteristics of families, and advocate for cooperative relationships between educators and families (Webber & Plotts, 2008).

Educators need to be aware how their past experiences, background, values, and beliefs can shape their opinions and lead to assumptions about the families they work with. Webber and Plotts (2008) described three categories within family units that can have a positive or negative impact on students with disabilities:

- **Family**: This involves family size, socioeconomic status, single vs. two parent homes, cultural diversity, and parental educational levels.
- **Education Environment**: This involves peer groups; social interactions; bullying or being bullied; and teacher, student, and family interactions.
- **Community**: This involves the geographical location, neighborhood dynamics, employment opportunities, resource accessibility, and recreational activities.

It is important to be careful making assumptions regarding family size, culture, socioeconomic level, and place of residence. For example, your colleagues may make derogatory statements about a group of students from a specific apartment complex. They may make over generalized comments about how their parents are uninterested in their child's education. As you gain experience teaching may lead you to realize while this may be true of a few families, it is not true of all.

Family Size. Size can be defined differently depending on each family's definition. As should be expected families are all different sizes. Some will be single parent families as a result of divorce, separation, death, or choice. In addition, the size of a family does not remain the same, but will often change over time (i.e., births, remarriages, and deaths).

Culture/Diversity. Family diversity is multidimensional. Thus, it is apparent in family membership; sociocultural and socioeconomic status, language, culture, and cultural identification; religion; race; ethnicity; values; and traditions. Families also differ in the ways they choose to perform everyday family functions (Lynch & Hanson, 2011). It is important to realize each of us has our own cultural background that influences the choices we make and serves as the foundation for our values and beliefs.

Socioeconomic Status. Socioeconomic status (SES) refers to an individual's or a family's position within a hierarchical social structure. SES depends on a combination of factors, such as occupation, education level, salary, wealth, and geographical location. A family's SES has an impact on the decisions and choices they make as well as on their life individually and as a family unit.

Geographical Location. Geographical factors can have significant impact on service delivery and family life, rural and urban factors specifically (Butera, 2005; Ridgley & Hallam, 2006). It is difficult for students to receive appropriate services when they are geographically far apart (Turnbull, Turnbull, Erwin, Soodak, & Shogren, 2015). Another difficulty in rural settings, it is difficult to hire and retain highly qualified teachers and other professionals (Theoharis, 2008). Comparing and contrasting rural and urban settings both have positive and negative aspects. Rural communities often provide more social support through informal networks, such as neighbors or churches. By contrast, living in an urban community can make parent-professional relationships difficult to establish (Turnbull et al., 2015).

Finally, some families have careers that require them to relocate frequently (i.e., military, construction workers, or migrant farmers). Relocating is difficult for all families especially those with a child with a disability. Establishing a new support system and services can be difficult. It can also be frustrating for faculty and staff while waiting for records and documents to arrive at the new school.

Family Experiences. Families of children with disabilities are similar to families who do not have children with disabilities. Both face challenges and experience life celebrations. While they both may have some similar experiences, there are some significant differences. For example, research suggests families with children with disabilities experience higher levels of **family stress**, employment struggles, and reduced rates of general well-being and quality of life compared to families without children with disabilities.

Families who care for a child with a disability typically experience significantly higher rates of chronic stress measured by employment, economic, and emotional factors. These families face additional challenges and stresses compared to families of children without disabilities including but not limited to (a) demands on time, (b) limited earning potential, (c) increased financial expenditures related to health care needs, (d) limited employment opportunities, and (e) emotional anxiety. In addition, time constraints limit opportunities for parents to have social interaction and advancing their education. Goudie, Fairbrother, Read, and Simpson (2010) divided family stress into the four categories described below:

- **Time Stress:** Parents are must work fewer hours because of increased time needed to provide and coordinate care for their child with a disability.
- **Employment Proximity:** Parents take lower paying jobs closer to home, which limit their employment opportunities, to be available to help with the care giving needs of their child.
- **Job Lock:** Parents take lower paying jobs with limited employment opportunities because of the health insurance benefits are better for their child.
- **Fatigue:** Parents are less available to work long hours and are less productive due to the physical and emotional exhaustion related to providing care.

Although there has not been significant research conducted on the implications for families caring for children with disabilities, it has been reported that raising a child with a disability causes marital strain and increases the probability of divorce or separation (Swaminathan, Alexander, & Boulet, 2006). As briefly described above, research has also indicated there is an impact on employment and income status. For example, mothers of children with disabilities are less likely to be employed outside the home and more likely to receive public assistance (Corman, Noonan, & Reichman, 2005) and fathers are more likely to work less hours compared to fathers who do not have children with disabilities (Noonan, Reichman, & Corman, 2005).

Unfortunately, to date, there are no known studies that have truly captured the overarching economic burden of caring for a child with a disability. Depending on the type of disability, medical devices and services needed, out-of-pocket expenses for the family can be expensive with much of what is required not being covered by traditional health care plans (Anderson, Dumont, Jacobs, & Azzaria, 2007). Anderson et al. (2007) also found that the annual financial impact of a disability for a family ranges from $108 to $8,742. Intuitively, families living in poverty who are raising a child with a disability are more likely to incur out-of-pocket expenditures of $500 or more (Parish, Shattuck, & Rose, 2009). It has also been reported that the average annual out-of-pocket healthcare costs were $535 per year for families raising a child with a disability compared to an average of $192 per year for families that do not have a child with a disability (Goudie et al., 2010). Finally, it was reported 1-in-6 families with children with disabilities had out of pocket medical expenditures greater than $1,300 per year (Goudie et al., 2010).

A limited resource for families of children with disabilities is time. It has been reported that time providing and coordinating services range from 4-to-84 hours a week (Smith, et. al., 2010). When parent provide extensive care over extended periods of time, get little sleep, spend little time socializing, and engage in few leisure activities, health-related symptoms for the parents quickly escalate (Moidrag & Hodapp, 2010). These health problems associated with chronic stress can prevent parents from being able to provide quality care, discourage a meaningful parent-child relationship, and even more generally raise public concern.

It is important to recognize, due impart to the amount of time spending providing care and coordinating services, parents of children with disabilities often lack social interaction and experience less social support compared to families without a child with a disability (Koshti-Richman, 2009). They also have higher levels of fatigue during the day, a greater number of daily stressful events, and receive less emotional support (Smith, Hong, Seltzer, Greenberg, Almeida, & Bishop, 2010). Unfortunately lack of social support has been linked to increased risk factors such as impaired psychological, physiological functioning, morbidity, and mortality (House, Landis, & Umberson, 1988). Further, social isolation and perceived lack of support often are associated with depression, sleep disorders, poor nutrition, and substance abuse (e.g., alcohol and tobacco). These systemic inflammations can significantly increase risk factors for disease such as type II diabetes, arthritis, and cancer.

Based on the aforementioned findings, it is easy to assume having a child with a disability would pose a serious strain on a marriage. While some research reports this to be true (see Meadan, Halle, & Ebata, 2010; Nealy, O'Hare, Powers, & Swick, 2012), it is not representative of all families. For example, one study indicated marital challenges do exist in some families; however, many families enjoy positive experiences raising a child with a disability (see Neely-Barnes & Dia, 2008).

CONCEPT OF FAMILY QUALITY OF LIFE

The concept of **family quality of life** attempts to illustrate the overall degree to which a family's needs are met, extent the they enjoy their time together, and the extent that they are able to participate in activities that are important to them (Poston, Park, Turnbull, Mannan, & Marquis, 2003). The family's quality of life focuses on the family's interactions. This includes their ability to solve problems together, to communicate openly with each other, to enjoy time together, and to have relationships with extended family members (Park, Hoffman, Marquis, Turnbull, Poston, & Mannan, 2003).

RELATIONSHIPS WITH EXTENDED FAMILY MEMBERS

Relationships vary among families in terms of adaptability to change in response to stressors or outside factors, and also in terms of degree of bonding among members. The outputs of family interaction address the fulfillment of their needs and their ability to complete family functions. Family functions include meeting (a) economic, physical, and health care needs; (b) recreation, socialization, and affection needs; and (c) self-identity, educational, and vocational needs (Turnbull, Summers, & Brotherson, 1984).

Relationships among extended family members can be complicated. For families of children with disabilities extended family members can become a great informal system of support in numerous ways. For some families it is not only a support system, but cultural norm that extended family members have a significant role in raising the children. Latinos, for example, tend to have a collective sense of family, often providing a valuable support network (Vega, Hough, & Romero, 1983). Before discussing how extended family members and close friends can improve support, it is important to consider the difficulties parents may face in taking the critical step of telling others.

When considering telling close family and friends their child has a disability, parents may worry how others will react or respond to the news. Often many will accept the information and begin offering support. There may be some that deny the disability exists or disagree with the diagnosis. Some reactions can be hurtful and uninformed. Letting others know about the disability can be challenging, but often is a great relief for all involved. Avoiding talking about it can send a message to extended family members there is a *secret* which can be accompanied with feelings of shame, embarrassment, and guilt.

Teachers should be cognizant that parents of students with disabilities, especially those with **autism**, oftentimes require informal support networks comprised of both family and friends to help meet the family's emotional needs and care for the child. In addition, the needs of families change as the child transitions into different phases of life. Synapse Organization (www.autism-help.org/family-friends-support-autism.htm) provides a tip sheet for ways friends and families can offer support. These tips are good to keep in mind (and may be offer as a suggestion) as you think about the families in your classroom.

- **Learn more about the disability**. The more knowledgeable extended family members and friends are about the disability, the better equipped they will be when providing support to the family and for the child. This is important because consistent approaches across environments are needed by children with disabilities. For example, if a child with autism goes to a grandparent's house who has taken the time to learn about the characteristics and the child's needs, the grandparents would have a better understanding of why social stories can be an effective strategy in different situations and would be receptive to using various strategies during throughout the visit.
- **Provide the parents with some respite**. All parents enjoy a break from parenting—a night out or some time to themselves on the weekend. This allows them time to regroup and continue to meet life's daily demands.
- **Change expectations**. Extended family members may have expectations of what life was to be like as a grandparent, aunt, or uncle. Grandparents, for example, may have had expectations of sharing hugs, *I love yous*, and bedtime stories. Parents may need to help extended family members readjust their expectations.

While there may be nothing educators need to do, they should be aware of the support network the family has in place. If needed, encourage a support system, share the importance, and offer suggestions. In addition, it is important not to make assumptions about family support systems. For example, do not assume all families from a culturally diverse background have the support of extended family members (Turnbull et al., 2015). Also, ask parents to share which family members are involved or they would like to be involved. Try to develop culturally sensitive ways for including them in the partnership (Turnbull et al., 2015).

FIRST PERSON TESTIMONIAL

Uncle Andrew's Perspective

Our family has learned so much from Max. Max has taught us all about having the odds stacked against us and exceeding every expectation. He has overcome many obstacles and gone from very low functioning (I remember when Raschelle told me she was not sure if he would ever be able to talk) to very high functioning. There is no better team in this world than Max and his mother. Together they have shown us what can happen with the correct tools and a wealth of knowledge. They continue to educate our family about advocacy for individuals with disabilities, adhering to high standards, and focusing on each other's strengths.

Whether I am giving his mom a heart attack by letting him drive my truck or going out squirrel and rabbit hunting, every second is full of enjoyment. I watch Max outwit anyone who crosses his path. From his hard work and dedication, I am amazed by the numerous awards and straight A's he earns on his report cards. He has received distinguished honors and taken a gifted class. I know that Max would not stop there, because he continues to exceed expectations without question. His development through the years is nothing shy of amazing!

Now we get to watch Max hit his teen years, and I laugh just thinking about him growing up so fast. While I leave all of the *little* things to the professionals, I will respectfully disagree with those who say he has problems with social skills. While yes, problems may arise socially and obsessing with things happen from time to time (like his current obsession with being cheap—it can be a good thing, but at times it can be frustrating—when the microwave won't start because he has unplugged it, yet again), these are tiny hurdles for Max to overcome. I believe Max will size you up pretty quick, and if you are lucky enough to be in his life, buckle your seatbelt and take full advantage. He may even be running this whole show one day! Max will be ready for the world, but will the world be ready for him? The possibilities are endless for Max.

Whenever the Theoharis family comes in town, Max joins the cousins in all of the activities. There have been times when we have had to be thoughtful about which activities all of them would enjoy. We have had to consider crowds, noise level, and the level of interactions with others. Max participates in each activity to his own ability and the cousins accept Max for Max. Max has developed a special relationship with each of us. With his great grandmother, they would high five whenever they saw each other (rather than hug). Then, she moved to squeezing his hand with a little shake and eventually she moved to pulling him close and giving him a hug and he willingly would hug her back.

As a young wild uncle and a young child with hurdles to cross, we grew together and will continue to grow through the years. Watching him now, I am truly amazed at how far he has come. Max does not realize quite yet that he has taught me so much more than I could ever teach him.

Max's Truck Story: Fifth Grade (11/16/10)

By

Max Theoharis

THE DAY I DROVE MY UNCLE'S TRUCK

One day after breakfast I went with Uncle Andrew to his work. His work was at a farm. He took me for a ride in his Dodge truck and he showed me how to drive. Then he got out of the truck and let me drive. He even took a video of it. My mom saw the video and she screamed. She was upset because she knew I didn't have a license. Well,…I did not run over Andrew or any of the animals.

Then I and Uncle Andrew went fishing. We rode a boat. The boat had foot peddles. We brought a tasty snack and ate them on the boat. I caught a few fish. I caught a one foot long catfish. It looked weird. Uncle Andrew took a picture. The fish was wiggling and then fell in the water. It went plop. It looked funny.

My mom called. I was sad she got mad and said, "YOU WILL NOT DRIVE UNTIL YOUR OLD ENOUGH!" I thought what she said was mean because she said it loud and sounded mad. Then she hung up. She worries a lot about stuff. Then me and Uncle Andrew went to Aunt Amanda's because we were done fishing. Then Andrew dropped me off. Amanda said, *hi*. Then I said, *hi*. I thought Uncle Andrew was nice since he let me drive his truck and go fishing.

It was a fun day because I drove fast and so did Uncle Andrew. He drove faster than me.

MAX'S SCENARIO

Max was our first child, not only was he our first, but he was the first grandchild, and nephew on both sides of our families. Aside from parenting books that described developmental milestones and the knowledge I had from my courses and textbooks there really was not anyone to compare his development to (our friends started having children right after Max was born and it had been a long time since I babysat). Max was absolutely perfect! He slept through the night by two months (I remember calling the doctor once, because he slept from 7 p.m. to 7 a.m. Only to be told they had never gotten a call from a parent their baby slept too much), and he wasn't overly fussy and was easy to calm. Max never really liked being passed off to new people, but I had read at some ages this was normal. Plus, Max spent his days with me or my sisters until the age of 2 (the time of his diagnosis). Until the age of 2, he was not really around other children unless there was a trip to the park or McDonald's Play Place.

At the age of 2, I began to notice Max was not responding to his name, and really did not seem to have much receptive or expressive language. I scheduled an appointment with an audiologist at the local children's hospital (it is not uncommon for parents of children with autism to begin with a hearing screening or exam). At the time of scheduling this appointment the administrative assistant asked if I would also like to schedule an appointment for speech and language. Since, I knew a hearing loss would impact language development and I was already seeing signs of language delays, I said *yes* and both appointments were made for the same day. There was a sense of relief when the audiologist explained the results. His hearing was in the normal range. There was no real concern when the speech language pathologist said she would recommend speech and language therapy. She stated, *He would only need therapy for a few months. It would catch him up and he would continue to progress with normal language development.*

I contacted the local health department in our area, and Max began speech therapy within a couple of weeks. When we were nearing what I thought should be the end of therapy (not because I noticed a change, but because we had been going for about six weeks), the therapist called me into her office for an update on his progress. This update included the suggestion to pursue further testing and evaluation. She had observed other behaviors that were characteristics of autism (e.g., repetitive behaviors, sensory issues, and stemming). I was overwhelmed with all of the information that had been shared in such a short amount of time.

My mind was going crazy trying to think about who to call, what changes this would mean for our family. Everything had changed in a short 10 minute conversation, but really everything was still the same. It is still difficult to explain and it was even harder to make sense of everything that was happening. My emotions were up and down and could change from minute to minute. This was still my Max I loved him dearly, but there were feelings of great sadness, guilt, and anger. There was denial (when he went for evaluations, or we had IEP meetings I knew the professionals were going to let me know a mistake had been made).

Although family and friends had begun having their own children, I was devastated because no mistake had been made. I was left with the weight of setting up evaluations and appointments for SPED services including speech and language, occupational, physical, and behavior therapies. I decided Max's diagnosis and therapies would remain a secret. I recognize now this was very irrational and I am not sure how I thought I could keep his behaviors and inability to communicate a secret. My rationale seemed logical: first, I wanted everyone to see him as Max and continue loving him as they had and holding him to the same expectations, second, I hated to have everyone worry if this all turned out to be nothing (still thinking, hoping, and praying this was a possibility). And maybe there was a third reason, maybe a little bit embarrassed. I had a degree in education (early childhood, elementary, deaf education with a lot of special education courses) and I felt clueless. Then, there was the social perception, what would people say and was I up for their opinions.

I quickly realized this secret could not continue. I had started hearing, *I don't remember Max ever doing that* or *Max doesn't do that.* Plus, maintaining Max's schedule was like managing a small business! I was taking him to appointments, trying to remember when therapist were coming to our house, and attending meetings. I needed the help and support of family and friends. Some friends left (or their life filled with other things) and new friendships developed. My family continued to love Max and continues to hold high expectations for him rather than making excuses.

From their support and willingness to make a commitment to him and love him when there were no hugs or *I love yous*, he has learned how to develop and maintain a few close relationships. He hunts with Uncle Andrew, ran a donut dash with Aunt Crystal, goes on outings that are spontaneous with Aunt Amanda, and frequents Sonic Happy Hour with Nana. He enjoys time with cousins. Each of these relationships took Max extensive time to develop, but thankfully everyone was willing to invest their time and energy. And these relationships he has built are equally important and significant to me as these individuals have also become part of my support system—that goes beyond *just being* a sister, brother, or mother. For me it helps to have people who understand (the best they can) and are willing to listen and provide support.

The importance of family to Max can be summed up in an 8th grade poem he wrote. The topic of family is intertwined through many of the lines of the poem.

Where I am From

By

Max Theoharis, 2/20/13, 8th grade

I am from trips to Sonic with 44 ounce cherry coke with nana
I am from taco Tuesday at Rancho Grande
I am from going to grandma's and having cool ice cream floats on hot summer days
I am from playing video games to watching TV
I am from "I told you so" and "I told you a million times"
I am from road trips to Kansas City to see friends and family
I am from going to Windstead's and celebrating birthday parties
I am from Christmas time with lots of presents and food
I am from Missouri to Pennsylvania and many places between
I am from friends and family

WORKING WITH SIBLINGS

Siblings of individuals with disabilities have been traditionally overlooked by parents, professionals, and researchers (Arnold, Heller, & Kramer, 2012). While siblings needs have been overlooked, individuals with disabilities and their parents have received extensive research in the field of SPED (Hodapp, Glidden, & Kaiser, 2005). Based on the dearth of existing research, findings suggest siblings' experience a mix of both positive and negative feelings (Gallagher, Powell, & Rhodes, 2006). More specifically, some research studies suggested that having a sibling with a disability has a negative impact on children's adjustment, while others reported positive effects, and others show no difference compared to children who do not have siblings with a disability (Hastings, 2003). Research has also indicated girls tend to be most affected by having a sibling with a disability in the family. The explanation provided in the past has been that girls may have felt the need or have believed they are expected to take on care responsibilities for their sibling. However, a review of research and data has not proven this to be true (Damiani, 1999). Thus, this information continues to show more research is necessary.

Another important factor for educators to keep in mind is the fact that siblings often become the next generation of caregivers when parents are no longer able to provide care (Heller & Kramer, 2009). As parents become less able to provide for the needs of their child with a disability (due to age), the involvement of siblings becomes more necessary. A review of the literature shows that most siblings expect they will take on a greater supportive role in the future (Heller & Arnold, 2010).

Educators working with students with disabilities play a huge role in making a difference in the lives of families. Often when teachers say they are working with families, this is interpreted to mean parents. Siblings are rarely considered by either the educator of the child with a disability or their own teacher as needing support. There are issues siblings of children with disabilities face that are different from their peers and need to be considered or addressed.

It is important to remember siblings of children with disabilities are children first. They need the benefits of childhood, the same as all other children, in order to become confident and productive citizens (Information for Professionals on Supporting Siblings, 2004). However, due to family circumstances this may not be the case or be possible. For example, many siblings often receive little parental attention and have less opportunities, compared to their peers, to participate in extracurricular and social activities. In addition, to the impact on social development, there may also be struggles with academics due to lack of sleep, stress, anxiety, or worry (Information for Professionals on Supporting Siblings, 2004).

Siblings may also make large contributions to caring for the child with a disability, helping with the functioning of everyday family life, or listen to adult concerns. It is also important to be aware some siblings maybe abused by their sibling and it may be tolerated by the family because the sibling *can't help it* (Information for Professionals on Supporting Siblings, 2004). Teachers also need to be aware siblings can be teased because their family is different and due to lack of understanding. Ultimately teachers can support the sibling by providing information and educating others. Children's books that include characters with disabilities can help introduce topics and promote discussion.

Thoughts of Siblings. Below are some thoughts and feelings of siblings family members and educators should be aware of. These can also serve as points for discussions:

- Siblings may wonder what caused their brother or sister's disability. They may also wonder if it is contagious.
- Siblings may feel that having to help care for their brother or sister with a disability may come before their own extracurricular activities or time with friends.
- Siblings may feel guilty about their negative feelings.
- Siblings may feel family members pay more attention to their brother or sister with a disability.
- Siblings may feel anger when their parents or family members spend extra time with their brother or sister with a disability.
- Siblings may worry how to share with their friends that their brother or sister has a disability. For example, they may not want to invite friends over to their house.
- Siblings may worry about their brother or sister's future. Will they be able to live on their own? Get Married? Have children? Will they have to care for their brother or sister if something happens to their parents?
- Siblings may feel their successes go unnoticed by family members, while their brother or sister with a disability gets considerable praise for less significant accomplishments.
- Siblings may feel that their brother or sister with a disability gets away with behaviors that would not be accepted of them.

MELAINA'S THOUGHTS (AGE 12)

To me Max is like a normal brother. We fight like other brothers and sisters. We share, play games together, and love each other, too. Max might have autism, but he acts like everyone else, but sometimes he needs help making friends or talking with other people. One time Max and I were on swim team together in Maryland. There were kids that said things that were not nice to Max. I told those kids they were not so great at swimming and to leave Max alone. I was only in second grade, but I knew it was wrong to make fun of other people.

I do not understand why people are so mean to others especially people with disabilities. Some kids just do not see that they are the same as us or try to be their friends. Now, that Max and I go to the same school, I see Max before and after school and sometimes during lunch. Sometimes, it is hard for me to watch Max sit by himself in the mornings before the bell rings. I know he has started making some friends. I see him talking to other kids. There are some really great things about Max. He is really smart, good at basketball, and he is amazing at 3D Puzzles. Max is a great brother.

Have you ever wondered what it would be like to have autism? I have. I have also wondered what Max wonders about and if he thinks about what it would be like to not have autism. What if Max thinks he is the only boy in the world that has autism? I have also wondered how autism is formed and how do people get autism. Other people may wonder this, too. My mom talked to me about it and when I have questions she tries to explain the answers. I wondered if autism is dangerous. I know Max. And I know, *no Max is 100% not dangerous.*

THEOHARIS FAMILY EXPERIENCE WITH COLLABORATION

Over the past 12 years (since Max began receiving services), we have worked with different professionals with different communication styles and different philosophies for working with families. For the most part, the relationships we have built with professionals have been positive, several continue to check-in on Max's progress even though there are numerous states between us. Often there is sadness, when the year comes to an end and we have to leave these professionals knowing we will be establishing new relationships in the fall when the new school year begins. This, however, is not always the case. There have been occasions, when we cannot wait for the year to end, so that we can have a fresh start.

What is the difference between these relationships? I have found there is a level of respect—a willingness to compromise to meet our needs. The years where the relationship is more positive are years, the teachers readily provide information (one year Max had a teacher who sent nightly emails to the class, another year daily notes went home to parents sharing what Max did that day—it was more of a checklist but was helpful). The times that were not so positive, were years I was constantly asking questions and seeking information from the teacher—feeling like I was *pulling teeth* to get information about Max's education—information that I should have access to, information that would be helpful to be able to support Max at home.

COLLABORATING WITH FAMILIES

There are several positive outcomes when professionals and families build positive collaborative relationships. Educators, parents, and students need to become partners with each other. Over time, they need to build trust. According to Turnbull, Turnbull, Wehmeyer, and Shogren, (2013):

> Without trust, the partnership is week or may not even exist. With trust, the partnership remains strong and can sustain all partners. They can move together to secure good outcomes for the student. But they cannot do it well and joyously without trusting each other. Collaborating with families has an impact on the climate and culture of schools and the academic and social achievement of students (p. 114).

Related to the Law. IDEIA (2004) and other educational laws are not explicit in explaining parents' legal rights in their child's education. That said, it does exist and can be explained (Turnbull, Stowe, & Huerta, 2007). The common-law doctrine is "parents have a duty to support their children and a corollary right to their children's services and earnings for as long as the children have legal status of minors" (Turnbull et al., 2007, p. 292). IDEIA (2004) recognized families as education decision-makers. This recognition has differed meanings among families, teachers, and **multidisciplinary teams**.

IDEIA (2004) mandated that parents are part of the team that makes decisions regarding SPED eligibility, placement, and services. It also stated parents will be regularly informed of their child's progress and will be given copies of evaluation reports. Part C of IDEIA (2004) mandated family-centered early intervention services which may include: family/parent education classes, support and counseling as decided by the team and written in the Individualized **Family Service Plan**. It should be noted, that with each reauthorization of IDEIA (2004) since it was originally passed in 1975 (see Chapter 2), the roles and responsibilities of parents and family members with a disability has become more significant (Bernheimer & Weisner, 2007; Turnbull, 2005).

Turnbull, Turnbull, Erwin, and Soodak (2006) stated there have been eight basic roles of parents (the final being the current):

1. Families are the cause of their child's disability.
2. Families as members of family-centered organizations created to support families' needs.
3. Families as developers of services for their child's needs (i.e., educational, recreational, vocational).
4. Families as essentially passive participants deferring to expert opinion.

5. Families as follow-through educators overseeing and ensuring expected education plans and interventions are followed-through.
6. Families as political advocates.
7. Families as education decision makers and collaborating with educators on educational plans.
8. Families as trust-driven collaborators (discussed below).

The final role not only includes parents, but also the child, extended family members, and close friends. This role understands the needs of an informal support system that is provided by family and friends.

SUCCESSFUL COLLABORATION

Educators must understand families and become familiar with their perspectives in order to know what supports they need as well as how to best collaborate (Friend & Cook, 2010). This chapter has outlined specific challenges families with children with disabilities face at different times and through different transitional phases. Educators need to be aware of the demands and challenges and consider them as they collaborate and develop a relationship with the family. In order to establish successful collaboration, educators need to be aware of communication strategies and factors of positive relationships.

Communication. Traditionally, teachers have communicated, for the most part, with mothers of children with and without disabilities, but there may be others (as described throughout this chapter) who are interested and willing to be a part of the child's education. It is the role of the professional to provide families with the information they need regarding their child's education, how to support the child, and ways to be effective participants in the decision making process (Friend & Cook, 2010).

Additionally, educators need to recognize information needs, answer questions, and provide resources and referrals when necessary. There can be times when information is complex, highly sensitive, or has multiple perspectives and opinions. During these times, it is important to be overly thoughtful in your communication with families. Thomas, Correa and Morsink (2001) offered the following suggestions:

- The location of the meeting should be safe, comfortable, and quiet.
- The number of professionals should be kept to a minimum.
- Talk with parents about the child's strengths and weaknesses.
- Ensure information is presented in a jargon-free manner, use examples of student work, assessments, and observations.
- Allow parent's time to process the information being presented.
- Be sensitive to families needing interpreters (review how to work with interpreters).
- Before the meeting discuss possible conflicts with the multidisciplinary team.
- Use conflict resolution strategies to clarify any possible conflicts with families.

With the challenges and stressors families of children with disabilities often face, it is important to find out the best way to provide them with information. Some parents may not have access to a telephone or internet at home or work or may have difficulty reading. This information is important so that the exchange of information can take place smoothly. It is also important to think about the type of information needing to be shared, some information can be shared in a short email or quick phone call, while other information is better shared in person.

When working with the family, it is important professionals demonstrate respect. To respect others is to value and affirm their strengths. Valuing and affirming strengths is critically important in forming partnerships with families (Turnbull et al., 2013). Commitment, feeling loyalty to one another, is also important when establishing a relationship with families. A committed educator will be available and accessible, go above and beyond what is expected, and be sensitive to the emotional needs of others (Turnbull et al., 2013). In addition, having confidence in another individual's word, judgment, and action—having the confidence that person will act in the best interest of the person who trusts him or her is a key factor in relationships and communication with families. Turnbull et al., (2013) added, "being reliable, using sound judgment, maintaining confidentiality, and trusting yourself" (p. 120) as four practices associated with being a trusted partner.

PROFESSIONAL ANALYSIS

Family Stress & Resiliency Framework

By

Bobbie Jo Kite, *Gallaudet University*

All families experience stress, but stress does not have to be viewed negatively; in fact, stress may promote growth. Changes may result in stress for families; however stress becomes problematic when it affects the family's rituals, rules, hierarchy, boundaries, roles, goals, and equilibrium (Ingoldsby, Smith, & Miller, 2004).

As Ingoldsby et al., 2004 outlined the boundaries of families greatly depend on how much involvement the family allows from the outside world in their lives. How is their worldview? Is the outside world good or bad? Can the world be trusted or not? Are the family members enmeshed as in having their identities closely tied to family's identities? Or do the family members value disengagement, which emphasize independence and autonomy?

The enmeshment and disengagement of family members are based on how they bond and buffer one another (Ingoldsby et al., 2004). How do family members bond with each other? How do they buffer which allows for some time alone? For example, when a family member sneezes and receives concerned attention from other family members (enmeshed) whereas a family member sneezes, and receives a *bless you* comment from other family members (disengaged).

The **Family Systems Theory** includes rituals and traditions (informal activities that shape family bonding which may occur on a daily, weekly, monthly, or yearly basis), rules (both explicit (chores posted) and implicit (do not start eating until everyone is seated at the table), hierarchy (power structure, parents make decisions), roles (dependent, enabler, peacemaker, mediator, hero, delinquent, clown, to name a few), goals (the way family live and carry out their vision) and equilibrium (seeking balance within family) (Ingoldsby et al., 2004; White & Klein, 2002).

We have covered components of how family functions and we will now focus on how families deal with stress using Reubin Hill's ABC-X model. Reubin Hill developed the model of family stress and crisis in 1930s after the Great Depression. From a systematic perspective each individual in the family has an interdependent relationship with every other member (White & Klein, 2002). This occurs in order to maintain equilibrium in the family. If a change is present in the family's life, the change will create a ripple effect throughout the family.

A. The Stressor Event. An event that changes an aspect of the family such as boundaries, rituals, rules, hierarchy, roles, goals, and equilibrium which may include positive and negative events (Ingoldsby et al., 2004). Not all events lead to stress (X), the family may be able to manage the stress level and return to a new equilibrium. Other factors may influence a family's perception of stressful events such as values, beliefs, culture, stage of family life cycle, disability, and accidents (White & Klein, 2002).

B. The Family's Resources. The family's resources may include individual and community's support and contributions. The resources may either be a buffer or increase the impact of stressor events. The resources may include time, monetary, knowledge, support system, network, and extended family members and friends (Ingoldsby et al., 2004).

C. The Meaning Attached to the Event (A) by the Family. How a family view the stressor event determines the meaning the family gives to the stress. The perception is subjective which means a family may view an event as an opportunity while the other may view the same event as overwhelming. Families who are able to reframe a stressful event in a positive way are better able to cope and adapt (Ingoldsby et al., 2004).

D. The Stress & Crisis. The stress represents a change in the family's system. How the family responded to the stressor event places a demand on other family members as of the result. The stress may lead to an imbalance in the equilibrium (Ingoldsby et al., 2004).

The crisis is defined as a disturbance that is so overwhelming that the family system is blocked and immobilized. The boundaries may no longer be maintained, the roles and tasks may no longer be performed (White & Klein, 2002).

There are many factors that could change a family's equilibrium, and it is crucial for all members involved (i.e., teachers, specialists, family members, community members) to recognize what each family needs and how to support them. For example, if a family member loses a job, the stress level is probably high for the family and will most likely impact the child in the classroom. If a child has been identified being on the autism spectrum disorders, the family might need specific resources to support their family members. The goal is to get the family on a new equilibrium.

The Resiliency Framework (Walsh, 2003) outlined resilience as the ability to withstand and rebound from life challenges, positive adaption in contexts of significant adversity and to *struggle well*, heal well and live and love fully.

How is this unique from Family Stress Theory by Reubin Hill outlined above? The resiliency framework focuses on *transformation* and *growth out of adversity* (Walsh, 2003). The key processes of the resiliency framework include the belief systems, organizational patterns and communication patterns.

The belief systems are how the crisis situations viewed by the family and shared beliefs of problem resolution. The organizational patterns of the family includes flexibility, connectedness and social and economic resources (Walsh, 2003). The aspects of the communication patterns are clarity, open emotional expression and collaborative problem solving (Walsh, 2003).

Keep this in mind, *the whole is greater than the sum of its parts* when working with families, especially when trying to understand a child's behavior, you have to think about what is happening with the child as a whole including the family.

SUMMARY & CONCLUSION

Family participation is a key component in the education for individuals with disabilities, and it is guaranteed by IDEIA (2004). Understanding the challenges families of children with disabilities face and how to communicate with families will help when establishing a working relationship that meets the needs of the child with a disability as well as the whole family. A variety of strategies can be used to maintain effective communication with families and build a positive collaborative relationship.

References

20 U.S.C. § 1400 et seq. (2004). Individuals with disabilities education improvement act.

Allen, R. I., & Petr, C. G. (1996). Toward developing standards and measurements for family-centered practice in family support programs. In G. H. S. Singer, L. E. Powers, & A. L. Olson (Eds.), *Redefining family support: Innovations in public-private partnerships* (pp. 57–86). Baltimore: Brookes.

Anderson, D., Dumont, S., Jacobs, P., & Azzaria, L. (2007). The personal costs of caring for a child with disability: A review of literature. *Public Health Reports*, *122,* 3–16.

Arnold, C. K., Heller, T., & Kramer, J. (2012). Support needs of siblings of people with development disabilities. *Intellectual and Developmental Disabilities, 50*(5), 373–382.

Bernheimer, L. P., & Weisner, T. S. (2007). Let me just tell you what I do all day: The family story at the center of intervention research and practice. *Infants & Young Children, 20*, 192–201.

Bodner-Johnson, B. (1986). The family environment and achievement of deaf students: A discriminate analysis. *Exceptional Children, 52*(5), 44–449.

Boyden, J. (1993). *Families: Celebration and hope in a world of change.* New York, NY: Facts on File, Incorporated.

Burgess, E. W. (1926). The family as a unity of interacting personalities. *The Family, 3,* 3–9.

Butera, G. (2005). Collaboration in the context of Appalachia: The case of Cassie. *The Journal of Special Education, 39*(2), 106–116.

Christensen, H. T. (1964). *Handbook of marriage and the family.* Skokie, IL: Rand McNally.

Corman, H., Noonan, K., & Reichman, N. E. (2005). Mothers labor supply in fragile families: The role of child health. *Eastern Economic Journal, 31*, 601–616.

Corman, H., Noonan, K., & Reichman, N. E. (2005). Mothers labor supply in fragile families: *The role of child health. Eastern Economic Journal, 31*, 601–616.

Damiani, V. B. (1999). Responsibility and adjustment in siblings of children with disabilities: Update and review. *Families in Society, 80*, 34–40.

Decker, L. E. (2001). Allies in education. *Principal Leadership (High School Ed.). 2*(1), 42–46.

Friend, M., & Cook, L. (2010). *Interactions: Collaboration skills for school professionals* (6th ed.). Boston, MA: Pearson.

Gallagher, P. A., Powell, T. H., & Rhodes, C. A. (2006). *Brothers and sisters: A special part of exceptional families* (3rd ed.). Baltimore, MD: Paul Brookes.

Goudie, A., Fairbrother, G., Read, D., & Simpson, L. (2010). Children with special health care needs in Ohio, CPRC Policy Brief: CCHMC.

Hastings, R. P. (2003). Brief Report: Behavioral adjustment of siblings of children with autism. *Journal of Autism and Developmental Disorders, 33*(1), 99–104.

Heller, T., & Arnold, C. K. (2010). Siblings of adults with developmental disabilities: Psychosocial outcomes, relationships, and future planning. *Journal of Policy and Practice in Intellectual Disabilities, 7*(1), 16–25.

Heller, T., & Kramer, J. (2009). Involvement of adult siblings of persons with developmental disabilities in future planning, *Intellectual and Developmental, 47*(3), 208–219.

Hodapp, R., Glidden, L. M., & Kaiser, A. P. (2005). Siblings of persons with disabilities: Toward a research agenda. *Mental Retardation, 43*(5), 334–338.

House, J. S., Landis, K. R., & Umberson, D. (1988). Social relationships and health. *Science 241*, 540–545.

Iceland, J. (2000). The "family/couple/household" unit of analysis in poverty measurement. Retrieved May 18, 2014, from http://www.census.gov/hhes/poverty/povmeas/papers/famhh3.html=2

Information for Professionals on Supporting Siblings (2004). Retrieved May 18, 2014, from http://www.sibs.org.uk/professionals/supporting-young-siblings/needs-siblings

Jackson, C. W., & Turnbull, A. (2004). Impact of deafness on family life: A review of the literature. *Topics in Early Childhood Special Education, 24*(1), 15–29.

Karpowitz, D. (1991). *Families in six perspectives.* Lawrence, KS: University of Kansas.

Kluwin, T., & Gaustad, M. G. (1992). How family factors influence school achievement. In T. N. Kluwin, D. F. Moores, & M. M. Gaustad (Eds.). *Defining the effective public school program for deaf students.* New York: Teachers College Press.

Koshti-Richman, A. (2009). Caring for a disabled child at home: Parents' views. *Pediatric Nursing, 21*(6), 19–21.

Lynch, E. W., & Hanson, M. J. (2011). *Developing cross-cultural competence: A guide for working with children and their families* (4th ed.). Baltimore, MD: Paul Brookes.

Meadan, H., Halle, J. W., & Ebata, A. T. (2010). Families with children who have autism spectrum disorders: Stress and support. *Council for Exceptional Children, 77*(1), 7–36.

Moidrag, N., & Hodrapp, R. M. (2010). Chronic stress and health among parents with intellectual and developmental disabilities. *Current Opinion in Psychiatry, 23*(5), 407–411.

Nealy, C., O'Hare, L., Powers, J., & Swick, D. (2012). The impact of autism spectrum disorders on family: A qualitative study of mothers' perspectives. *Journal of Family Social Work, 15*, 187–201.

Neely-Barnes, S. L., & Dia, D. A. (2008). Families of children with disabilities: A review of literature and recommendations for interventions. *Journal of Early and Intensive Behavior Interventions, 5*, 93–107.

Neely-Barnes, S. L., & Dia, D. A. (2008). Families of children with disabilities: A review of literature and recommendations for interventions. *Journal of Early and Intensive Behavior Intervention*, *5*, 93–107.

Noonan, K., Reichman, N. E., & Corman, H. (2005). New fathers' labor supply: Does child health matter? *Social Science Quarterly, 86*, 1399–1419.

Parish, S., Shattuck, P., & Rose, R. (2009). Financial burden of raising CSHCN: Association with state policy choices. *Pediatrics, 124*, 435–442.

Park, J., Hoffman, L., Marquis, J., Turnbull, A. P., Poston, D. J., Mannan, H. (2003). Toward assessing family outcomes of service delivery: Validation of family quality of life survey. *Journal of Intellectual Disability Research, 47*, 367–384.

Poston, D., Park, J., Turnbull, A. P., Mannan, H., & Marquis, J. (2003). Family quality of life outcomes: A qualitative inquiry launching a long-term research program. *Retardation, 41*(5), 313–328.

Poston, D., Turnbull, A., Mannan, H., Marquis, J., & Wang, M. (2003). Family quality of life: A qualitative inquiry. *Mental Retardation, 41*(3), 313–328.

Ridgley, R., & Hallam, R. (2006). Examining the IFSPs of rural, low income families: Are they reflective of family concerns? *Journal of Research in Childhood Education, 21*(2), 149–162.

Smith, L. E., Hong, J., Selzer, M. M., Greenberg, J. S., Almeida, D. M., & Bishop, S. L. (2010). Daily experiences among mothers of adolescents and adults with autism spectrum disorder. *Journal of Autism and Developmental Disorders, 40* (2), 167–178.

Swaminathan, S., Alexander, G., & Boulet, S. (2006). Delivering a very low birth weight infant and the subsequent risk of divorce or separation. *Maternal and Child Health Journal, 10*, 473–479.

Theoharis, R. & Fitzpatrick, M. (2011). Max's family experience: Web-resources for working with special education students and their families. *Critical Questions in Education* 1(2), Web Link: http://education.missouristate.edu/AcadEd/99553.htm#max.

Thomas, C. C., Correa, V. I., & Morsink, C. V. (2001). *Interactive teaming: Enhancing programs for students with special needs.* (3rd ed.). Columbus, OH: Merrill Prentice Hall.

Turnbull, A. P., & Turnbull, H. R. (2001). *Families, professionals, and exceptionality: Collaborating for empowerment* (4th ed). Upper Saddle River, NJ: Merrill Prentice Hall.

Turnbull, A. P., Turnbull, H. R., Erwin, E. J., & Soodak, L. C., (2006). Families, professionals, and exceptionality: Positive outcomes through partnership and trust (6th ed.). Boston, MA: Pearson.

Turnbull, A. P., Turnbull, H. R., Erwin, E. J., Soodak, L. C., & Shogren, K. A. (2015). *Families, professionals, and exceptionality: Positive outcomes through partnership and trust* (7th ed). Upper Saddle River, NJ: Merrill Prentice Hall.

Turnbull, A., Summers, J., & Brotherson, M. J. (1984). *Working with families with disabled members: A family system approach.* Lawrence, KS: Kansas University Affiliated Facility.

Turnbull, A., Turnbull, H. R., Wehmeyer, M. L., & Shogren, K. A. (2013). *Exceptional lives: Special education in today's school* (7th ed.). Boston, MA: Pearson.

Turnbull, H. R. (2005). Individuals with disabilities education act: Accountability and personal responsibility. *Remedial and Special Education, 26*, 320–326.

Turnbull, H. R., Stowe, M. J., & Huerta, N. E. (2007). *Free appropriate public education: The law and children with disabilities* (7th ed.). Denver, CO: Love.

Vega, W., Hough, R., & Romero, A. (1983). Family life patterns of Mexican Americans. New York: Brunner/Mazel.

Walraven, R., Fitzpatrick, M. Valverde, A., Allen, C., & Rodriguez, J. B. (2010). Analyzing systems for students with emotional and behavior disorders: Bridging the gap via a home visit model. Border Walking Journal, 8(1), 33–42.

Webber, J., & Plotts, C. A. (2008). Emotional and behavioral disorders, theory and practice. Pearson Education, Inc.

Wedig, M. M., & Nock, M. K. (2007). Parental expressed emotion and adolescent self-injury. Journal of American Academy of Child and Adolescent Psychiatry, 46(9), 1171–1178.

7 The Impact of Climate & Culture of Schools

Chapter Objectives

After studying this chapter readers should be able to:

- Define school climate and culture.
- Compare and contrast the role of principals and teacher leaders.
- Summarize the purpose and explain the importance of collaboration.
- Explain how climate and culture can either positively or negatively impact the educational outcomes for students with autism.

Chapter 7 Subject Index:

1. Administrators
2. Autism
3. Belief
4. Climate and Culture
5. Collaboration
6. Communication
7. Community
8. Community Engagement
9. Cultural Reciprocity
10. Inclusion
11. Individualized Education Plan
12. Individuals with Disabilities Education Improvement Act
13. Instructional Leaders
14. Learning Community
15. Least Restrictive Environment
16. No Child Left Behind Act
17. Norms
18. Paraeducators
19. Principals
20. Relationships
21. S.T.E.P.
22. Self-Injurious Behaviors

23. Shared Governance
24. Special Education
25. Teachers as Leaders
26. Traditions
27. Values

INTRODUCTION

Although it is hard to explain, **principals**, teachers, families, and students often experience an undefinable positive or negative sense about the schools in which they belong. These tacit feelings can be defined as **climate and culture**. Climate and culture are extremely important, powerful, and critical elements of every school and is created by the combined **beliefs**, **values**, morals, etc. of adults and students within the building.

According to Peterson and Deal (1998), the culture of schools incorporates the underlying stream of **norms**, values, beliefs, and **traditions** that have been established over time and serve as a mechanism for faculty and staff to work together, face challenges, and seek solutions. Similarly, climate and culture influences and impacts everything that takes place within the building including but not limited to (a) dress codes; (b) conversations and interactions between faculty, staff, students, and families; (c) risk taking, problem solving, and adapting; (d) implementation of strategies; (e) emphasis placed on student learning and professional development; and (f) willingness to accept differences. These connections and variables help foster **relationships** and serve as the foundation for establishing a sense of **community** within and outside the classroom and school setting. Intuitively, schools which display and maintain the precepts of fairness, equality, justice, respect, cooperation, and compassion greatly enhance community development (Bushnell, 2001; Osher & Fleischman, 2005).

It is the responsibility of **administrators**, teachers, and families to identify, develop, and maintain strong, positive, and student-centered school cultures. Without these elements, reforms will be unsuccessful, faculty and staff dedication and enthusiasm will plummet, and student learning outcomes will be negatively impacted (Peterson & Deal, 1998). For example, some schools over time have become unproductive and toxic environments. Peterson and Deal (1998) described these schools as places where staffs are extremely fragmented, a place where the purpose of meeting the needs and serving students has changed to focus on meeting the needs and serving adults. Toxic schools are places where negativity dominates conversations, interactions, and planning. Typically, no one wants to work in this type of school.

In sharp contrast to venomous environments, many schools have strong, positive cultures. These schools tend to have faculty and staff who are dedicated to a shared sense of (a) purpose; (b) collegiality, improvement, and hard work; (c) celebrating student success, (d) dedication; and (e) family commitment which have a direct correlation on achievement, happiness, and humor (Peterson & Deal, 1998). As alluded above, school leaders (e.g., principals, teachers, and families) have the responsibility to foster, shape, and maintain a school climate and culture made up of positive values (Peterson & Deal, 1998).

The following scenarios provide two different examples of climate and culture of schools, one negative and one positive. Both illustrate the significant impact the community of principal, educators, staff, students, and families has on the sense of the school environment.

MAX'S SCENARIO SCHOOL CULTURE: PERSPECTIVE I

When it was time for Max to start kindergarten, we scheduled a tour of the neighborhood elementary school. I felt it would be an important part of Max's transition to elementary school to ease his anxiety and help him become familiar with the school. When I called the school to schedule the visit, I asked the principal, Mrs. Wilson, if Max could join us. She went into a long drawn out explanation as to why this would not be a good idea.

I arrived on time for the tour, rang the buzzer outside the front door, and walked through a second set of locked glass doors. I was greeted by the administrative assistant who was seated at her desk on the other side of the door. She asked, what I needed and the purpose of my visit. She motioned me inside and asked me who I was there to see. She was busy working on other tasks, if she had looked up when she greeted me, she would have seen my eagerness to be there, but her focus did not leave her task. I was let in, handed my visitor badge, and told to wait for the principal.

Aesthetically, the office was cold, there were no chairs or reading materials. I kept myself busy reading official notices that had been posted on a bulletin board in the office until the principal introduced herself 15 minutes later. After the introductions, we proceeded with the tour, which took place during school hours, so I was able to see some interactions between the teachers, staff, and students.

We began the tour in the kindergarten hall which was lined with student artwork. Mrs. Wilson made a point of sharing the work was of *general education* students. As we continued with the tour, we passed several school employees and students. Mrs. Wilson did not have any interactions with these individuals (no smiles or greetings were exchanged and no introductions were made). When we approached the nurse's office there was a sense of mild chaos. A frantic teacher was looking for a custodian, while the nurse motioned students and adults to the other side of the hall. As we walked by, Mrs. Wilson did nothing to assist with the situation or calm the upset students, sick child, or the staff.

At the opposite end of the building, away from the kindergarten hall where we started the tour, I began to wonder what else there was for me to see. I saw the cafeteria, where Max would eat lunch, the multipurpose room, where he would have PE and learn new games, and the classrooms where he would have music and art. Perhaps, we were making our way to the playground I saw when I drove in—the playground where Max and his new friends would play. I soon realized this was not where we were heading. We paused for a short minute for me to peer into two 10' by 10' classrooms. The first room was designated for speech therapy, physical therapy, and occupational therapy. The other was a **special education** (SPED) classroom.

While **inclusion** has become a key component of reform efforts to improve SPED and the services for students with disabilities (McLeskey, Henry, and Hodges, 1998; Schumm & Vaughn, 1995; Schmidt, Rosendal, & Greenman, 2002), the principal explained this would be Max's classroom when he arrived in the fall. *The classroom,* she said, *is where children with disabilities can be helped.* Having a background in SPED, I could not believe what I was hearing. I could not help but wonder if this was similar to the historical practices of segregating students with disabilities from their nondisabled peers that families and advocates worked so hard to prevent and improve upon (Bredberg & Davidson, 1999; Pamelazita & Bruschbacker, 2003).

I asked about other options with the hope of Max remaining in the general education classroom with his peers. I offered the option of an aide written into his **Individualized Education Plan** (IEP) similar to what he had experienced in preschool. The principal told me that simply would not be possible. She went on to explain, ***Paraeducators*** *at my school work with struggling readers, not special education students.* Mrs. Wilson's comments did not promote an inclusive environment which (a) guarantees physical access, (b) allows opportunities for the best academic and social experiences, and (c) provides a nurturing atmosphere. Without the critical elements of an inclusive environment being established, students with disabilities are denied full participation, access, involvement, and an appropriate and equitable educational experiences (Pivik, McComas, & LaFlamme, 2002).

Mrs. Wilson's lack of understanding about the needs of students with disabilities and their families, SPED, and **Individuals with Disabilities Education Improvement Act** (IDEIA, 2004) was apparent during our short time together. Her attitude suggested a lack of commitment to *all* children. These interactions also indicated her lack of awareness and concern for her impact on the climate and culture of the school.

Max's IEP meeting was held a few weeks later. The team members had very distinct opinions about the educational placement that could best meet *all* of his needs. We considered his strengths and weaknesses, wrote goals and objectives, and contemplated the **least restrictive environment**. It was my feeling and the thought of many of the IEP team members, that Max should attend a school where he would be part of a community, welcomed and accepted. I believed this would be important for Max's academic and social success. I also felt like the effort I had put into preparing for Max's kindergarten year had been unsuccessful and had been a waste of time.

The following section provides an overview of how a principal, teachers, and staff interacted with students with disabilities and their families, accepted *all* students with disabilities, and were active participants in the SPED process, thus, upholding the spirit of IDEIA (2004) and **No Child Left Behind Act** (NCLB, 2002). This scenario illustrates how their understanding impacted the climate and culture of the school in positive and meaningful ways which benefited *all* internal and external stakeholders.

MAX'S SCENARIO SCHOOL CULTURE: PERSPECTIVE II

Two weeks after the IEP meeting, I received a phone call from the school Max would attend in the fall. The administrative assistant had some questions and needed additional information. Then, she asked if Max and I would like to tour his new school. She also offered for us to meet Max's SPED teacher and eat lunch with her, her students, and the principal. I was so excited and appreciated the thoughtful invitation; however, looming thoughts of the last school tour were ever present. I was eager but also anxious and nervous about the upcoming tour and introductions.

We were greeted at the front door by the principal, Mr. Jones. He bent down, said hello, and introduced himself to Max. He reached out to shake his hand, while Max did not make eye contact, he did stick out his hand. The three of us headed off for the tour. Mr. Jones kept making sure Max was included in the conversation. We stopped by what would be his new classroom in the fall and met his new teacher. She spoke with Max and asked him questions about what he liked to do. While she was talking to Max, Mr. Jones spent time with the other children in the classroom. During my short observation, it was clear that Mr. Jones was a frequent classroom visitor.

We neared the end of the tour, Max was getting restless and anxious and I was getting nervous. Then, Max ran screaming through the library. I was mortified and was sure I knew what Mr. Jones would say next and we would be off to find another school for fall. To my surprise, Mr. Jones waited patiently while I got Max calmed down. Then, he said, *I can see Max has had enough. The tour has worn him out. Why don't we schedule lunch for another day?* Relieved, shocked, and amazed, we shook hands and I thanked him for the tour. He told Max he was excited he would be coming to his school and sensing my nervousness reassured me Max would do just fine.

Max began the kindergarten year without any problems. On several occasions, I had to stop by the school to drop off papers or lunch that did not make it into his backpack. During these visits, I would see Mr. Jones laughing and engaged in conversations with students. Once, I saw him walk Max back to class, asking questions and listening as if he were really interested in his response. Max, I am happy to report, had a successful kindergarten year. While he continued to need support for fine motor skills, he was reading at the first-grade level and was above his peers in math. Additionally, based on the advice and support of Mr. Jones, Max was ready for full inclusion and would begin his first-grade year in a general education classroom with paraprofessional support.

To help ensure the success of students with disabilities and inclusion, it is important that administrators demonstrate behaviors that promote and advance the integration, acceptance, and success of students with disabilities in general education classes. Mr. Jones' attitude resulted in the increased opportunities for Max to be included with his nondisabled peers. It resulted in school faculty and staff being willing to positively support and meet the needs of students with disabilities. His interactions with families, students, teachers, and staff had a clear link to building a foundation that resulted in a positive and effective climate and culture of the school. In order for inclusion to be successful, school administrators must exhibit a positive attitude and commitment. Research also indicates principals, with similar philosophies to Mr. Jones, are more likely to place students with disabilities in less restrictive placements (Praisner, 2003).

Each of these areas were evident throughout both Max's kindergarten and first grade years. Mr. Jones was consistent in his interactions—he demonstrated the same level of kindness, commitment, and leadership abilities throughout our time together as he did during our initial meeting. During Max's annual IEP meeting (e.g., Mr. Jones was an active participant). He shared ideas, made recommendations, and asked for clarification.

A few months later, Max was invited to another student's birthday party. The party was held at a local child friendly restaurant. The SPED teachers and paraprofessionals all attended, and so did Mr. Jones. He was interacting with all of the children playing games, eating pizza, and socializing with the adults. These are just a few examples that illustrate Mr. Jones commitment and understanding for students, families, faculty and staff, as well as the recognition of the impact it has on the climate and culture of a school.

While both of these scenarios offer the principal as the main character in setting the tone for the climate and culture of a school, it is important to recognize that school leaders at every level (i.e., principal, teachers, staff, students, and families) are responsible for shaping school culture. For schools to be effective a high level of satisfaction must exist among all community members. Teachers and staff must have a role in the school's decision making process. Students must believe and trust the educators and feel good about the choices being made regarding the school and what is happening (Halawah, 2005). No significant change or improvement can take place without all stakeholders working together. The next sections look at the school climate and culture established by these individuals, their roles, and the impact on student achievement.

THE ROLE OF THE PRINCIPAL

In addition to providing building level leadership, Halawah (2005) suggested establishing safe and secure climates are critical first steps for building administrators to help ensure positive environments. To achieve this objective, principals typically set a series of goals, expectations, and priorities for themselves and their community. Ultimately a principal's values, attitudes, **communication** skills, and leadership abilities influence the overall culture of a school (Smith, 2006). More importantly is the level of support felt by SPED teachers, service providers, and students with disabilities and their families. Principals need to be aware that their attitudes, interactions, and philosophies related to SPED programs, teachers, staff, students, and families are factors that impact attrition and retention rates of educators (Theoharis, 2008).

Principals can build upon pre-existing strengths by reevaluating and reflecting on current traditions that encourage a sense of community, foster achievement, and celebrate success (Benton & Bulach, 1995). They play an important role in establishing school discipline, with both effective leadership and personal example. Effective principals are liked and respected verses disliked and feared. Principals must have knowledge and understanding of effective communication strategies (discussed below).

The climate of a school has an impact on a principal's ability to be effective. It also interferes with the outcomes of both teachers and students. Improvement in the climate and culture of the school enhances the principal's ability to be effective, teachers' performance, and students' achievement and behavior (Halawah, 2005). These improvements can only occur if the principal, teachers, and students are empowered. They must all identify and implement instructional strategies that will result in working towards and achieving the school's vision and mission (Korir & Karr-Kidwell, 1996).

TEACHERS AS LEADERS

The two scenarios are very different and illustrate the impact on school administrator's overall attitude, leadership abilities, and commitment to the climate and culture of their building. Strong positive school climate and cultures (i.e., Mr. Jones' school) exists because there is a shared sense of what is important, common philosophy of care and concern, similar values, and a community effort of ensuring *all* students learn. While research has shown school climate and culture is one of the most important factors of any educational system, many schools (i.e., Mrs. Wilson's school) continue to lack the critical aspects because they are not valued or seen as significant.

School principals and teachers are in positions to influence the change process. As **instructional leaders**, administrators articulate the schools mission, support an instructional climate, oversee curriculum and instruction, evaluate teaching, and monitor student progress (Krug, 1992). Teachers and specialist also play a key role in affecting change. Both general and special educators must be leaders for inclusive education. Teachers work closest with students and their families, so they have the most direct impact on the educational program. For significant improvement to happen, teachers must become *change agents* (Walther-Thomas, Korinek, McLaughlin, Williams, 2000). Teachers must see themselves as leaders committed to making a difference and confident in their ability to do so (Fullan, 1993).

Current school reform literature and research continues to include some conceptualization of teacher leadership as a way to increase student achievement and learning outcomes (Burke, Marx, & Lowenstein, 2012). The integration of **learning community** models that focus significantly on teacher leadership has resulted in the recognition that learning to effectively lead in changing environments requires a new set of knowledge and skills (Burke & Marx, 2011). York-Barr and Duke (2004) conducted a review of the literature that found that teacher leadership is an umbrella term that has different meanings and connotations among various stakeholders. For some, it is forward ideas from the mid-1990s concerning site-based management and participatory leadership. While others believe, teacher leadership is a term used to represent the specific types of pedagogical decision-making that educators engage in while leading their classrooms (Lieberman, 1995). Given the term has multiple meanings for different individuals, it is difficult to ascertain roles and responsibilities when trying to envision new relationships and alternatives when addressing the challenges associated with having *all* students reach high expectation and levels of achievement.

Katzenmeyer and Moller (2001) defined teacher leadership after a review of the literature, careful consideration, and discussion with teacher leaders and administrators. They stated the definition is an evolving work in progress. The definition they provided, "Teachers who are leaders lead within and beyond the classroom, identify with and contribute to a community of teacher learners and leaders, and influence others toward improved professional practices" (p. 5).

A professional teacher is competent and comfortable in the classroom while facilitating students' learning. Teacher leadership is initiated by being recognized as a capable teacher in the classroom (Katzenmeyer & Moller, 2001). Next, teacher leaders accept being a facilitator leader to others in the field; they recognize that they can transfer their classroom skills to their interactions with peers. Teacher leaders can be an agent of change beyond the classroom by accepting more responsibility for helping colleagues to achieve success for all students and for school programs.

Shared governance allows teachers to have an active leadership role and to participate in meaningful ways in the decision making process. They are teacher leaders. All stakeholders have representation in development, implementation, and evaluation of programs (Walther-Thomas et al., 2000). Planning teams participating in shared leadership address concerns proactively. These individuals make reasonable decisions related to teaching assignments and curriculum and design schedules that facilitate meaningful classroom support and positive environments. Overall, shared leadership promotes more trust, dedication, **collaboration**, and problem-solving. Without shared leadership, stakeholders often feel excluded from the decision making process (Walther-Thomas et al., 2000). This could result in less involvement and communication with many participants offering little commitment or investment in change and improvement.

Collaborating. Friend and Cook (2010) provided a definition that characterizes collaboration distinctive characteristics. They stated, "Interpersonal *collaboration* is a style for direct interaction between at least two co-equal parties voluntarily engaged in shared decision making as they work toward a common goal" (p. 7). Effective collaboration is based on continuing participation of two or more professionals who are devoted to working together to achieve common goals. Many successful collaborative relationships begin from the shared concerns of like-minded individuals (Villa, Thousand, Nevin, & Malgeri, 1996). Usually, these collaborators possess different skills and offer a variety of contributions to create, strengthen, and maintain these partnerships (Friend & Cook, 1996). They stated, the term collaboration continues to often be misused. It is important to recognize as schools have changed overtime, collaboration has become an integral component (Barth, 2006; Murray, 2004). Today, administrators are encouraged to use and model a collaborative leadership approach and educators are supported to apply collaboration models to improve student learning (McCullen, 2006; Friend & Pope, 2005). In addition to the multifaceted challenges schools encounter, none are as critical as creating a culture of collaboration (Friend & Cook, 2010).

Collaborative cultures are environments where teamwork, partnerships, cooperation, and trust are valued and supported. In inclusive schools, all members of the school team (i.e., administrators, educators, service providers, specialists, staff, students, & families) work together to create a positive school climate and culture, improve student learning outcomes, and make all educational programs stronger. In collaborative cultures that promote shared resources, value and celebrate personal and team efforts, there is an opportunity for growth, success, and leadership. These environments encourage and lend themselves to innovative ideas and risk taking (Walther-Thomas et al., 2000). Schools that do not operate with or promote collaborative cultures are often competitive and stressful environments. Without a collaborative culture there is limited trust and valued participants often do not share their ideas for fear of how they will be received by others.

In order to create the collaborative environment, each individual who is a part of the school must have the disposition, knowledge, and skills to collaborate in order to have a positive impact on the culture of the school. Administrators, general and SPED teachers, related service providers, and other professionals need to know how to collaborate and work with colleagues, paraprofessionals and families (Friend & Cook, 2010). This is true for all grade levels. Friend and Cook (2010) have identified the following as *defining characteristics* of collaboration:

- is voluntary;
- involves equality among participants;
- is founded on shared goals;
- relies on shared responsibility for both decision making and participation;
- entails sharing resources;
- requires shared accountability for student learning outcomes and achievement.

Additionally they stated successful collaborative experiences result in *emergent characteristics* which include:

- Participants who collaborate value the interpersonal approach.
- Participants who collaborate trust each other.
- A sense of community emerges from collaboration.

In addition to the *emergent characteristics,* there are several reasons for the significance of collaboration. First, the overall trend is expanding and increasing the multifaceted responsibilities of school personnel which become more realistic and easier to manage when professionals group their knowledge, talents, and skills together (Neus & Sterns, 2005). Walther-Thomas (1998) reported working together collaborators create a sense of synergy that allows them to accomplish more than they could individually. Second, stems from the **No Child Left Behind Act** (2001). NCLB sets high standards for achievement and has established clear accountability for *all* students. Finally, reason is the continued movement for inclusive practices (Patterson, 2005).

Collaboration is a vital factor for school administrators, educators, staff, and other service providers to think about and reflect on as they incorporate differentiated instruction, meet the requirements of high-stakes testing, and create and apply professional development strategies (Friend & Cook, 2010). Professionals also agree that effective and long-term commitment among collaboration stakeholders is an essential component of effective inclusion (Bauwens & Hourcade, 1995; Cramer, 1998; Creasey & Walter-Thomas, 1996; Thousand, Nevin, & Malgeri, 1996). Fundamentally, meaningful inclusion is not possible without effective collaboration (Skrtic, 1991). It is important to note collaboration is a key part of the SPED process and can be illustrated through every phase—initial referral and evaluation, IEP development, accommodations, modifications, and service delivery, conflict resolution, and family involvement and participation.

While some view SPED collaboration as a compartment of the whole school collaboration, it is important to give some attention to its rich history and its policy and practice. Even before the first SPED law was enacted in 1975, SPED teachers were consulting with general education teachers to provide indirect services to students with disabilities (McKenzie, 1972). Tharp and Wetzel (1969) reported school psychologists were urged to support teachers with students with learning and behavioral disabilities. After P.L. 94-142 (1975) became law, collaboration was a part of both the mandate for least restrictive environment and the provision for family participation. Through each revision of the law, the focus of collaboration has increased (Friend & Cook, 2010). While collaboration has had a considerable amount of focus, extensive confusion has accompanied the evolution of SPED collaboration (Smith & Leonard, 2005). Some schools use the terms *collaboration* and *inclusion* synonymously and interchangeably, even though they are very different (collaboration is a style of interaction and inclusion is the belief system that establishes a foundation for how students are educated). Other schools confuse collaboration with service delivery models such as co-teaching.

Another area unique to SPED collaboration is the partnerships formed among the professionals who provide services and related services to students with disabilities. This collaboration assists students in generalizing skills across environments and helps ensures interventions are implemented in both SPED and general education settings (Friend & Cook, 2010). SPED teachers may have frequent communication with speech language pathologist, counselors, or deaf and hard of hearing teachers.

Arguably adults working together to reach common goals would bring about positive benefits like improving student achievement and learning outcomes and increasing teachers' abilities and knowledge. However, due to the complexity and the numerous factors within programs, it is difficult to report if it is collaboration alone that makes a difference. There continues to be a need for more research specifically related to collaboration, nevertheless two research studies have indicated it does make a difference. Shannon and Blysma's (2004) research indicated four themes that characterized schools: (a) quality teaching and learning, (b) effective leadership, (c) support for system-wide improvement, and (d) collaborative relationships. They reported collaborative relationships are essential to a nurturing professional culture, clear understanding of roles and responsibilities, and colleague support and trust. Caron and McLaughlin (2002) examined how individual schools are successful in improving student outcomes. Six elementary and middle schools participated in the study. One of the key findings was that collaboration in different forms (i.e., collaborative planning, consultation, and co-teaching) were significant factors. These schools possessed an overarching culture of collaboration which included trust, high-expectations, and a sense of community.

Communication. When interacting with other professionals and families some teachers have a natural instinct for what to say and when to say it, while others seem to say the wrong things or do not know what to say. Finally, most educators fall somewhere in the middle. It is important to recognize no matter where you fall on the communication continuum, communication skills can be improved.

In order to build or strengthen school climate and culture and establish a collaborative environment, communication is essential. Structures and procedures need to be in place which allows all members of the community to participate and have equal say in decisions and policies that impact them (Furman &

Starratt, 2002). Communities need to have structures that promote teachers, students, and families, thinking, discussing, and making decisions together. In addition, there needs to be time to socialize, meet, and talk, as well as communication structures and guidelines that encourage and continue productive dialogue (Burrello, Hofffman, & Murray, 2005). Teachers need opportunities for professional development to enhance and build knowledge, skills, and dispositions in order to better respond to new practices in curriculum, pedagogy, and assessment (Burrello, Hoffman, & Murray, 2005). While these improved practices are occurring conditions need to be created where educators can share their practices publically, collaborate with colleagues and families, and discuss with others about student achievement and school related issues. These conversations should take place both formally and informally.

Establishing opportunities for productive communication is not enough. According to Furman and Starratt (2002) it also requires openness to improvement and change, an ability to listen, understand, empathize, respect, trust, negotiate, debate, problem-solve, and resolve conflicts while staying focused on the overall mission and goals. The focus should remain on attaining the goals and establishing an environment where everyone can openly express their thoughts, opinions, and feelings without argument or judgment (Furman & Starratt, 2002).

In school environments, information is shared and received through multiple channels. And, at any given point numerous messages may be happening through different modes simultaneously. Sending the same message through several channels can be reinforcing and strengthen the message. This can be a simple smile when giving a complement (Friend & Cook, 2010). While this can increase the strength of the message and add validation the message is being received correctly, it can also complicate communication. Discrepant messages are common miscommunications. It is important for school faculty and staff to be aware and guard against miscommunications. Sitting in a meeting your colleague, for example, says they agree with your ideas for the end of the day bus dismissal. While stating they think your ideas will help the dismissal process go more smoothly, lend for a quicker transition, and increase the safety for all students, your colleague is frowning and shaking his head with disgust. This is a discrepant message that causes confusion and miscommunication.

The focus thus far has been on face-to-face communication, but as you know communication is not limited to face-to-face interactions. Emails, voicemail, instant messages, text messages, and hand-written notes are other ways educators communicate. When thinking about which method is best to share the message, it is important to think about the type of message you are sending and how it will be received. Finally, it is also important to think about the preferred method of communication, for example, because of time and scheduling a family might prefer email verses phone calls for everyday communication and for a more important message or one that requires an immediate response a phone call would be more appropriate.

Careful thought and consideration should be given regarding which mode of communication is the most effective based on the message being delivered, situation, and circumstances. Below is a summary of Bullard's (2003) communication strategies:

- Take time to learn about effective communication, including listening. Read books attend a conference or workshop.
- Reflect on your personal interactions. Apply what you have learned related to communication strategies, reflect on what went well and what you could do different next time in order to improve communication.
- Pre-plan interactions. Think about who you will be communicating with, what problems will you be seeking to solve, what communication strategies will be most effective.
- Ask questions for clarity and to seek information. It is natural to work from a personal frame of reference, it is important to seek ways to bring clarity to communication and see others perspectives. Ask open-ended questions rather than questions that lend themselves to only a yes or no response. Try not to ask questions that contain the answer you are expecting. When appropriate, ask others about their feelings and opinions.

- Practice active listening. Focus on what others are saying not on you. Put away what you are working on and give the individual your full attention. Pay attention to the individual's facial expressions, gestures, and tone. Try not to be judgmental as you listen to the speaker. Sort out the main points being stated. You may need to summarize the points in your mind as you listen to the other person's perspective. Ask if you can take notes to help you remember important details.
- Nonverbal and verbal responses. Nonverbal responses include facial expressions, gestures, tone of voice, and the space between you and the other person (Turnbull & Turnbull, 2001). The other person pays as much attention to nonverbal responses as they do the message being stated. Verbal responses are also important. Use encouragers, such as *yes* or *uh huh*. Use *verbal following* repeat the key points of the speaker stated in your response. This helps to check for understanding.
- Avoid making evaluative comments. *You should have*… or *This will never work because*… these comments can stop communication or result in other negative outcomes.
- Avoid giving advice. Be cautious to jump in with advice. It is best to work together to evaluate and seek solutions to the problem, share in the planning, and the course of action.
- Avoid commanding statements. These statements can lead to anger and resistance.
- Avoid making statements that diminish the other person. These statements make you appear superior to the other person. When you provide information to others make sure not to use language that will put down others. Similarly, avoid comments that will lessen how the other person feels such as, *it is not so bad.*

While there are strategies that help promote good communication, there are also things that can block communication (Bullard, 2003). Communication is essential for both personal and professional activities. The skills of communication are critical for performance of instruction, administrative duties, planning, and other intervention responsibilities as you work with other professionals and families (Friend & Cook, 2010).

Problem Solving. A lot of communication teachers have with other adults' centers around problems that need solutions (Bullard, 2003). Having a framework to solve problems can be beneficial. This helps to ensure problems are well-defined, effective solutions are presented and considered, and general consensus is reached on a proposed solution. When it has been determined that a specific problem needs to be addressed, the problem-solving process can begin.

Clearly, defining the problem is a critical first step. The purpose of defining the problem allows for the best possible solutions. This step of defining the problem can be complicated. More specifically, research supports defining the problem is the most important step (Jayanthi & Friend, 1992). Bergan and Tombari (1975) reported it is not uncommon to spend half of the time defining the problem. It can be tempting to rush to the solution and skip this step, but this could lead to possible misunderstandings (Bullard, 2003). Defining the problem needs to begin with all participants agreeing and recognizing the specific problem. The problem needs to be defined clearly so that discrepancy of the current situation and the desired outcome are apparent. This is related to the concept of working towards a common mission and mutual goals.

Next, the participants will want to gather facts and data. This will help when thinking about possible solutions. Data may include test results, student records, observations, interviews, and discussions with other school staff, students, and family members. After defining the problem and gathering information, the next major step in problem solving is generating possible solutions. During this step, it is important to accept all possible ideas without being critical or evaluating them. Evaluating solutions during this phase could stifle creativity and limit the ideas presented. It is important during all brainstorming sessions ideas are being recorded.

Potential solutions need to be evaluated and analyzed. This could be a list of positives and negatives or advantages and disadvantages. Determine what resources are available and what resources will be needed. Keep these in mind as you continue with the discussions. The participants should select a solution, assign responsibilities for carrying out the solution and develop a timeline for evaluating the results of the solution (Bullard, 2003).

The evaluation of the solution should determine whether the implemented solution assisted in reaching the established goal and the intended outcome. If the evaluation step shows the solution is not successful, the participants should discuss modifying the solution, consider one of the other proposed solutions, or review the problem and make sure it has been defined correctly. Timelines are important as decisions are made on how to proceed during this phase and moving forward.

Problem solving is a central process used in collaboration activities. Many professional activities which educators are responsible for present some type of problem or challenge. Problem solving is perhaps the most fundamental component of successful communication (Friend & Cook, 2010). One mistake educators often make is that they spend so much time problem solving alone, they sometimes assume that they have the skills needed to problem solve without others. It is important to recognize problem solving with others requires additional skills compared to problem solving alone (Chiu, 2000).

COMMUNITY ENGAGEMENT

Community engagement is the extent to which the school has developed and cultivated a partnership or constructive relationship with its community (Uline & Tschannen-Moran, 2008). This area focuses on the degree in which the school can rely on support from family and community members, as well as the extent in which the school provides the community with information about its accomplishments, needs, and activities. Schools with strong community engagement are committed to meeting the needs and concerns of (a) families and community members and (b) provides the needed support. This ability to actively engage the community has been found to be correlated to student achievement (DiPaola & Tschannen-Moran, 2005). Conversely, Hoy and Sabo (1998) suggested that schools that are successful and keeping families and community members on the side lines have negatively impacted student achievement.

IMPACT OF SCHOOL CLIMATE & CULTURE

A positive safe and orderly school climate is a characteristic that consistently shows good achievement and academic success. Positive climate and culture, supportive relationships, research-based teaching strategies, and effective classroom management strategies promote student connectedness, reduce behavior problems, decrease dropout rates, close achievement gaps, and retain teachers. It also encourages successfully including students with disabilities. Schools with leaders who are self-aware, reflective, and follow both short-term and long-term plans regarding the climate and culture of the school tend to result in an improved academic environment and become an ethical foundation for the students (Keiser & Schulte, 2009).

Increasing academic performance, shaping social and emotional skills, and retaining highly qualified teachers and staff are all related to the positive school climate. However, trying to understand the complex patterns and subtle norms which provide the foundation for the established climate can be difficult to understand (Osher & Fleischman, 2005).

School climate is also an assessment of social dynamics with in a building. More than four decades of research offers a strong link between school climate and student achievement (see Anderson, 1982; Hoy & Feldman, 1987; Hoy & Sabo, 1998). Research on effective schools, restructuring, and instructional leadership indicate the impact of leadership on student achievement, learning, and improvement (Hallinger & Heck, 1996). This impact and the effect of leadership on student learning cannot be overstated (Halawah, 2005). Buffie (1989) reported student achievement is likely to be greatest where administrators, educators, families, and students work together.

FIRST PERSON TESTIMONIAL

Josh's Journey

By

Jeremy Covey, Oak Grove R-VI High School Assistant Principal

Josh, a student with **autism** who is prone to running, was making the transition from middle school into our high school in the fall of 2013. Given the culture, expectations, and routines are completely different; our IEP multidisciplinary team met to develop a schedule and plan we believed would make him as successful as possible. Prior to the beginning of the school year, we brought his parents on a tour of the building while his teachers took him through his daily schedule.

The year started off really well, but similar to *virtually all* best laid plans adjustments had to be made as the year progressed. For example, we had a few hiccups that mainly occurred during his 1st hour Transitional Skills Class with one of our SPED teachers. Anytime the teacher would hold Josh's feet to the fire on an assignment, he would ask to go to the bathroom. Instead, Josh would go directly to the nurse's office and ask to go home sick. Anytime he would not be allowed to go home he would have major meltdowns and begin to cry loudly, curse at our nurse, and sometimes engage in **self-injurious behaviors**. I would try to intervene by talking with Josh and there were times I would get one of our female SPED teachers to help tag team the situation.

Thankfully, she seemed to develop a good relationship with him, so that anytime we were having a difficult morning I would ask her to mediate. The majority of the time she did amazing work with Josh and could get him back on track so that he could have a successful day. Anytime Josh was having a tough day, she was always willing to reach out to his parents to see if we can find out what the true issues were. We could usually narrow bad mornings at school to bad mornings or a change in his routine at home.

The hiccups seemed to be happening more frequently with Josh towards the end of the first semester. He began to run multiple times a week and made more visits to the nurse's office when he was *sick*. We had a few major incidents during this time. For instance, Josh had run about a fourth of a mile from the school before his Transition Skills teacher and I caught up with him. As we got closer, he pulled out a pencil and told us to *get back*, I did not really feel threatened because I truly do not believe it is in his nature to be violent. I took his wrist with the pencil in it and he dropped it and began to cry. I had called our Student Resource Officer and he took Josh in his car and brought him back to school once he calmed down and was ready to talk.

Another major incident occurred in my office after an attempted run. I was working as he was deciding if he was going to go back to class or work in my office the remainder of the day. He wanted to argue and I would not engage in an argument. I continued to focus on work; however, our principal came into assist and proceeded to argue with him. I was called out of the office for another discipline issue, but before I left Josh started crying and said *I want to go home, I hate this place*. This was something he frequently would say whenever things were not going his way.

He had also dropped to the floor that day and tried to choke himself with the bottom of the chair he was sitting in. Once we got him calmed down a bit I left to deal with the other situation. I came back to the office expecting to find Josh still there. He was not in my office, as I was walking down the hall I met our principal. I asked if Josh had made a choice and if things went smoothly. He said *Yes, they went smoothly after he mooned me*. Apparently during the conversation our principal asked Josh what he wanted to do and he stood up and said *this* as he mooned our principal.

As we dug a little deeper late in the semester as the behavior became worse we discovered on a phone call home that mom and dad had separated and were divorcing. As a kid of divorce and a parent of divorce nothing will rock a kid's world more. Josh and his need for routine and stability was experiencing a whole new world. Every day was different for him and he did not have the skills to know how to process and adapt to the new world in which he had no control over. We met as a team with Josh and his parents and came up with a new game plan for Josh. We changed his first hour class to our female SPED teacher whom had developed a positive relationship with Josh. This offered him stability and routine to get his day started in a positive manner. He was in an environment that would offer Josh the patience and one-on-one assistance that would make each day successful.

The second semester went very smooth with one minor hurdle. Josh had been to the doctor and they changed his medicine to help level Josh off and make his days better. This change along with being with a different parent each night was tough for Josh. He was coming to school very tired. Finally after several different attempts to get Josh awake I finally did something to perhaps *bribe* him. I told him if he could stay awake for one week of school I would buy him McDonald's for lunch. After a week I owed Josh lunch. He ordered a whole $3 worth of food. This was a very big deal to Josh, we had zero problems with sleeping or behavior the remainder of the year. I made it a point to check in with him 3 times a week first hour and each and every day at lunch. Each day was different, but Josh and I have developed a positive relationship.

I truly believe with the help of each stakeholder that is vested in Josh's education we can make his next three years of high school very successful. It is a matter of us all communicating Josh's personal and educational needs with one another and especially with Josh's parents and for Josh. We have to stress to Josh that being an advocate for himself will benefit him for a lifetime. However, we have to give Josh the skills necessary to do just that. I think that our collaboration with Josh and his parents throughout the year helped Josh make a successful transition to high school.

Although I do believe things could have gone better, however, as many of you know in the educational world, adjustments had to be made on the fly. The multidisciplinary team did the best we could for Josh based on the information that we had at the time. We made adjustments to the plan as we went. I know that things will continue to improve for Josh as I develop a better/closer relationship with him and work towards making him college or career ready based on his future interests.

PROFESSIONAL ANALYSIS

Cultural Reciprocity: Promoting an Inclusive School Culture

By

Dr. Tracey R. Nix, University of Wisconsin

In Chapter 7, the authors eloquently discussed the role of the principal, educators as leaders, community engagement, and the impact of school climate and how each of these are woven together to effectively cultivate an inclusive school culture. I write this review to further strengthen their argument by introducing the posture of **cultural reciprocity** as a method to create culturally responsive educators within an inclusive school climate.

As a caveat, it is important to acknowledge that I do not limit culture to include only race or ethnicity. Culture is defined with a broader scope and includes (a) shared norms, (b) values, (c) beliefs, (d) behaviors, (e) traditions, (f) ideals, and (g) rules that are followed by a group of people over time (Banks, 2004). More importantly, culture influences factors such as how people interact with one another, language, social behaviors, religious affiliation, disability views, gender, sexual orientation, race, ethnicity, and attitudes (Timm, 1995; Turnbull, Turnbull, Shank & Smith, 2004). For example, while Max's family is Caucasian, his family beliefs, values, and traditions are influenced by their views on disability, religion, and social behavior. These beliefs were principal in finding a school that cared about Max's social well-being within the school as well as in the classroom. Therefore, as you read about the posture of cultural reciprocity, understand that family's culture is not one dimensional, but rather is comprised of a myriad of factors that shape and influence the family's behaviors.

The premise of cultural reciprocity is that people first become aware of their own cultural beliefs, values, and assumptions before addressing those of others (Kalyanpur & Harry, 2012). Cultural awareness within a school is important because the values and beliefs that are formed over time guide how the school functions. However, these cultural norms can often be taken for granted and the educators believe that their school's behaviors, beliefs, and values represent the dominant culture (Kalyanpur, & Day, 2012).

Kalyanpur and Harry (2012) suggested that there are three levels of cultural awareness: overt, covert, and subtle. People whose awareness is at the overt level recognize obvious external differences (e.g., dress, race, language, etc.) and no extra effort is required to form a relationship. Covert awareness identifies the differences that are not obvious by outward signs (e.g., communication styles, behaviors, etc.). It requires professionals to be more sensitive and observant in order to understand the family's culture. However, the covert level is limited because professionals may not seek to understand the family or they may find an explanation of the behavior that makes sense from their own cultural perspective, but not in accordance with the families' culture. The third level, subtle awareness, is the recognition of our values and beliefs that are rooted in our actions. Subtle awareness is more challenging because it requires educators to evaluate what they believe and why they believe it while not taking for granted, assuming, or demanding that others must comply.

The three levels of cultural awareness relate to cultural reciprocity because the goal is to move educators from the covert level to the subtle level of awareness. Kalyanpur and Harry (2012) demonstrated how to increase cultural awareness when educators work with families from diverse backgrounds who have children with disabilities by implementing what they call the posture of cultural reciprocity.

Next, I describe cultural reciprocity using the following acronym **S.T.E.P.** (**S**elf-awareness, **T**ake time to gather and learn, **E**stablish respect, and **P**articipate and collaborate) as a mnemonic for the process (Trainor, 2012). It should not be interpreted as a simple four-step plan to be accomplished overnight, but rather an ongoing universal approach that helps educators be reflective, particularly when working with families with different cultural norms and influences (Kalyanpur & Harry, 2012). Because cultural reciprocity is a universal approach and unique to each situation, I will apply it to the administrators' and educators' role and consider how these steps, if applied appropriately, could have helped Mrs. Wilson build a positive school climate.

THE POSTURE OF CULTURAL RECIPROCITY

Step 1: Self-awareness. The first step to cultural reciprocity is to identify your own cultural values. Principals should identify the cultural values that are embedded in their interpretation of school culture, student's needs and in their recommendation of service. For instance, Mrs. Wilson, in scenario I, created a school culture that segregated children with disabilities. Step one suggests that Mrs. Wilson should reflect upon why she expects students with disabilities to be educated in an isolated setting. Seeking self-awareness helps the principal to identify if their school practices are rooted in personal biases or a specific U.S. culture. Self-awareness is ongoing and as administrators engage new families in the community, they should continually reflect on their own beliefs, question school practices, and determine if they are working toward an inclusive and welcoming school community.

Step 2: Take time to gather and learn. Principals should take time to recognize the values of families in the school community. This means that administrators and teachers would need to gather information about family beliefs regarding their customs and traditions, perceptions about professional roles, priorities, educational practices, and work ethics (Lynch & Hanson, 2002). While Mrs. Wilson was giving Raschelle a tour of the school, this would have been an opportunity to informally communicate to learn more about their family's educational values, particularly their beliefs toward the inclusion of Max in the general education classroom. While understanding cultural values outside of your own may be difficult, taking the initiative to view situations from the lens of parents of a children with a disabilities shows understanding, empathy, care, and cultural sensitivity (Kalyanpur & Harry, 2012). Step two is very important in creating culturally responsive educators because it facilitates communication and positive relationships with families.

Step 3: Establish Respect. Educators should acknowledge and respect families' beliefs and cultures even if they differ from their own. This requires sharing the basis for their professional belief and assumptions that may be rooted in the mainstream culture and then acknowledging and respecting the families beliefs (Kalyanpur & Harry, 2012). Mrs. Wilson could have applied step three if she would have explained her position about the inclusion of students with disabilities while respecting that Max family's perspective was different. Once the differences are understood, Mrs. Wilson could have begun finding commonalities between the two views. However, in order for Mrs. Wilson to have established respect with the family, she would have had to first be aware of her own beliefs (step one) and then learned about the family's beliefs (step two). When administrators share their beliefs about critical school practices and are willing to accept the family's differences it is a precursor to building a positive school climate. More important, respecting family's values and beliefs allows the administrator to learn more about how those beliefs impact their child's services.

Step 4: Participate and Collaborate. Educators should discuss and collaborate with the family to determine the most effective way to adapt their professional interpretations and recommendations to the value system of the family. In fact, collaborating with the family to meet the needs of the child is a student-centered approach that is the responsibility of the principal. As the administrator, Mrs. Wilson could have developed an alternative plan for Max's transition into the school that is acceptable to her while not compromising the families' beliefs about inclusion (Kalyanpur & Harry, 2012). Educators can meet the needs of the child by considering the family's uniqueness, strengths, and challenges. Furthermore, when administrators collaborate with families who have children with disabilities, it encourages acceptance of all students and allows the family to be active participants in the process.

The purpose of cultural reciprocity is to present a nonbiased approached to help people recognize that how they act and what they believe can be different from others' ways of acting. It is a method that aligns with the author's strategies for effective communications and problem-solving as a means to build relationships with families. While educators have a range of communication styles and abilities (Thoeharis, 2014), educators would benefit from continually being self-aware of their professional behaviors regarding working with families whose cultural beliefs and values are different from their own. When educators take time to gather and learn about families, it is not necessary for them to know all aspects of every family's culture. It is necessary, however, to respect the information that is gathered and then use that information to collaborate with a family to create an optimal educational experience for their child (Harry, Kalyanpur, & Day, 1999; Robinson, 2012). Furthermore, administrators have a responsibility to create a school climate that is culturally responsive to the needs of all their families. This endeavor is no small task; however, it can be accomplished if administrators are culturally responsive and open to change.

SUMMARY & CONCLUSION

School leaders' role in the crafting of the climate and culture is all-encompassing (Peterson & Deal, 1994). The things they say, their nonverbal actions, their behavior, and their success all impact and shape a school's culture. Without the attention, focus, determination, and commitment school cultures can become toxic and unproductive environments.

The intent of this chapter was to use a broad term for school leaders. It is not the sole responsibility of the principal to set the tone for the climate and culture of a school, but also teachers, staff, students, and their families. It is important to recognize that self-awareness and self-reflection by both teachers and students can lead toward an improved school climate and cultural proficiency (Gehrke, 2005).

References

Anderson, M. E. (1991). Principals: How to train, recruit, select, induct, and evaluate leaders for America's schools. Eugene, OR: ERIC Clearinghouse on Education Management, University of Oregon.

Banks, J. (2004). Multicultural education: Characteristics and goals. In J.A. Banks & C. A. Banks (Eds.), *Multicultural Education: Issues and Perspectives* (5th ed.) (pp. 3–30). NY: Wiley.

Barth, R. S. (2006). Improving relationships within the schoolhouse. *Educational Leadership,63*(6), 8–13.

Bauwens, J., & Hourcade, J. J. (1995). *Cooperative teaching: Rebuilding the schoolhouse for all students.* Austin, TX: Pro-Ed.

Benton, E., & Bulach, C. (1995). How an elementary school improved school climate. *ERS Spectrum, 13*(3), 32–38.

Bergan, J. R., & Tombari, M. L. (1975). The analysis of verbal interactions occurring during consultation. *Journal of School Psychology, 13,* 209–226.

Bredberg, E., & Davidson, I. F. W. K. (1999). Ethical reasoning used by teachers of children with severe and profound intellectual disabilities: A preliminary investigation. [Electronic version]. *International Journal of Disability, Development, and Education, 46*(1), 88–107.

Buffie, E. G. (1989). The principal and leadership. *Phi Delta Kappa Educational Foundation,* Bloomington, Indiana.

Bullard, C. (2003). *The itinerant teacher's handbook.* Hillsboro, OR: Butte.

Burke, W., & Marx, G. E. (2011). Maintaining, reframing, and disrupting traditional expectations and outcomes for professional development with critical friend groups. *The Teacher Educator, 46*(1), 32–52.

Burke, W., Marx, G. E., & Lowenstein, E. (2012). Leading, leadership, and learning: exploring new contexts for leadership development in emerging school environments. *Planning and Changing, 43*(1), 113–126.

Burrello, L. C., Hoffman, L. P., & Murray, L. E. (2005). *School leaders building capacity from within: Resolving competing agendas creatively.* Thousand Oaks: Crowin Press.

Caron, E. A., & McLaughlin, M. J. (2002). Indicators of Beacons of Excellence schools: What do they tell us about collaborative practices? *Journal of Educational and Psychological Consultation, 13*, 285–313.

Chiu, M. M. (2000). Effects of status on solutions, leadership, and evaluations during group problem solving. *Sociology of Education, 73,* 175–195.

Cramer, S. F. (1998). *Collaboration: A success strategy for special educators.* Boston: Allyn and Bacon.

Creasey, M. S., & Walther-Thomas, C. S. (1996). Using planning teams to implement inclusive education effectively. *Preventing School Failure, 41*, 39–43.

Deal, T. E., & Peterson, K. D. (1994). *The leadership paradox: Balancing logic and artistry in schools.* San Francisco: Jossey-Bass.

DiPaola, M. F., & Tschannen-Moran, M. (2005). Bridging or buffering: The impact of schools' adaptive strategies on student achievement. *Journal of Education Administration, 43*, 60–71.

Friend, M. & Cook, L. (2010). *Interactions: Collaboration skills for school professionals* (6th ed.). Boston: Pearson.

Friend, M., & Cook, L. (1996). *Interactions: Collaboration skills for school professionals* (2nd ed.). New York: Longman.

Friend, M., & Pope, K. L. (2005). Creating schools in which all students can succeed. *Kappa Delta Pi Record, 41*(2), 56–61.

Fullan, M. (1993). *Change forces: Probing the depths of educational reform.* Bristol, PA: The Falmer Press.

Furman, G., & Starratt, J. (2002). Leadership for democratic community in schools. In J. Murphy (Ed.), *The educational leadership challenge: Redefining leadership for the 21st century* (pp. 105–133). Chicago: The University of Chicago Press.

Gehrke, R. S. (2005). Poor schools, poor students, successful teachers. *Kappa Delta Pi, 42*(1), 14–17.

Halawah, I. (2005). The relationship between effective communication of high school principal and school climate. *Education, 126*(2), 334–344.

Harry, B., Kalyanpur, M. & Day, M. (1999). *The posture of cultural reciprocity: A practical approach to collaborative relationships with families from culturally diverse backgrounds.* Baltimore, MD: Paul Brookes.

Hoy, W., & Feldman, J. (1987), Organizational health: The concept and its measure, *Journal of Research and Development in Education, 20*(4), 30–37.

Hoy, W., & Sabo, J. (1998). *Quality middle schools open and healthy,* Corwin Press, Sage: Thousand Oaks, CA.

Jayanthi, M., & Friend, M. (1992). Interpersonal problem solving: A selected literature review to guide practice. *Journal of Education and Psychological Consultation, 3*, 147–152.

Kalyanpur, M., & Harry, B. (2012). *Cultural reciprocity in special education: Building family-professional relationships.* Baltimore, MD: Brookes.

Katzenmeyer, M., & Moller, G. (2001). *Awakening the sleeping giant: Helping teachers develop as leaders* (2nd ed.). Corwin Press, Sage: Thousand Oaks, CA.

Keiser, K. A., & Schulte, L. E. (2009). Seeking the sense of community: A comparison of two elementary schools' ethical climates. *The School Community Journal, 19*(2), 45–58.

Korir, J. & Karr-Kidwell, P. J. (2000). The relationship between self-esteem and effective educational leadership (ERIC Document Reproduction Service ED 443 142).

Krug, S. E. (1992). Instructional leadership: A constructivist perspective. *Educational Administrative Quarterly, 28*(3), 430–433.

Lieberman, A. (1995). *The work of restructuring schools: Building from the ground up.* New York: Teachers College Press.

Lynch, E. W., & Hanson, M.J. (2002). *A guide for working with children and their families: Developing cross-cultural competence.* Baltimore, MD: Brookes Publishing Company.

McCullen, C. (2006). High five: Building capacity for school excellence. *Principal Leadership, 7*(3), 33–37.

McKenzie, H. S. (1972). SPED and consulting teachers. In F. Clark, D. Evans, & L. Hammerlynk (Eds.), *Implementing behavioral programs for schools and clinics.* Champaign, IL: Research Press.

McLeskey, J., Henry, D., & Hodges, D. (1998). Inclusion: Where is it happening? [Electronic version]. *Teaching Exceptional Children, 35*, 50–54.

Murry, C. (2004). Clarifying collaborative roles in urban high schools: General educators' perspectives. *Teaching Exceptional Children, 36*(5), 44–51.

Neus, A., & Scherf, P. (2005). Opening minds: Cultural change with the introduction of open-source collaboration methods. *IBM Systems Journal, 44*, 215–225.

Osher, D., & Fleischman, S. (2005). Positive culture in urban schools. *Educational Leadership, 62*(6), 84–85.

Pamelazita, W. & Buschbacher, L. F. (2003). Understanding and intervening with the challenging behavior of young children with autism spectrum disorder [Electronic version]. *Language, Speech, and Hearing Services in Schools, 34*(3), 217–227.

Patterson, K. (2005). What classroom teachers need to know about IDEA '97. *Kappa Delta Pi Record, 41*, 61–67.

Peterson, K., & Deal, T. (1998). How leaders influence the culture of schools. *Educational Leadership, 56*(1), 28–30.

Pivik, J., McComas, J., & LaFlamme, M. (2002). Barriers and facilitators to inclusive education. *Exceptional Children, 69*(1), 97–107.

Praisner, C. (2003). Attitudes of elementary school principals toward inclusion of students with disabilities. *Exceptional Children, 69*(1), 97–107.

Robinson, A. H. (2012). Using creativity and collaboration to develop innovative programs that embrace diversity in higher education. *Collected Essays on Learning and Teaching, 5.*

Schmidt, R. J., Rozendal, M. S., & Greenman, G. G. (2002). Reading instruction in the inclusion classroom: Research-based practices [Electronic version]. *Remedial and Special Education, 23*(3), 130–140.

Schumm, J. S. & Vaughn, S. (1995). Getting ready for inclusion: Is the stage set? [Electronic version]. *Learning Disabilities Research & Practice, 10*, 169–179.

Shannon, G. S., & Blysma, P. (2004). *Characteristics of improved school districts: Themes from research.* Olympia, WA: Office of the Superintendent of Public Instruction.

Skrtic, T. (1991). *Behind SPED: A critical analysis of professional knowledge and school organization.* Denver: Love Publishing.

Smith, R., & Leonard, P. (2005). Collaboration for inclusion: Practitioner perspectives. *Equity & Excellence in Education, 38*, 269–279.

Smith, S. (2006). *School Leadership: Handbook for Excellence in Student Learning.* Thousand Oaks: Crowin Press.

Theoharis, R. (2008). Factors related to attrition: A study of one Midwestern university special education program's graduates. *Dissertation.*

Thousand, J. S., Villa, R. E., & Nevin, A. I., (Eds.). (1994). *Creativity and collaborative learning: A practical guide to empowering students and teachers.* Baltimore: Brookes.

Timm, J. T., (1995). *Four perspectives in multicultural education.* Belmont, CA: Wadsworth Publishing Company.

Trainor, (2012). Culturally responsive transition planning: The use of federal workforce development system resources. Presentation at CEC Division on Career Development and Transition Conference. Adapted with permission.

Turnbull, A., & Turnbull, H. R. (2001). *Families, professionals, and exceptionality* (4th ed.). Columbus, OH: Merrill-Prentice Hall.

Turnbull, A., Turnbull, R., Shank, M., & Smith, S. (2004). *Exceptional lives: Special education in today's schools* (4th ed.). Upper Saddle River, NJ: Merrill/Prentice-Hall.

Uline, C., & Tschannen-Moran, M. (2008). The walls speak: The interplay of quality facilities, school climate and student achievement. *The Journal of Educational Administration, 46*(1), 55–73.

Villa, R. A., Thousand, J. S., & Rosenberg, R. L. (1995). Creating heterogeneous schools: A systems change perspective. In M. A. Falvey (Ed.), *Inclusive and heterogeneous schooling.* Baltimore, MD: Brookes.

Walther-Thomas, C. S. (1998). Co-teaching: Benefits and problems that teachers and principals report over time. *Journal for Learning Disabilities, 30*(4), 395–407.

Walther-Thomas, C. S., Korinek, L., McLaughlin, V. L., & Williams, B. T. (2000). *Collaboration for inclusive education: Developing successful programs.* Boston: Allen & Bacon.

York-Barr, J., & Duke, K. (2004). What do we know about teacher leadership? Findings from two decades of scholarship. *Review of Educational Research. 74*(3), 255–316.

8 Related Services for Students with Autism

Chapter Objectives

After studying this chapter readers should be able to:

- Compare and contrast the similarities and differences between appropriate education and reasonable accommodations.
- Identify 3-to-4 related services that are available for students with ASD.
- Summarize the function of multidisciplinary teams when considering appropriate related services.
- Describe how students with ASD can benefit from SPED and related services.

Chapter 8 Subject Index:

1. Appropriate Education
2. Autism Spectrum Disorders
3. Education for All Handicapped Children Act
4. Free Appropriate Public Education
5. Individuals with Disabilities Education Improvement Act
6. Individualized Education Plan
7. Individualized Family Service Plan
8. Intellectual Disabilities
9. Local Education Agency
10. Multidisciplinary Team
11. Occupational Therapist
12. Physical Therapy
13. Savant Syndrome
14. Special Education
15. Speech-Language Pathologists
16. Splinter Skills
17. State Education Agency

INTRODUCTION

As noted throughout this book, the **Individuals with Disabilities Education Improvement Act** (IDEIA, 2004) require students with disabilities to receive **special education** (SPED) which consists of specially designed instruction and services. Specifically for children with **autism spectrum disorders** (ASD) have a heterogeneous set of skills and several significant areas requiring improvement (Thomas, Ellis, McLaurin, Daniels, & Morrissey, 2007). As discussed in Chapter 4, a successful **individualized education plan** (IEP) must take into account the characteristics of each student in order to identify meaningful instructional strategies (see Chapter 11) and related services.

RELATED SERVICES DEFINITION

Students with disabilities are entitled to receive a **free and appropriate public education** (FAPE) and related services, as appropriate. Related services are noninstructional support services such as therapy, counseling, and transportation. The term related services is defined in IDEIA (2004):

> Related services means transportation, and such developmental, corrective, and other supportive services (including speech pathology and audiology services, interpreting services, psychological services, psychological services, physical and occupational therapy, recreation, including therapeutic recreation, social work services, school nurse services designed to enable a child with a disability to receive a free appropriate public education as described in the individualized education program of the child, counseling services, including rehabilitation counseling, orientation and mobility services, and medical services (except that such medical services shall be for diagnostic and evaluation purposes only) as may be required to assist a child with a disability to benefit from special education, and includes the early identification and assessment of disabling conditions in children. Exception: The term does not include a medical device that is surgically implanted, or the replacement of such device (602(26)(A)).

Related services are support services that may be required in order for the child to *benefit* from SPED. It is important to note the word *benefit* (Bowe, 2007). Only related services that are *essential* for a child to receive benefit from instruction and make appropriate progress towards their goals must be provided. This means, while some services might help the student, they are not necessary for the student to benefit from SPED. Therefore, these services are not required.

Related service needs should be determined by the **multidisciplinary team**. Sometimes, it can be difficult for the team to come to consensus on the type and amount of service needed. While a student might benefit from more intense and comprehensive services the school is only required to provide appropriate services.

DEFINING APPROPRIATE EDUCATION

Before delving into how IDEIA (2004) defined an **appropriate education**, it is important to consider *Board of Education v. Rowley* (1982). The case did not involve a student who had autism, rather one who was deaf. This case specifically was a dispute about the meaning of *appropriate education* and was the Supreme Court's first decision regarding SPED and their first opportunity to interpret the FAPE mandate.

In this case, the Course was asked to decide whether the **Education for All Handicapped Children Act** (1975) required a **local education agency** (LEA) to provide an interpreter for Amy Rowley, a student at Furnace Woods School in the Hendrick Hudson Central School District (Turnbull, Stowe, & Huerta, 2007). Amy's parents filed a complaint against her school district, when the district refused to pay for an interpreter. Her parents believed the district was out of compliance with the *Education for All Handicapped Children Act* (1975), because their daughter did not have an interpreter meant she did not have access to FAPE.

Her parents won the case at the federal level, because they stated although Amy was doing better than the average student, she was not learning as much as she could because of her disability (Yell, 2012). Due to the difference in her achievement and potential achievement, the district court ruled Amy had in fact been denied FAPE. Following the federal court trial, the school district appealed to the Supreme Court.

The Supreme Court considered two questions: (a) what is FAPE, and (b) what is the role of state and federal courts in reviewing SPED decisions (Yell, 2012)? The Court sided with the school district—agreeing, that the Education for All Handicapped Children Act (1975) did not require LEA to provide an interpreter for Amy Rowley. The belief was that while the *Education for All Handicapped Children Act* (1975) does place an affirmative duty on the LEA and **state education agency** (SEA) to ensure FAPE is provided to all students with a disability, the LEA satisfies the requirement by providing personalized instruction with sufficient support that allows the student to benefit educationally from the instruction (Turnbull, Stowe, & Huerta, 2007).

Furthermore, Supreme Court Justice Rehnquist stated that FAPE included educational instruction designed to meet the unique needs of a student with a disability, supported by services as needed in order to permit a student to benefit from instruction (Yell, 2012). Therefore, the purpose of FAPE was determined to provide students with disabilities, a basic opportunity which included access to specialized instruction and related services individually designed to result in educational benefit. The Supreme Court rejected the argument school districts were responsible for providing the best possible education for all students with disabilities.

IDEIA (2004) defined *appropriate education* using two criteria: standards and individualization (20 U. S. C. Sec. 1401(9)). The *standards* criterion is one that includes special education and related services (a) that are provided at a public expense without charge to the family; (b) are implemented under public direction and supervision; (c) meet the expectations and standards of the SEA; and (d) includes an appropriate pre-k-12 education (Turnbull, Stowe, & Huerta, 2007).

The *individualized* criterion focuses on the IEP. Each student must have an IEP written specifically to meet his or her educational needs and each infant/toddler must have an **individualized family service plan** established to meet the needs of the child and family. Turnbull et al. (2007) stated criterion are difficult to comprehend in isolation from their history and from IDEIA (2004) as a whole. Together, they provide the foundation for inquiry into what is and is not appropriate education.

This means, when students with a disability receive a related service, those services must be included in the student's IEP and they must be provided to the student at no cost. There have been court cases (*Max M. v. Illinois State Board of Education,* 1986; *Seals v. Loftis,* 1985) in which the courts have ruled school districts must reimburse families for the unilateral provision of related services when it is determined services were necessary for education benefit and the services were not provided by the school (Yell, 2012).

COMMONLY NEEDED SERVICES FOR STUDENTS WITH AUTISM

Children with ASD have distinct deficit in language and communication, social interactions, and often exhibit unusual body movements such as hand flapping and body rocking (American Psychiatric Association, 2000). They also have difficulty participating and attending to social stimuli (Dawson, Meltzoff, & Osterling, 1995). In addition, many also engage in various forms of challenging behaviors, such as self-injury, disruption, and aggression (Simpson & Myles, 1998). Although, impacted in all three areas (communication, socialization, and behavior) no two children with ASD are the same (APA, 2000).

The American Speech-Language-Hearing Association (ASHA, 2007) reported there is great heterogeneity among the ASD population. This is seen in the broad range of cognitive, social, communication, adaptive, and motor abilities. Some children with ASD have **intellectual disabilities** while others function within the normal range. Regardless of intellectual functioning, children with ASD have a developmental disability that impacts social and communication skills and affects home, school, and work and community environments—their ability to participate within each (ASHA, 2007).

Research suggests that interventions that target specific areas of need, such as social skills, language acquisition, and behavior management can greatly improve the lives of children with ASD (National Research Council, 2001). Therefore, it is important for professionals and families to understand the characteristics of autism and the specific needs of the individual student before considering related services.

The next sections of this chapter will focus on these specific characteristics, how they are intertwined as well as the related services to support these areas. Additionally, gross motor, fine motor, sensory, and intellectual functioning will be discussed. This chapter specifically looks at the needs of a child with autism and who provides the services; see Chapter 11 for strategies.

MAX'S SCENARIO SCHOOL CULTURE: MANAGING A SMALL BUSINESS

Soon after Max was diagnosed with autism, he began receiving services (some in our home, some in clinics, and some in a special pre-school setting). As a mother of two small children, it was difficult to keep up with daily routine and family life, as well as manage all of Max's appointments. Sometimes I would compare the craziness to managing a small business—keeping up with time sheets, setting up meetings, and ensuring everyone had the most current and accurate information.

When Max first began services, he received speech and language, **physical therapy**, occupational therapy (for both fine motor and sensory), behavior therapy, and special instruction. These services continued into elementary school, but the goals, amount of time, and the placement varied as his needs changed.

I worked closely with the related service providers. They let me know what skills they were working on and how I could help Max generalize and use those same skills in different environments. For example, at home, I would stick pennies in play dough to help him work on his pincher grasp. When we would walk on the sidewalks, he would jump with two feet off the curb to work a physical therapy skill. Roll down hills, crabwalk, drinking thick milk shakes all worked on sensory integration. I added language to every part of our day—labeled items, sang songs, made up silly words, parallel play, modeled, read stories, asked questions—and answered my own questions. I worked hard to reinforce what Max was learning and the skills he was working on at home and in the community.

Since related services were directly connected to Max's areas of need, they proved to be a lot of work and challenging for him—sometimes extremely stressful. Many students with autism do not indicate in a meaningful ways when they are experiencing difficulty coping. Quite often, they might not know they are in a stage of crisis (Myles & Southwick, 1999). This was often the case for Max. The **occupational therapist** or the SPED teacher would report just getting out the smocks for a project would cause a meltdown for Max. Max would know this meant a sensory activity such as shaving cream on the tables or finger painting.

Due to the behaviors Max was experiencing, he also received behavior therapy. He received services in the community—his therapist would consult with his soccer or swim coach as well as work with Max in these different settings. She had a meeting with those that worked with Max at our church so that his needs would be met there and she provided our family with support in our home. Related services have contributed to the progress Max has made in his academics, communication, social interactions, behavior, fine and gross motor skills, sensory integration, and intellectual functioning at home, school and in the community.

COMMUNICATION & LANGUAGE

Children with autism typically struggle with communication and language development. Communication and language abilities cover a broad range—from no-or-limited language to very complex communication (National Research Council, 2001). Children with autism have difficulty with communication and language in the following areas: (a) alternating focus and maintaining on a topic different from their specific interest (e.g., wanting to discuss their specific interest), (b) inability to use and understand natural gestures to support language, (c) pronoun reversals, (d) echolalia (e.g., repeating language they hear others say either immediately after it is said or repeating it at a later time), and (e) expressive and receptive language (e.g., understanding and using literal and figurative language) (Arnett, Fitzpatrick, & Theoharis, 2013).

One important factor to note that impacts communication and language skills of children with autism is the fact that many do not watch those they are communicating with nor do they automatically turn their heads towards sounds. For children with autism, the complexities of language must be explicitly and directly taught, because applying meaning to their experiences naturally is a challenge. In the past, it was believed that about half of children with autism would learn to communicate in meaningful ways (Prizant, 1983). However, today, with research-based practices and early intervention services 85-90% of children with autism learn to use meaningful communication (Koegel, 2000).

Speech-language pathologists (SLP) have a key role in the screening, evaluation, assessment, diagnosis, and services for individuals with autism. A SLP is often a critical and regular member of the IEP team. A child may need speech and language services in a one-on-one setting when being taught a new skill or concept, but need a small group environment when working on social skills. The SLP also educates other professionals and families how to teach and support language skills throughout the day and in different environments (Janzen, 2003). The SLP or an augmentative or alternative communication specialist may provide technical assistance to augment the child's current communication and possibly select or adapt electronic communication to match the child's specialized and individualized needs. The responsibility may also include providing training to families and other professionals related to how to use the device and use the device with the child.

PROFESSIONAL ANALYSIS

A Coach's Perspective of Working with Kids with Disabilities

By

Greg Walker, Swim Coach

I have found that working with children, including those with disabilities, is extremely rewarding. As a swim coach, I have been privileged to be able to work with and help all different kinds of children with and without disabilities.

It is amazing how kids will not only accept, but also include those who may have difficulties. Typically, they do not treat individuals with disabilities much differently. In addition to observing the kids, I have witnessed this from young adults as well. Whether it was inviting everyone on the team to dinner, or allowing a kid to score a goal the results tend to be positive.

A lot of the time, having a kid with disabilities on the team brings the team together. There have been so many times where the team rallies around that kid, and it makes everyone better. Not just as a person, but I think mentally and emotionally too. I do not think there is anything more rewarding than seeing a smile on the face of someone who has been challenged from the day they were born.

Having children with disabilities on a team makes the children around them grow. Sometimes kids do not really know, or see, what it is like to have disabilities. They do not quite understand. But when someone their age has a disability, and they witness this every day, they realize when they begin to grow mentally and as an overall person.

For example, when I was in high school there was a girl with Down syndrome on my swim team. She was easily the person to most likely make your day. Our team would get closer when she swam. Everyone, and I mean everyone would make sure they watched her swim. And in those moments, everyone is watching, and feeling the same thing and I do not think there is a better, more rewarding way to become closer as a team.

As a swim instructor, I have come across many kids with different kinds of disabilities. Even though they may not learn the same way, the results end up the same. All children have things they really like, or may even be obsessed with. If you find that, learning becomes much easier for them. Finding what they love or like can be tricky sometimes. Some children are quiet, some are loud, and some are not afraid to tell you how it is. When you can relate school, or swimming lessons to something they may like, say trains, learning becomes ten times more fun for them, and teaching becomes ten times easier.

FIRST PERSON TESTIMONIAL

The Boy with the Mischievous Smile

By

Barbara Sullivan, MA CCC-SLP

Recently Max's mother, Raschelle contacted me. Years had passed since I had worked with Max as his Speech-Language Pathologist, I remembered well the intelligent, humorous boy with the mischievous smile. I was excited to hear how well Max is doing and I felt a little proud that I got to play a small part in his story.

When Max began coming to the Clay County Public Health Center in March of 2002 for his speech and language therapy, he was just over two years old. His diagnosis at that time was a delay in receptive and expressive language skills, but he also demonstrated several *red flag behaviors* consistent with ASD.

For example, Max avoided eye gaze, flapped his hands, perseverated on words/phrases, demonstrated echolalia, tactile defensiveness, struggled greatly with transitions, and, at times, would become auditorily/visually over stimulated and attempt to elope from the area. Of course, not all of these behaviors were present all of the time. Max spent time playing peacefully with cars, trains, or action figures without demonstrating any of these behaviors. He would engage in parallel play and did not always mind my *intrusion* into his play scheme, even when I would attempt to change it in order to elicit language and imitation of sounds.

Throughout our sessions, Max worked on increasing his utterances, creating novel utterances, labeling, acknowledging others, transitioning, and responding to his name. Visual schedules using pictures were used to help Max understand what was being asked of him as well as what to expect next. It was the summer of 2002 when Max was diagnosed with high functioning Autism. Although the diagnosis did not change how I worked with Max or his family, it answered some of their questions and opened up the possibility of extra help via state funding for children diagnosed with ASD.

During our initial sessions I interpreted his smile to mean he was feeling shy or even trying to be friendly. However, I soon learned that it usually meant that Max had a plan. Sometimes the plan was to attempt to get hold of another toy, a sticker, or even to hide the object I had been using. Occasionally he was looking for an opening to flee. It was during those early sessions when I discovered Max's fabulous sense of humor and I began to understand just how much he observed even when it appeared he was not even aware of his surroundings.

I was lucky enough to work with Max twice a week for a little over eight months before he transitioned at age three to services through his school district. After that, I worked with Max twice a week for eight weeks for the next four summers.

Each June, when Max came back for summer therapy, I noticed how much he had grown physically, academically, and socially. We continued to work on his receptive and expressive language skills, focusing on asking and answering questions appropriately, telling about remote events, and transitioning not only physically, but also mentally. Imbedded into these sessions were more indirect social skills lessons such as turn taking, acknowledging a communication partner, responding appropriately, and learning to wait. He steadily increased his skills in all areas and worked on honing his very sharp sense of humor, which was typically accompanied by that smile.

During the summer of 2005 it was noted that Max had begun to demonstrate some aggressive behaviors and would perseverate on asking *why* frequently in order to avoid work. Behavior goals were implemented with parental input in order to address these concerns. This was a hard summer for Max.

Looking back, I see it as a time of transition for a child with great growth in language skills yet still struggling to grasp everything that was expected of him both socially and academically.

By the summer of 2006, at age 6:8 years, Max's receptive and expressive language skills were formally assessed and found to be within normal limits. However he continued to struggle with his social, or pragmatic, language skills. Max loved humor and could be very funny; however he was overindulging in humorous antics/responses and not staying on task. As Max had moved from picture reinforcers to written out schedules and activities, a list of four rules for speech as well as the consequences for not following rules was printed off and sent home. These rules were read at the beginning of each session.

After the first six sessions, Max no longer needed the reinforcement of the rules as he followed them and demonstrated very few inappropriate behaviors the rest of the summer. Once Max learned to better control his behavior, he was able to focus on and progress in his goals of understanding and using simple idioms, analogies, and learning to admit he needed help or did not know something. Admitting he needed help was huge for Max as this is a very hard thing to do, even for typically developing children.

Max still had his mischievous smile, but he had expanded it to not only mean he had a plan, but also to share a joke, greet, and to reciprocate a friendly smile. The growth I saw in him over those 4-1/2 years was rewarding and indicated a future full of possibilities.

During the time I worked with Max, I also worked with several other young (i.e., 2-5 years old) children who had either been diagnosed with ASD or demonstrated many characteristics consistent with the diagnosis. All of these children had their own unique personalities and ways of learning. As a clinician, my job was to find what worked best for them to make progress. I conducted therapy under tables, with my back turned partially, while jumping, using quiet voices, loads of wait time, and various other tactics to elicit language to build communication skills.

Having experiences with these children and interactions with their families in this clinic setting gave me a great foundation on which to build when I moved into the public school setting. Since then, I have worked with numerous students from 3-21 years of age who have varying types and severity of ASD and its related diagnosis. Based upon what I learned from Max, the other children at the clinic, and the students I have worked with in public education, I see that although every student is different and has their own unique learning style, some things are fairly consistent. In general, these include the need for visual schedules and/or reinforcers to help process information, structure in order to aid in prediction, minimize auditory and visual stimulation (i.e., busy environments), allow them time to demonstrate their skills, and appreciation of their strengths and use those to build a bridge to the more difficult skills.

Another important lesson I have learned is that, for the most part, no matter how hard a parent, clinician, teacher, or other adult tries to help encourage a child with ASD to be social and learn skills, they cannot make them *want* to do it. That is when the power of a peer cannot be underestimated. Many students with ASD will imitate another child or student long before they will imitate the same modeled behavior from an adult.

Flexibility in using various approaches has helped me when working with children diagnosed with ASD. Keeping in mind that just as each child is different, approaches should be varied and adapted as needed. What works for one student may not be very successful for others.

Children diagnosed with ASD can learn and have friends. I have seen many students with the diagnosis go on to be successful adults, not just academically, but also personally and professionally. Those of us who get to work with these students all feel a little bit of pride in every small step they make, knowing it helps them move that much closer to reaching their potential.

Way to go Max, keep reaching higher!

Social Interactions. A typical social development is a key characteristic of autism (Dawson, Metzoff, & Osterling, 1995). When children are being diagnosed with autism, families are often asked to think back to when their child was a baby or toddler and describe how they reacted to being touched, cuddled, or picked-up. Often the responses are not how babies or toddlers typically respond. Some children do not discriminate among different relationships—families, teachers, and strangers are all treated as similar relationships. APA (2000) established four criteria for diagnosing atypical social development in children with autism: (a) lack of nonverbal behavior, (b) lack of peer relationships, (c) lack of spontaneous shared interest with others, and (d) lack of reciprocity. These characteristics overlap with the characteristics of communication and language and are closely related. In addition, it is a challenge for many children with autism to know the emotional state of others, express their own emotions, and form relationships with peers and adults (Dawson et al., 1995).

At one end of the spectrum of challenges in relating to others, especially peers, is a reserved child, who intentionally avoids social interactions, then there is the child who may be described as passive, who will tolerate social situations with encouragement and prompting, and can initiate social interaction, but primarily only to access something he or she wants. The next child may interact with others, but the interactions may be awkward and are typically with adults rather than peers (Buron & Wolfberg, 2008). There is evidence that children across the spectrum rarely establish long term or typical friendships (Orsmond, Krauss, & Seltzer, 2004).

There are three main reasons it is difficult for children with autism who lack social skills to build and sustain relationships with others—theory of mind, central coherence, and joint attention. Children with autism have not developed an awareness and understanding of their own beliefs, perspectives, and intentions, nor do they see how theirs differ from others (Arnett et al., 2013). This creates difficulty in understanding the emotions and desires of others and their ability to show empathy (Baron-Cohen & Wheelwright, 2004). Children with ASD often show deficits in joint attention—a social skill that begins to emerge during infancy. When two individuals use nonverbal communication (e.g., gestures and eye gaze) during conversation, it allows them to share their space using the same point of reference. This is an important component of language and social development. Central coherence is the ability to focus on both details as well as wholes. Individuals with autism appear to place more heightened focus on details rather than wholes. The lack of joint attention is one reason children with autism struggle to learn what is happening in their environment naturally (Wolfberg & Shculer, 1993).

It cannot be assumed that children with ASD fully or accurately understand a particular problem, situation, or expectation (Janzen, 2003); due to the fact they have difficulty with executive function which impacts their ability to sequence the required steps to solve problems and achieve objectives. Therefore, they experience difficulty completing tasks that require self-regulated planning and flexibility. Many children with ASD may have difficulty breaking down chunks of information, analyzing, making comparisons, integrating details in order to understand cause and effect relationships, generalizing concepts, developing broader ideas, and understanding the perspective of others (Janzen, 2003).

It is important when thinking about the socialization needs of the child with ASD to think about the placement—individual setting, small group, or large group setting. It is also important to think about how socialization goals can be included in daily activities—walking into the classroom and responding to a classmate's greeting. For example, an SLP can provide support and consultation to other professionals and family for working on socialization goals, but socialization is something *all* related service providers need to be aware of when establishing a plan for the child.

Behavior. There are several areas of behavior to address concerning children with ASD (e.g., aggression and self-injurious behavior, repetitive and unusual behavior patterns, sameness and perseverance). While these areas are characteristic of the disability, not all children may experience them to the same degree or at all. It is important to remember that when behavioral difficulties occur, the child is giving a message. This is true for *all* children, behaviors are messages. However, for children with limited language, difficulty expressing their wants and needs, and an inability to understand social situations and their environment, it is important that others be cognizant of the messages their behaviors send. They typically appear to be a function of: (a) lack of social skills and social understanding, (b) lack of general understanding with the environment, (c) high stress or anxiety level, (d) lack of control over the environment, (e) an obsessive and single minded pursuit of their own specific interest, (f) inability to understand the needs and feelings of others, or (f) a defensive panic reaction (Myles & Southwick, 1999).

Therefore, the behavior problems of children with ASD are associated with a more generalized inability to function in a world they perceive to be irregular and intimidating. Researchers and practitioners have developed a list of additional possible behavior functions that include: (a) escape or avoidance, (b) attention from peers or adults, (c) emotional state (e.g., anger, depression, frustration, or confusion), (d) power or control, (e) intimidation, (f) sensory stimulation, (g) fear—including fear of failure, (h) request for something (Myles & Southwick, 1999). Understanding which function the behavior is serving is one of the initial steps to setting up an effective intervention.

On a behavioral continuum—children through adulthood—with ASD may range from withdrawn to active (Myles & Southwick, 1999). Regardless, of where they are on the continuum, they are often viewed as socially awkward, self-centered, inflexible, and lack empathy and understanding.

Aggression & Self-Injurious Behavior. Aggression and self-injurious behavior are analogous in the fact that both types of behaviors cause harm. The first, aggressive behaviors are directed towards others and are problematic in all environments. Some children with autism cause harm to themselves, self-injurious behaviors, such as head banging, biting, or scratching. Children with self-injurious behaviors are at serious risk for causing permanent harm to themselves (Arnett et al., 2013). Both of these types of behaviors can continue unto adulthood (Hyman & Towbin, 2007).

Repetitive & Unusual Behavior Patterns. Repetitive and unusual behavior patterns are characteristics of children with ASD. Repetitive behavior is when a child repeats a movement or verbalization. They may exhibit a pattern of repetitive behaviors such as flapping their hands during a favorite activity or rocking their body while sitting. These movements could also include humming or making other noises or clicking a pen. A child with autism may spend extensive amounts of time engaged in these distracting behaviors. This can make it difficult for them to participate in other activities as well as learn new skills and concepts. Another important consideration for teachers, are the social stigmas that accompany these behaviors. The social stigmas may inhibit others from interacting with the child in an appropriate and meaningful ways which prevents the child from being included in school and community activities (Loftin, Odom, & Lantz, 2007).

Sameness & Perseverance. Children with autism have a need for strict adherence to routines and insistence on sameness that gives them a sense of predictability, structure, and security. When there is an interruption in their daily or normal routine, an unexpected assembly at school for example, the child can become stressed or anxious. They may also have a need for items to be placed in the same place and may become upset with change. What may seem like insignificant changes in routine or placement can be significant causing meltdowns.

Unlike other children, children with ASD are not deliberately misbehaving or seeking attention. This makes it difficult for professionals and families to know how to improve behaviors, especially in settings where multiple things are happening (e.g., teaching math and managing a classroom or doing laundry). Sometimes to help understand the behaviors of children with autism a behavior specialist maybe needed.

A behavior specialist will observe the environment and the child with autism and gather data about what seems to cause difficult behaviors and what seems to be calming. After gathering this information, the behavior specialist can suggest changes with the environment, interventions, and accommodations. This is not a quick and easy process. Data is gathered again to see how the intervention is working and then the intervention is modified as needed.

Gross Motor. Some children with autism may need help with developing age appropriate motor skills (such as throwing, catching, jumping, hoping, climbing, or skipping) or have low muscle tone. Physical therapy can help children with autism work towards these goals. They also may help with treating the impairments that impact motor function; such has problems with respiratory control or coordination, improving posture, or developing a fitness program. A physical therapist may serve on the multidisciplinary team and provide a related service to children with autism. Physical therapists can provide services in a variety of settings: school, home, community, hospital, or clinic.

Fine Motor. Some children with ASD may have difficulty with fine motor tasks such as picking up small objects, tying their shoes, hand writing, and buttoning their shirt. Occupational therapists provide services to children in schools, home, and community or in a clinic. They work to modify activities so that children with autism can participate fully and successfully in all daily activities, self-care, and social situations. Occupational therapist may develop strategies and provide services, collaborate with other professionals, provide family support, and consult with other community organizations.

Sensory Integration. Sensory sensitivity (i.e., hyperresponsive or hyporesponsive) is an area of autism that little is known and more research is needed. Harrison and Hare (2004) reported that between 70-80% of children with autism have difficulty or have unusual reactions to sensory stimulation. Children with ASD maybe either hypersensitive or hyposensitive to sensory input from their environment.

Hypersensitive means the child is overresponsive to the input from their environment. They may not be able to tolerate certain noises (such as a fire truck siren) or they can hear sounds others are not able to hear (such as butterfly wings) or visual stimuli (such as florescent lights). Some children may dislike the feel of certain textures (e.g., grass on bare feet or tags in clothing). Because of taste, texture, or smell some children with autism may refuse to eat specific foods (Arnett et al., 2013).

Hyposensitive means a child is underresponsive to input from their environment. They may appear oblivious to sensory stimuli that an individual would typically have a reaction. To an observer, children who are hyposensitive, these children may demonstrate the characteristics of children who are deaf or blind. In fact, several diagnoses for autism begin with hearing evaluations, because the child is displaying the characteristics related to hearing loss. In addition, some children with autism do not feel pain. Finally, it is not uncommon for a child with ASD to show a combination of both hypersensitive and hyporsensitive responses to sensory stimulation within the environment (Arnett et al., 2013). A child may, for example, be hypersensitive to sounds and dislike loud noises such as the school bell, but have a hyposensitive response to touch and not notice when they fall and scrape their knee.

Children with ASD, who respond to sensory input with either a hypersensitive or hyposensitive response, may respond negatively when overloaded with certain types of sensory stimuli (Myles & Southwick, 1999). Families and professionals have reported behavior problems (including meltdowns) associated with sensory stimuli including the child's fear of anticipated by unpleasant sensory stimuli. While reports on sensory integration problems are for the most part anecdotal, research does support family observations (Myles & Southwick, 1999). Research conducted by Myles, Hagiwara, Dunn and colleagues (2004) reported that families and teachers frequently observed the following behaviors: (a) difficulties focusing with varied stimuli, (b) prefers quiet activities and games, (c) has difficulty paying attention, (d) prefers certain tastes and foods, (e) has difficulty with change, (f) has low frustration, and (c) seems anxious.

An occupational therapist understands the neurology of sensory processing and motor functioning (Janzen, 2003). Occupational therapists are especially helpful in assessing and finding solutions related to sensory overload, attention, stereotypic behavior, and self-injury. They may provide individual therapy and collaborate and consult with other professionals and family members. An occupational therapist may provide instruction and give suggestions on how to adapt natural, developmentally appropriate activities so that appropriate sensory stimulation and motor skills are provided throughout the child's environment and during daily activities. An occupational therapist should be a regular member of the multidisciplinary team during early development and intervention services and as a child needs continue during later development.

Intellectual Functioning. The intellectual abilities of children with ASD span across a full range. However, epidemiological surveys show that 70-80% of those with autism also meet the criteria for intellectual disabilities (Coolican, Bryson, & Zwaigenhaum, 2008). Of those individuals, half are in the severe to profound range of intellectual disabilities. Some researchers and professionals differentiate those with intellectual disabilities from those without by using the terms low-functioning and high-functioning autism (Arnett et al., 2013). It should be noted, it is common practice for those with low functioning autism also to receive a diagnosis of intellectual disability as though there are two co-occurring diagnoses rather than a modifier to indicate the level of functioning (Buron & Wolfberg, 2008). Buron and Wolfberg (2008) also stated, "When autism is at its most severe, there is essentially no capacity to attach meaning to sensory information" (p. 58). This reduction in information-processing with preservation of the autism characteristics presents itself as an intellectual disability. Some cognitive processing problems seem to be specific to autism. Children with autism may experience challenges with coding and categorizing information (Scheuerman & Webber, 2002).

Two other some-what common intellectual functioning characteristics are **savant syndrome** and **splinter skills**. Savant syndrome describes an individual ability to display giftedness in a specific area such as mathematical calculations, memorizing dates in history or musical skills while functioning in all other areas with an intellectual disability (Heaton & Wallace, 2004). Researchers estimate about 10% of individuals with autism have savant syndrome. Splinter skills are when a child has excellent performance in some skills which are unexpected due to their performance in other areas. It is estimated between 10-15% of children with autism have splinter skills (Heaton & Wallace, 2004).

Often times, the SPED teacher is responsible for helping ensure the child has access to the general education curriculum and accommodations and modifications are in place, so that the student can be successful with the content. While it is the SPED teacher and not a related service provider who is primarily responsible, it does not mean related service providers are unaware of the child's needs in this area or that they do not address these skills while they are introducing other concepts. For example, the SLP can reinforce vocabulary that matches the social studies curriculum. Whereas the OT can have the child work math problems using different types of paper and writing utensils such a pencil, pen, marker, or crayons.

COLLABORATING WITH PROFESSIONALS

When professionals and families work together it enhances generalization skills. Children with ASD often have difficulties being able to use skills learned in one context, environment, or with one person to other contexts, and other individuals (Buron & Wolfberg, 2008). A collaborative partnership amongst all professionals and family can enhance the effectiveness of the services, skills, and concepts of related services as strategies are implemented at school, home, and in the community.

Getting all of the service providers on the same page to organize and plan goals, accommodations, implementation, and data collection, so that skills and concepts can be generalized to multiple contexts is difficult to say the least. In many cases, arranging a schedule (difficult to do in many cases without administrative support) is not the only thing needed in most cases (Friend & Cook, 2010). Brownell and Walther-Thomas (2002) noted another factor of scheduling that needs to be considered is how the schedule will impact other service providers and programs within the school. This matter is extremely important when considering elementary and middle schools in which most individualized services happen in the general education classroom. Consider the list of professionals who could be going into a general education classroom to work with teachers and students (Friend & Cook, 2010):

- Special Education Teachers;
- Speech/Language Therapist;
- Occupational Therapist;
- Physical Therapist;
- Counselors;
- Social Workers;

- Psychologist;
- Paraeducators;
- Title I Reading & Math Teachers;
- Parent Volunteers;
- Bilingual Educators.

Coordinating these efforts can be difficult for a classroom teacher. This section only draws awareness to the pragmatic issues of collaboration when a large number of professionals are involved as well as outline the benefits for children with autism when all service providers are aware of the goals and strategies everyone is working on and who is responsible.

SUMMARY & CONCLUSION

The challenges and assets of children with autism are varied. The areas of cognition, communication and language, socialization, sensory issues, and behavior each present characteristics that differentiate these children from their typically developing peers. When their environment is structured in ways that meets their needs, it can reduce stress and anxiety for students with ASD.

Related service professionals can help make accommodations and modifications as well as work on teaching skills in a specific area that can be generalized to different environments. The roles and responsibilities of the related service providers may overlap. As the child improves their language and communication abilities, this will reduce behaviors. Developing a visual schedule, helps to reduce anxiety and promote language and communication.

References

American Psychiatric Association. (2000). *Diagnostic and statistical manual of mental disorders* (6th ed.). Washington, DC: Author.

American Speech-Language-Hearing Association. (2007). Scope of practice in speech-language pathology [Scope of Practice]. Retrieved June 18, 2014, from www.asha.org/policy

Anderson, M. E. (1991). *Principals: How to train, recruit, select, induct, and evaluate leaders for America's schools*. Eugene, OR: ERIC Clearinghouse on Education Management, University of Oregon.

Arnett, S., Fitzpatrick, M., & Theoharis, R. (2013). *Foundations of special education: Understanding students with exceptionalities.* Dubuque, IA: Kendall Hunt.

Baron-Cohen, S., & Wheelwright, S. (2004). The empathy quotient: An investigation of adults with Asperger syndrome or high functioning autism, and normal sex differences. *Journal of Autism and Developmental Disorders, 34*(2), 163–175.

Bowe, F. G. (2007). *Early childhood special education birth to eighth* (4th ed.). Clifton Park, NY: Thomas Delmar Learning.

Brownell, M. T., & Walther-Thomas, C. (2002). An interview with Dr. Marilyn Friend. *Intervention in School and Clinic, 37*, 223–228.

Buron, K. D., & Wolfburg, P. (2008). *Learners on the autism spectrum: Preparing highly qualified educators.* Shawnee Mission, KS: Autism Asperger Publishing Co.

Coolican, J., Bryson, S. E., & Zwaigenbaum, L. (2008). Brief report: Data on the Stanford-Binet Intelligence Scales (5th ed.) in children with autism spectrum disorders. *Journal of Autism and Developmental Disabilities, 38*, 190–197.

Dawson, G., Meltzoff, A., & Osterling, J. (1995). *Children with autism fail to orient to naturally occurring social stimuli.* Poster presented at the 1995 meeting of the Society for Research in Child Development, Indianapolis, IN.

Friend, M., & Cook, L. (2010). *Interactions: collaboration skills for school professionals* (6th ed.). Boston: Pearson.

Harrison, J., & Hare, J. D. (2004). Brief report: Assessment of sensory abnormalities in people with autistic spectrum disorders. *Journal of Autism and Developmental Disorders, 34*, 727–730.

Heaton, P., & Wallace, G. L. (2004). Annotation: The savant syndrome. *Journal of Child Psychology and Psychiatry, 45*, 899–911.

Hyman, S. L., & Towbin, K. E. (2007). Autism spectrum disorders. In M. L. Batshaw, L. Pellegrino, & N. J. Roizen (Eds.), *Children with disabilities* (6th ed., pp. 325–343). Baltimore: Paul H. Brookes.

Janzen, J. E. (2003). *Understanding the nature of autism: A guide to the autism spectrum disorders* (2nd ed.). San Antonio: PsychCorp.

Koegel, L. (2000). Interventions to facilitate communication in autism. *Journal of Autism and Developmental Disorders, 30*(5), 383–391.

Loftin, R. L., Odom, S. L., & Lantz, J. F. (2007). Social interactions and repetitive motor behaviors. *Journal of Autism and Developmental Disorders, 38*, 1124–1135.

Myles, B. S., & Southwick, J. (1999). *Asperger syndrome and difficult moments: Practical solutions for tantrums, rage, and meltdowns*. Shawnee Mission, KS: Autism Asperger Publishing Co.

Myles, B. S., Hagiwara, T., Dunn, W., Rinner, L., Reese, M., Huggins, A., & Baker, S. (2004). Sensory issues in children with Asperger syndrome and autism. *Training in Developmental Disabilities, 39*(4), 283–290.

National Research Council. (2001). *Educating children with autism.* Washington, DC: National Academy Press.

Orsmond, G. I., Krauss, M. W., & Seltzer, M. M. (2004). Peer relationships and social and recreational activities among adolescents and adults with autism. *Journal of Autism & Developmental Disorders, 34*(3), 245–256.

Prizant, B. M. (1983). Language acquisition and communicative behavior in autism: Toward and understanding of the "whole" of it. *Journal of Speech and Hearing Disorders, 48*, 296–307.

Scheuerman, B., & Webber, J. (2002). *Autism: Teaching DOES make a difference.* Belmont, CA: Wadsworth-Thompson Learning.

Scheuermann, B., & Webber, J. (2002). *Autism: Teaching does make a difference.* Independence, KY: Cengage Learning.

Simpson, R. L., & Myles, B. S. (1998). Understanding and responding to the needs of children with autism. In R. L. Simpson, & B. S. Myles (Eds.), *Educating children and youth with autism: Strategies for effective practice.* Austin, TX: Pro-ED.

Thomas, K. C., Ellis, A. R., McLaurin, C., Daniels, J., & Morrissey, J. P. (2007). Access to care for autism related services. *Journal of Autism and Developmental Disorders, 37*(10), 1902–1912.

Turnbull, H. R., Stowe, M. J., & Huerta, N. E. (2007). *Free appropriate public education: The law and children with disabilities* (7th ed.). Boston, MA: Pearson.

Wenkart, R. D. (2000). *Appropriate education for students with disabilities: How courts determine compliance with IDEA.* Horsham, PA: LRP publication.

Wolfberg, P., & Schuler, A. (1993). A case illustration of the impact of peer play on symbolic activity in autism. Paper presented at the annual meeting of the Society for Research in Child Development, New Orleans, LA.

Yell, M. L. (2012). *The law and special education.* Boston, MA: Pearson.

9 Paraeducators

Chapter Objectives

After studying this chapter readers should be able to:

- Explain how policies have helped and hindered paraeducators.
- Compare and contrast *the various roles and responsibilities* of paraeducators.
- Discuss the similarities and differences between terms paraeducator and paraprofessional.
- Identify3-to-5 key factors while working with paraeducators in the classroom and school settings.

Chapter 9 Subject Index:

1. Free Appropriate Public Education
2. Elementary and Secondary Education
3. Individuals with Disabilities Education Act
4. Local Education Agency
5. No Child Left Behind Act
6. Special Education
7. The Education for all Handicapped Children Act
8. The Individuals with Disabilities Improvement Act

INTRODUCTION

A Rose by Any Other Name. The term paraeducator is used throughout this chapter, but the position has many titles (e.g., instructional aides, teacher's aide, para-professional, teacher's assistant). If broken into parts and analyzed, the second part, educator, is a noun commonly used. However, the prefix must be comprehended and understood why *para* is preferred as a descriptor for this position.

The prefix *para* is appropriate when naming an occupational role that is considered ancillary or subsidiary to the noun it is attached, such as para-legal. Despite being subordinate to a profession requiring significant schooling and training, it is a role that demands the individual to receive ample professional development to fulfill. Therefore, paraeducators are secondary to certified teachers, supportive of the certified teacher, but must be trained how to provide the supplementation.

The dictionary defines *para* as "at or to one side of, beside, side by side." Thus, paraeducators are the personnel who serve at or to one side of an educator, even beside an educator. When this title is used in some areas it is often reflective of the different responsibilities of the position (i.e., teacher's assistant in contrast to para-professional or paraeducator), or it may just denote the individual choices of a demographic location within the United States. These personnel emerged due to a need in the public schools;

crises calls for quick solutions. During crises, there is little time to coordinate a title, much less define the role, or create standards of expectations. The demand was there and paraeducators met that demand.

Age, Rank, & Serial Number. Currently there are 780,000 instructional and non-instructional paraeducators employed in the U.S. Public Schools, so they total 34% of the uncertified personnel within the school system. Of this number 91% are working directly with formative aged students (i.e., preschool, kindergarten, & elementary), but most work with students in their early, formative years. Seventy-five percent of them are supporting students with disabilities. Eighty-one percent of them are considered full-time employees, yet full time often is defined as when students are in session and does not include time for professional development. Some professional development offerings are available through the schools, but much of their training has to be attained on their own time. Eighty-three percent of those hired have job responsibilities which promote and include school safety, such as recess duty and lunchroom responsibilities.

Ninety-four percent of them are female with an average age of 50 years. Seventy-seven percent of them live and work in the same community, often the same community their own children attend. Eighty percent of them are married and frequently are mothers themselves. Their retention rate is 70%, so schools often complain about the turnover rate, and the constant need to rehire and retrain. Yet 61%, when asked, state they would like to stay in the position until retirement age. When one takes into consideration their average age of 50, then 11 average years on the job is fitting.

Typically paraeducators do not receive formal training for their job, though 29% have a two-year college degree. However, an associate's degree may not have included any coursework concerning teaching methods. Additionally 39% have taken some college towards an associate's degree. Twenty percent have a bachelor's degree, 5% even have a master's or higher degree, but these degrees often do not pertain to education.

The typical hourly wage for paraeducators is between $8-and-$9 an hour with an average salary of $18,052. Generally, the paraeducators' position is the lowest paid position within a **local education agency** (LEA) or school district. On average they work 6.7 hours daily (when the pupils are in school), and this is often referred to as full-time employment despite the fact that the common definition of full-time is an 8-hour-day. Benefits, such as insurance or sick leave are inconsistent from one LEA and/or state to another.

The conditions of their jobs imply that the role is undefined, as 21% work without a job description, 15% who have a job description that is so generic is does not describe their role, and 46% are requested to fulfill roles that are not included into that description. Sixty-one percent are not consulted about the formation of their job description, so often the match between their skills and the job expectations is poor (French, 2003; NEA, 2007).

WHY ARE THEY HIRED BY SCHOOLS?

Public education is continuously charged with the task of preparing students with and without disabilities to be productive members of society. Due to the individuality of humans, insuring all students with disabilities the rights to a **free and appropriate public education** demands forethought, adaptation, reflection, reform, and diligence. When the recent past is reviewed our government's attempts to think ahead, to adjust slightly towards the better, to look back readdressing missed components, and to restructure education is evident. Students at risk for failure due to disabilities, racial differences, poverty, and English language acquisition have been addressed conscientiously and with diligence. Education, which 75 short years ago was limited to some, is now embracing all students. Paraeducators resulted from an outcome of public education's endeavor to answer the challenges of educating *all.*

Legislations, such as **Head Start**, **Title I**, the **Individuals with Disabilities Education Improvement Act** (IDEIA, 2004), and **No Child Left Behind Act** (NCLB, 2002) have all addressed teacher quality as a necessary means to improving the excellence of education. This intensification resulted in an unpredicted outcome, as the number of highly qualified teachers was not available to meet mandated expectations. Scrambling to provide students with disabilities their rightful support, LEAs hired uncertified personnel to assist this limited number of highly qualified teachers. A practice evident for years in the medical field (e.g., doctors assisted by nurses who were in turn assisted by aides), provided schools with a quick solution to an immediate need. The needs were so numerous that with each and every new legal authorization a surge of paraeducators' employment was evident, so that the increase of paraeducators' employed since 1969 is 1,178% (Reinfelds, 2012).

WHAT DOES THE LAW STATE CONCERNING THEIR (PARAEDUCATORS) ROLE FOR MY CHILD?

As previously stated, the number of legislation from 1975 to the present has been numerous and represents a diligent attempt to reform education to include all students rather than a few. Reviewing all of these mandated pieces of legislation might be interesting, but not necessarily relevant to the current topic of paraeducators. Only a review of the key mandates that show our government responding to this surge of personnel is provided below.

ESEA & IDEA. Title I of **Elementary and Secondary Education** (ESEA, 1994) was an extensive stature attempting to add funding for education. It was the first mandate that specifically addressed the uncertified personnel in the schools. This policy defined paraeducators' role as provision of direct instruction to students under the supervision of a teacher, whose primary responsibility was the provision of instructional services to students. It expected a collaborative relationship between those teachers and the paraeducators through professional development and participation in academic planning. It made it the responsibility of LEA for paraeducators to have a high school diploma prior to employment, but it also stated that paraeducators needed the knowledge and skills necessary to assist pupils with achieving their academic goals.

The Education for all Handicapped Children Act (P.L. 94-142, 1975), was reauthorized in 1990 and retitled the ***Individuals with Disabilities Education Act***. It was reauthorized again in 1997 and addressed paraeducators. It mandated paraeducators to be included in the professional development expectations for teachers in 1990. Although ESEA (1994) and IDEA (1997) were explicit, it was understood that paraeducators must either have or be given the skills needed to support achieving students.

NCLB. NCLB (2002) attempted to address paraeducators specifically, and recognized the need for policy and regulations. The role of paraeducators was refined: to reinforce and augment the teacher's effort by providing students instructional support under the direct supervision of a highly qualified teacher. It specified that this role did not include introducing new skills, concepts, academic content to pupils, or designing instruction for pupils; this remained the teacher's role. The pre-employment expectation of a high school diploma was risen to two years of study at an institution of higher education, an associate's degree, or to meet a rigorous standard of quality by passing an assessment showing knowledge of and abilities in the instruction of reading, writing, and mathematics readiness. It also limited the numbers of paraeducators hired without also increasing the numbers of highly qualified teachers on staff. This policy had its limitations, as it's scope of influence was bound to only those receiving funding for explicit reasons, but even with these boundaries, its' influence is evident as many states and LEA have decided that all paraeducators in their employment must comply with these expectations.

WHAT INFLUENCED THESE MANDATED EXPECTATIONS FOR PARAEDUCATORS?

This review of policy implies that while the lack of highly qualified teachers resulted in the use of paraeducators, the support they offered had enough merit to address their quality legally. Inclusion within policy implies that paraeducators have been included as a viable member of public education. But the demand for paraeducators was not lead by policy, but instead policy is in response to the demands of many. Legislation occurred because people requested such; a review of the professional literature shows that parents, students, and teachers have demanded all of the current policy components, and are calling for more.

WHAT ARE THESE INFLUENCERS CONCERNED WITH NOW?

Three topics emerged when the literature is reviewed: roles, relationships, and responsibilities. The first topic, clearly defining the role of both the paraeducators, as well as the teachers supervising those paraeducators, impacts student success. Well-defined roles are needed to insure that the support needed by students is in place. The second topic, creating a collaborative relationship between paraeducators, teachers, and parents, also benefits the level of success for students with disabilities. The advantage of working relationships where each party contributes toward this success is a given. Once the roles are defined, and a relationship has been established, the third topic, responsibilities can easily be observed. Yet once the responsibilities are listed it is important to match those responsibilities with the skill level of the paraeducators. If the match is not possible, then professional development must be offered to raise the skill level to, indeed, match the responsibility listing. Knowing who must accomplish what towards the establishment of a positive learning environment for a student and knowing that the person entrusted with the responsibility has the skill to do so can only enhance student success.

Roles. Using paraeducators as providers of direct instruction to students under the supervision of a teacher (ESEA, 1994) was refined to reinforce and enhance the teacher's effort (NCLB, 2002). Direct instruction implied that paraeducators were able to teach, yet research between 1994 and 2001 illustrates why this implication needed refinement. The professional petitions (French, 1999; French & Pickett, 1997; Pickett, 1999), the parental pleas (French & Chopra, 1999), the pressure from paraeducators (Minondo, Meyer, & Xin, 2001; O'Connor & French, 1998) and the stress from students (Maag, Vasa, & Reid, 1998; Marks, Schrader, & Levine, 1999; Skar & Tamm, 2001) contributed to this refinement. While it may seem logical, there is also the ethical issue to consider: paraeducators, uncertified to teach, should not provide direct instruction to students. When the role of both the paraeducators and the teachers are established and understood, teachers cannot neglect their role as the educator, and paraeducators will not overstep their role to reinforce and supplement the teacher's effort.

Proximity Harm. The current mandated definition of the paraeducators' role has not addressed a concern current literature has focused on. While the role of paraeducators is to enhance student success towards their academic plans, students do not always view this supplement as positive (Broer, Doyle, & Giangreco, 2005). Students sometimes view this support as an invasion of their liberties and seem too parental-like (Skar & Tamm, 2001). Observation of students in the classroom has illustrated possible reasons why pupils feel this way. The highest concern is expressed when an individual student is limited to the one-to-one model of support, but this may occur with any inadequately trained paraeducators. Observation shows, when an adult remains by the pupil's side throughout the academic day (even if a team of adults are rotating support), many issues emerge (Giangreco & Broer, 2007; Suter & Giangreco, 2008).

First, the pupil is often separated physically from their peers. This may not be intentional, but when the paraeducator remains in close proximity to the student, this limits others from being close (Giangreco & Doyle, 2002). If viewing a classroom (empty of students), this proximity concern is evident. If one adult chair is next to the student desk, yet no other pupils have adult chairs near their desk, then that whoever is assigned that pupil desk is being singled out as different. Inclusion of a pupil with his or her peers has not occurred; the peers will respond to this nonverbal communication of *different* by treating the pupil differently. Naturally, this stigma creates a second concern, interaction with peers is reduced (Giangreco, Edelman, Luiselli, & MacFarland, 1997; Malmgren & Causton-Theoharis, 2006). The third concern may also be a natural result of close proximity by an adult. The pupil can become unnecessarily dependent upon adult assistance (Blacher & Rodriguez, 2007). Given adult proximity has been shown to increase pupil's attention to task (Werts, Zigmond, & Leeper, 2001) offering professional development to paraeducators which increases the skills of how an adult can use proximity without invading a pupil's space, and, therefore, foster independence in a student can address these three concerns easily.

A fourth concern when one-to-one assignments are observed is the limited access the pupil has with the teacher (Giangreco, Broer, & Edelman, 2001; Harris, 2011; Young & Simpson, 1997). The teacher will talk to the paraeducator, rather than the student; the presence of the paraeducator seems to lower the teacher's ownership for the pupil. The teacher makes several assumptions including but not limited to (a) the paraeducator is communicating adequately with the parent concerning the pupil's academic progress, (b) the paraeducator knows and understands the pupil's academic goals, and (c) the paraeducator is adequately trained to offer the appropriate directive instruction to the pupil. Not only is the pupil missing directive instruction from the teacher, the paraeducator is not being given adequate instructions from that teacher as to what best practice is concerning this directive instructional need (Giangreco, Yuan, McKenzie, Cameron, & Fialka, 2005). While teachers are usually pleased to have the assistance of paraeducators (McNally, Cole, & Waugh, 2001) they often express a reluctance to supervise paraeducators because they may not have been prepared to do so (Drecktrah, 2000; French, 2001), or due to a preparedness they were assigned to supervise several paraeducators working elsewhere in the building rather than under their direct supervision (French, 1998).

Connecting or Overstepping. Paraeducators have become important connectors for schools. Parents report that they value their relationship with the paraeducators as paraeducators help to connect and participate with the education processes (French & Chopra, 1999). It is often the paraeducators who maintain daily contact regarding their child's performance at school (Downing, Ryndak, & Clark, 2000). In fact, often hiring of paraeducators by the school in response to parental pressure to do so (French & Pickett, 1997). However, when using the one-to-one model the familiarity between the parent and the paraeducator frequently became overly dependent, and paraeducators overstepped the boundaries of their role. Paraeducators can even become negative towards the parent due to a sense of ownership toward the student (Chopra & French, 2004).

Relationships. For a collaborative relationship to form between parents, students, paraeducators, and teachers several variables must be understood by all. First is the requirement of parity, in that all must know and understand their role within the team, but that role definition does not diminish their value to the team. Equality of importance to the student's success should be felt by all members of the team. Recently, the importance of this equality has been quite evident in the literature (see Carnahan, Williamson, Clarke, & Sorensen, 2009; Giangreco, Edelman, & Broer, 2001).

Parity is not occurring if the team is limited, without everyone at the table (Carter & Hughes, 2006; Hughes & Valle-Riestra 2008; Patterson, 2006; Riggs, 2004). Paraeducators are critical members of the academic team (Daniels & McBride, 2001) in that they have information to add to the interaction, but also their ability to implement the academic goals demand team membership. As to need to maintain communication in order to collaborate, the teacher/parent teaming is enhanced through paraeducators' involvement (Chopra & French, 2004; Chopra, Sandoval-Lucero, Aragon, Bernal, Berg De Balderas, & Carroll, 2004). If there are regularly scheduled meetings, the team, over time, will learn to appreciate each other's role and equality will occur naturally. All too often the time to meet together is difficult to schedule, so inadequate communication hampers the teaming relationship (French & Chopra, 2006; Morgan & Ashbaker, 2004; Morgan, Ashbaker, & Young, 2001) and isolation (Downing et al., 2000). Adequate communication cannot occur during lunch, during students' instructional time, or even when on recess duty, but requires regularly scheduled meetings (Hauge & Babkie, 2006).

Responsibilities. The responsibilities of paraeducators vary from individual to individual, based upon specific student needs. As noted above, NCLB (2002) mandated paraeducators either pass a test showing skill in reading, writing, and mathematics or two years of higher education. Their responsibilities are so varied that any pre-employment preparation may not prepare them for their duties. Therefore, professional development on the job is quite important (Moshoyannis, Pickett, & Granick, 1999). Yet, often this does not occur (Giangreco, Broer, & Edelman, 2002). Teachers those are unsure of how to provide paraeducators with training. In order to provide professional development to paraeducators, the teacher needs to provide the pupil's lesson plan to the paraeducators, observe the paraeducators reinforcing the academics planned, meet with the paraeducators to provide the paraeducators feedback and reinforcement, and then offer the professional development for the skills the observation indicated as needed (Reinfelds, 2012). This is an on-going process which promotes a positive growth trend.

MAX'S SCENARIO

Currently in education, there is an increasing utilization of paraprofessionals (Pickett, Likins, & Wallace, 2003). I would say Max's educational experiences are reflective of this statement. Max has experienced paraprofessionals in a variety of settings (special education classrooms, general education classrooms, large group, small group, during non-academic times such as recess, lunch, and related arts classes).

In 1st grade, Max had lots of areas he was working on—some academic skills, speech and language, motor skills, social skills, and behavior. He had paraprofessionals with him most of the day, but their primary responsibility was not to focus on Max. They were where Max was, but attended to the needs of all students. Every once and a while, I would go to the school and observe Max at different times (I like to have a clear picture of Max in different environments and a visual to go with the Max they describe during IEP meetings. I had no idea how Max would react to being around 20 other students at one time, so I would go and observe.)

One day when I went to observe Max during lunch and recess. Max was eating lunch at the end of the table. There were other kids sitting at the table with him, but Max did not seem to notice. He really did not even look up or engage in conversation.

During recess, Max played basketball and for the first 5 minutes he was playing alone. Then two other students joined. One of them made a comment to Max when they walked up, but he did not seem to acknowledge what appeared to be a greeting. The two of them had their own basketball and played together and Max continued to play alone in the same space. After several minutes, the two kids ran off to play somewhere else.

After the observation, I spoke with his **special education** (SPED) teacher. We agreed, Max needed more direct support during nonstructured times such as lunch and recess. Paraprofessionals were provided during these times—with the primary purpose to support Max's social interactions. They helped small groups of children that sat near Max at lunch engage in conversation—this proved to be beneficial for all of the students that sat near Max.

During recess, they helped Max take turns and join games other kids were playing. These were meaningful activities where Max learned as much as he was learning in the classroom. It also gave him a chance to practice skills he was working on in speech and with the SPED teacher. He was able to begin to generalize the skills he was working on in the classroom to different environments.

Over the years, I have not had many interactions with the paraprofessionals that have worked with Max. During IEP meetings, members of the IEP team would describe the support and interactions Max had with paraprofessionals. On one occasion, however, I walked into the school and was greeted by one of the paraprofessionals I knew worked with Max. I had a quick and what I thought was a generic question, so I asked her. She was there and without thought I quickly asked the question. Her response surprised me. It was not a bad or rude response, but it was a response that let me know that my question was a little more complex than I had originally thought and she clearly understood confidentiality. It was evident that she and her supervisor had had conversations about confidentiality and working with families. I respected her response and found Max's SPED teacher to ask my question.

Since, Max began his education journey paraprofessionals have had a part. There are many more examples that could be provided, but the main point is that he has been more successful because of these individuals.

FIRST PERSON TESTIMONIAL

Ride Mary, Ride: Laughter the Universal Language

By

Laura Farina, *Founder & President of Bohemian Roots Creative Art Center*

I worked with a four-year-old boy with autism named Derick. He was in an early childhood program in a small rural school district with 17 other students. There was a main teacher, a para, and I was Derick's one-on-one. The classroom was large enough to accommodate the number of students and it had numerous activity centers for them to interact with. Although there were countless scenarios that could be shared, I will focus on how, over time, he socially accepted me into his world.

Derick required a one-on-one because he did not interact well with others. He displayed social isolation, perseveration, trust issues, parallel play, and other common characteristics of individuals with autism. For example, on the first day of school the teacher introduced me as, Ms. Laura. Derick promptly renamed me, Mary. I assured him my name was Laura, but he insisted on calling me Mary for the remainder of the school year. Additionally he had a small plastic container of therapy putty he called *Jiggle*. Although he never played with *Jiggle*, it was his constant companion that could never be left behind.

After months of trying to connect with Derick, the walls of social isolation finally began to breakdown as we entered late October to early November. On a Wednesday, right after their mid-morning snack, Derick started playing alone on a preschool sized Fisher Price® Train Set. I was standing adjacent to him watching him scoot along the carpet.

At one point, he rode up to another Train Set and started patting the seat and said, *Ride, Mary, Ride*. I informed him I was too big, but he insistently patted the seat and continually said *Ride, Mary, Ride*. I began weighing the pros and cons of sitting on, and perhaps breaking, the teeny tiny train verses the months of attempting to build a trusting relationship with Derick. Despite the size differential, I opted to gingerly sit down and scoot alongside him around the classroom.

While riding side-by-side, we exchanged a brief look of trust and began laughing gleefully. The commotion around the classroom stopped as the teacher, other paras, and students watched us. This was the first time he had interacted with anyone since the beginning of school. From that moment on, I knew I was welcomed into his world.

SUMMARY & CONCLUSION

The support paraeducators provide has value, but improvements are needed and warranted. Federal policies serve as an umbrella; however, each individual state forms its own interpretation of guidelines. Therefore it is vital for parents and teachers to be knowledgeable about the supports that are provided within their state. Thus, both parents and teachers can continue playing a pivotal role in supporting paraeducators. For example, they should communicate with policy makers requesting additional mandates regarding providing clearer guidelines for roles and responsibilities, training, and professional development opportunities.

References

20 U.S.C. § 1400 et seq. (1990). Individuals with disabilities education act.

20 U.S.C. § 1400 et seq. (2004). Individuals with disabilities education improvement act.

Blacher, J., & Rodriguez, T. (2007). Holding on to their kitestrings: Paraprofessional support in inclusion settings. *The Exceptional Parent, 37*(10), 74–76.

Broer, S. M., Doyle, M. B., & Giangreco, M. F. (2005). Perspectives of students with intellectual disabilities about their experiences with paraprofessional support. *Exceptional Children, 71*(4), 415–430.

Carnahan, C. R., Williamson, P., Clarke, L., & Sorensen, R. (2009). A systematic approach for supporting paraeducators in educational settings: A guide for teachers. *Teaching Exceptional Children, 41*(5), 34–43.

Carter, E. W., & Hughes, C. (2006). Including high school students with severe disabilities in general education classes: perspectives of general and special educators, paraprofessionals, and administrators. *Research and Practice for Persons with Severe Disabilities, 31*(2), 174–185.

Chopra, R. V., & French, N. K. (2004). Paraeducator relationships with parents of students with significant disabilities. *Remedial and Special Education, 25*(4), 240–251.

Chopra, R. V., Sandoval-Lucero, E., Aragon, L., Bernal, C., Berg De Balderas, H., & Carroll, D. (2004). The paraprofessional role of connector. *Remedial and Special Education, 25*(4), 219–231.

Daniels, V. I., & McBride, A. (2001). Paraeducators as critical team members: Redefining roles and responsibilities. *National Association of Secondary School Principals Bulletin, 85*(623), 66–74. Retrieved February 7, 2007 from http://bul.sagepub,com/content/85/623/66.

Downing, J. E., Ryndak, D. L. & Clark, D. (2000). Paraeducators in inclusive classrooms. *Remedial and Special Education, 21*(3), 171–181.

Drecktrah, M. E. (2000). Preservice teachers' preparation to work with paraeducators. *Teacher Education and Special Education, 23*(2), 157–164.

French, N. K. (1998). Working together: Resource teachers and paraeducators. *Remedial and Special Education, 19*(6), 357–369.

French, N. K. (1999). Paraeducators: Who are they and what do they do? *Teaching Exceptional Children, 32*(1), 65–69.

French, N. K. (2001). Supervising paraprofessionals: A survey of teacher practices. *The Journal of Special Education, 35*(1), 41–53.

French, N. K. (2003). Managing paraeducators in your school. Thousand Oaks, California: Corwin Press, Inc.

French, N. K., & Chopra, R. V. (1999). Parent perspectives on the roles of paraprofessionals. *The Association for Persons with Severe Handicaps, 24*(4), 259–272.

French, N. K., & Chopra, R. V. (2006). Teachers as executives. *Theory Into Practice, 45*(3), 230–238.

French, N. K., & Pickett, A. L. (1997). Paraprofessionals in special education: Issues for teacher educators. *Teacher Education and Special Education, 20*(1), 61–73.

Giangreco, M. F., & Broer, S. M. (2007). School-based screening to determine overreliance on paraprofesionals. *Focus on Autism and other Developmental Disabilities, 22*(3), 149–158.

Giangreco, M. F., & Doyle, M. B. (2002). Student with disabilities and paraprofessional supports: Benefits, balance, and band-aids. *Focus on Exceptional Children, 34*(7), 1–12.

Giangreco, M. F., Edelman, S. W., & Broer, S. M. (2001). Respect, appreciation, and acknowledgment of paraprofessionals who support students with disabilities. *Exceptional Children, 67*(4), 485–498.

Giangreco, M. F., Edelman, S. W., Luiselli, T. E., & MacFarland, S. Z. C. (1997). Helping or hovering? Effects of instructional assistant proximity on student with disabilities. *Exceptional Children, 64*(1), 7–18.

Giangreco, M. F., Yuan, S., McKenzie, B., Cameron, P., & Fialka, J. (2005). "Be careful what you wish for…": Five reasons to be concerned about the assignment of individual paraprofessionals. *Teaching Exceptional Children, 57*(5), 28–34.

Girangreco, M. F., Broer, S. M., & Edelman, S. W. (2002). "That was then, this is now!": Paraprofessional supports for students with disabilities in general education classrooms. *Exceptionality, 10*(1), 47–64.

Harris, B. A. (2011). Effects of the proximity of paraeducators on the interactions of braille readers in inclusive settings. *Journal of Visual Impairment and Blindness, 105*(8), 467–478.

Hauge, J. M., & Babkie, A. M. (2006). Develop collaborative special educator—paraprofessional teams: One para's view. *Intervention in School and Clinic, 42*(1), 51–53.

Hughes, M. T., & Valle-Riestra, D. M. (2008). Responsibilities, preparedness, and job satisfaction of paraprofessionals: Working with young children with disabilities. *International Journal of Early Years Education, 16*(2), 163–173.

Maag, J. W., Vasa, S. F., & Reid, R. (1998). Frequency of interventions used by paraeducators with students with emotional and behavior disorders. *Psychological Reports, 82*(3), 1121–1122.

Malmgren, K. W., & Causton-Theoharis, J. N. (2006). Boy in the bubble: Effects of paraprofessional proximity and other pedagogical decisions on the interactions of a student with behavioral disorders. *Journal of Research in Childhood Education*, *20*(4), 301–312.

Marks, S. U., Schrader, C., & Levine, M. (1999). Paraeducators experiences in inclusive settings: Helping, hovering, or holding their own? *Exceptional Children*, *65*(3), 315–329.

McNally, R. D., Cole, P. G., & Waugh, R. F. (2001). Regular teacher's attitudes to the need for additional classroom support for the inclusion of students with intellectual disability. *Journal of Intellectual & Developmental Disability*, *26*(3), 257–273.

Minondo, S., Meyer, L. H., & Xin, J. F. (2001). The role and responsibilities of teaching assistants in inclusive education: What's appropriate? *The Journal of the Association for Persons with Severe Handicaps*, *26*(2), 114–119.

Morgan, J., & Ashbaker, B. (2004). An interview with … Joyce Hinckley on the front line. *Intervention in School and Clinic*, *39*(3), 168–171.

Morgan, J., Ashbaker, B., & Forbush, D. (1998). Strengthening the teaching team: Teachers and paraprofessionals learning together. *Support for Learning*, *13*(3), 115–117.

Morgan, J., Ashbaker, B., & Young, J. R. (2001). Teaming, supervision, and evaluation: Teacher-paraeducators team perspectives of their teaching. Paper presented at the Annual Meeting of the American Association of Colleges for Teacher Education. Retrieved from ERIC database. (ED454200).

Moshoyannis, T., Pickett, A. L., & Granick, L. (1999). The evolving roles and education/training needs of teacher and paraprofessional teams in New York City Public Schools: Results of survey and focus group research. New York: Paraprofessional Academy. Retrieved from ERIC database. (ED436827).

National Education Association (2007). Retrieved July 19, 2014 from http://www.nea.org/home/19035.htm.

O'Connor, J., & French, R. (1998). Paraprofessionals' attitudes toward inclusion of students with disabilities in physical education. *Perceptual and Motor Skills*, *86*(98), 98.

Patterson, K. B. (2006). Roles and responsibilities of paraprofessionals: In their own words. *Teaching Exceptional Children Plus*, *2*(5), Article 1. Retrieved August 9, 2014 from http://escholarship.bc.edu/education/tecplus/vol2/iss5/art1.

Pickett, A. I., Likins, M., & Wallace, T. (2003). *The employment and preparation of paraeducatiors: The state-of-the-art* 2003. New York: National Resource Center for Paraprofessionals in Education and Related Human Services, City University of New York.

Pickett, A. L. (1999). Paraeducators: Factors that influence their performance, development, and supervision. Retrieved August 9, 2014 from http://wwwericdigests.org/2000-4/factors.htm.

Reinfelds, C. L. (2012). The need for paraeducators and policy relagated to their supervision: A search for supervisor competencies (Unpublished doctoral dissertation). University of Kansas, Lawrence, KS.

Riggs, C. G. (2004). To teachers: What paraeducators want you to know. *Teaching Exceptional Children*, *33*(3), 78–83.

Skar, L., & Tamm, M. (2001). My assistant and I: disabled children's and adolescents' roles and relationships to their assistants. *Disability & Society*, *16*(7), 917–941.

Suter, J. C., & Giangreco, M. F. (2008). Numbers that count: Exploring special education and paraprofessional service delivery in inclusive-oriented schools. *The Journal of Special Education*, *20*(10), 1–13.

Werts, M. G., Zigmond, N., & Leeper, D. C. (2001). Paraprofessional proximity and academic engagement: Students with disabilities in primary aged classrooms. *Education and Training in Mental Retardation and Developmental Disabilities*, *36*(4), 424–440.

Young, B., & Simpson, R. (1997). An examination of paraprofessional involvement in supporting inclusion of students with autism. *Focus on Autism & Other Developmental Disabilities*, *12*(1), 31–40.

10

Technology Integration

Chapter Objectives

After studying this chapter readers should be able to:

- Discuss the two dimensions of the Technology-Related Assistance for Individuals with Disabilities Act.
- Rationalize why students with ASD benefit from using a variety of technologies.
- Explain the similarities and differences between various technologies.
- Identify why communication is vital to the human condition.

Chapter 10 Subject Index:

1. Assistive and Instructional Technology
2. Assistive Technologies
3. Augmentative and Alternative Communication Devices
4. Autism Spectrum Disorder
5. Individualized Education Program
6. Individuals with Disabilities Education Improvement Act
7. Information/Educational Technologies
8. Market Media Mediums
9. Picture Exchange Communication System
10. Sign Language
11. Speech-to-Text and Text-to-Speech Software
12. Technology
13. Technology Integration
14. Technology-Related Assistance for Individuals with Disabilities Act
15. The Education for All Handicapped Children Act
16. Video Modeling
17. Virtual Reality

INTRODUCTION

Technology has become omnipresent (Fitzpatrick, 2010) and McDonald and Hannafin (2003) suggested that recent technological advances have had the most significant impact on society compared to any other era. Historically, developments and applications of computer based technologies have assisted student's compensate for their disability (Bryant & Bryant, 1998; Fitzpatrick, 2005; Jones, Kirkup, & Kirkwood, 1993; Lewis, 1998; Raskind & Higgins, 1999). Specifically, within the last 15-to-20 years advances in **information/educational technologies** (I/ET) and **assistive technologies** (AT) have improved educational supports for students with and without disabilities (see Fitzpatrick & Brown, 2008; Fitzpatrick & Theoharis, 2010; Wehmeyer, Palmer, Smith, Davies, & Stock, 2009).

Unfortunately despite the positive impact of **technology integration**, the field of education continually encounters the challenge of ensuring *all* students are prepared for the technological advances of the 21st century and beyond (Brown & Fitzpatrick, 2010). Although there is a growing trend of school districts migrating towards a one-to-one computer initiative (see Fairbanks, 2013; Storz & Hoffman, 2012; Tonks, Weston, Wiley, & Barbour, 2013), the difficulties guaranteeing *all* students are prepared for technological advances should not be surprising. Especially when considering the precepts of Moore's Law (1965) which essentially stated information technology doubles every 18 months. From this perspective, it is virtually impossible for any public educational institution to sustain the infrastructure to continually invest in the latest versions of available hardware, software, and other newly developed resources. At best, the vast majority of school districts around the nation struggle to maintain their current technology strategic plan which poses several conundrums for district personnel.

The focus of this chapter provides a synopsis of technology and related programs in the K-12 environment for students on the **autism spectrum disorder** (ASD) and includes overviews of (a) **assistive and instructional technology**, (b) **video modeling**, (c) **virtual reality**, and (d) **augmentative and alternative communication devices**. It should be noted that it is beyond the scope of this chapter to provide implementation guidelines for all the various technologies available. Rather this serves as a preview of digital-based applications which have shown to enhance the academic, social, emotional, and behavioral outcomes of students with ASD.

THE TECH ACT

According to Sandholtz, Ringstaff, and Dwyer (2000) the introduction of computers in the classroom led to unparalleled expectations that technology would revolutionize education, because they make continual learning a reality and have dramatically changed how knowledge is accessed (Schneider, Glass, Henke, & Overton, 1997). In 1988, Congress passed the **Technology-Related Assistance for Individuals with Disabilities Act** which was reauthorized in 1999 (34 CFR § 300 et seq.).

The Tech Act was the first piece of legislation which (a) focused on making AT available to individuals with disabilities (Fein, 1996), (b) defined both AT devices and AT services (Fitzpatrick, 2005), and (c) authorized Federal funding of state-based delivery systems for implementing these services and devices into the classroom (Edyburn, 2000). As discussed in Chapter 2, the reauthorization of the **Education for All Handicapped Children Act** (P.L. 94-142), now entitled **Individuals with Disabilities Education Improvement Act** (IDEIA, 2004), mandated that a students' **individualized education program** (IEP) team consider assistive technology when developing an IEP.

As discussed above the Tech Act defined AT with two dimensions, devices, and services. The first dimension, AT devices, is defined as:

> any item, piece of equipment, or product system, whether acquired commercially off the shelf, modified, or customized that is used to increase, maintain, or improve the functional capabilities of a child with a disability (20 U.S.C. § 1401(1), 1997, 2004).

The second dimension of AT is services which address the actual implementation of the assistive technology devices (20 U.S.C. 1401(2), 1997, 2004). For example, it is not uncommon to believe an individual would benefit from a specific piece of equipment to assist in gaining access to the general education curriculum. However, it is another thing to ensure that the entire process involved with (a) assessment, (b) planning, (c) implementing, (d) monitoring, and (e) purchasing of devices is followed according to Federal guidelines.

ASSISTIVE & INSTRUCTIONAL TECHNOLOGY

All students with disabilities, especially those with ASD, typically need specialized instruction and instructive technologies to help address their unique learning styles. Thus, the potential for integrating AT and E/IT devices into the general and special education classrooms is substantial (Quenneville, 2001).

Although legal mandates have led to greater access to and use of AT for students with disabilities (Fitzpatrick & Brown, 2008), AT should be viewed on a continuum from low-to-high tech. For example, (a) pencil grip, (b) booster seat, (c) handheld magnifier, and (d) canes or walkers are traditionally considered low-tech devices. Conversely hardware such as (a) adaptive feeding aids, (b) augmentative communication devices, (c) visual aids, and (d) wheelchairs are viewed as high-tech devices. Additional AT devices include but are not limited to (a) telecommunication devices, (b) high-resolution monitors, (c) speech digitizers, (d) synthesizers, and (e) electronic communication aids (Duhaney & Duhaney, 2000).

Educational technology can be defined as "a combination of the processes and tools involved in addressing educational needs and problems, with an emphasis on applying the most current tools" (Roblyer, 2006, p. 9). I/ET—specifically for computers—can take many forms, including speech output, word-prediction, and speech recognition software. Duhaney and Duhaney (2000) asserted that educators must be able to acknowledge and recognize the importance of these and other instructional technology devices as powerful tools for improving the outcomes for students with disabilities.

VIDEO MODELING

Over the last two decades, the use of video instruction has increased exponentially. Grounded in Bandura's (1969, 1977) theory of observational learning (a.k.a. modeling), both researchers and educators have embraced video modeling as an intervention strategy appropriate for *all* students, especially those with ASD. Unlike **Market Media Mediums**—such as Hollywood blockbusters (e.g., *Star Wars*, *Lord of the Rings*, etc.) or episodic television shows (e.g., *The Simpsons*, *WWE RAW*, etc.)—which are predicated on the ideal of standardization (see Fitzpatrick, 2010), Wilson (2013) suggested video modeling is used to target a specific learning opportunity.

Although there are copious variations, at its core, video modeling uses performers to demonstrate specific desired outcomes which can include but are not limited to daily living tasks (e.g., tying shoes or brushing teeth), interpersonal or social skills (e.g., saying hello or playing at recess), and academic and behavioral expectations (e.g., completing classwork or waiting in line). Intuitively, video modeling can be used to ameliorate simple-to-complex tasks individually or within a group setting and research indicates many positive results (see Boser, Goodwin, & Wayland, 2014; Mechling & Ayres, 2012; Reichow & Volkmar, 2010; Tetreault & Lerman, 2010; Wang & Spillane, 2009).

VIRTUAL REALITY

According to some, *We're livin' in a land of virtual reality* (Glabicki, 1996, Track 4) to others the *Futures made of virtual insanity* (Smith, 1996, Track 1). Regardless of perspective, it is difficult to dispute that **virtual reality** (VR) is an ever present force in contemporary society.

Market Media Mediums have a rich history of blurring the edges between fiction and ever present future (see Fitzpatrick, 2010). For example, science fiction novels are the foundation for many of Hollywood's biggest movies and are much more accessible to the masses comparatively to printed text. From Stephen King's *Lawnmower Man to* the *Matrix* franchise, the goal of VR is to allow participants to become integrated into an exciting, highly engaged digital rich environment. For better or worse, online social community platforms, such as *Second Life* and *World of Warcraft*, take us one step closer to integration.

Evidence suggests that individuals with ASD have an innate ability to interact within controlled environments provided by computer-based technologies (see Moore, McGrath, & Thorpe, 2000; Moore & Taylor, 2000). Specifically for students with ASD, VR technology has shown to be effective for practical training and game-playing purposes. Similarly Moore, Cheng, McGrath, and Powell (2005) reported that collaborative virtual environments have great potential for individuals with autism.

AUGMENTATIVE & ALTERNATIVE COMMUNICATION

By nature, humans are communal creatures and communication is an integral component of social interaction. For example, reflect on the moment you woke up until you return to bed, how many face-to-face, texting, emails, and phone conversations did you have throughout the day? Now consider how different your life would be if you were unable to converse or interact with your friends, family, significant other, classmates, coworkers, etc. Ponder the potential number of conundrums, difficulties, and frustrations that would arise from being socially integrated, yet isolated, from communicating with those around you.

As discussed in previous chapters, students with ASD often experience difficulties with verbalization and oral expression. During the 1980s and early 1990s researchers began exploring the viability of AAC interventions in an attempt to increase communication for students with ASD (Shane, Laubscher, Schlosser, & Flynn, 2012). AAC provide individuals who do not have the capacity for verbal speech or writing to communicate their thoughts, ideas, needs, and wants using AAC interventions. Below are a truncated summary of three select AAC systems.

Picture Exchange Communication System. Bondy and Frost (1994) developed the **Picture Exchange Communication System** (PECS) to help enable students with autism acquire functional communication skills. It is a popular communication training program for students with ASD (Flippin, Reszka, & Watson, 2010; Preston & Carter, 2009).

PECS teaches users, including students with ASD, to learn how to request for a specific concrete desired item (Bondy & Frost, 1994), which according to Chiang and Carter (2008) fosters a sense of spontaneity. Unlike other AAC systems which require a wide range of prerequisites, there are very few requirements for effective use of PECS. For example, students should demonstrate the ability to (a) imitate both verbal and motor movements, (b) maintain eye contact, (c) attend to task (i.e., seat time), (d) discriminate between pictures, (e) follow simple prompts, and (f) clearly indicate which visual item (i.e., picture) they desire (Bondy & Frost, 2002).

Speech-to-Text & Text-to-Speech Software. Although many students with ASD are nonverbal, **speech-to-text** (STT) software programs can greatly enhance the academic achievement of students on the higher end of the spectrum. Similarly, **text-to-speech** (TTS) and reading software programs provide students on the lower end of the spectrum access to otherwise inaccessible content. Given that STT and TTS programs are typically proprietary, the following is a snapshot of available software Dragon NaturallySpeaking®, Kurzwil 3000®, Premier Literacy®, and Read&Write Gold®. Please note the objective of this section was not to propagate one industry standard program over another, nor was it to delve into the intricate similarities and differences between each software package. Rather the goal was to provide a baseline for readers to conduct further research into STT and TTS systems.

Sign Language. Historically, students with ASD have benefited from the use of **sign language** (see Bonvillian & Nelson, 1976; Carr, 1979; Carr, Binkoff, Kologinsky, & Eddy, 1978; Yoder & Layton, 1988). Unlike spoken language interventions which are often difficult to remember (Seal & Bonvillian, 1997), Gaines, Geaper, Monahan, and Weickgenant (1988) reported that students with ASD typically retained sign language skills for longer periods of time. Not surprisingly, as with any instructional strategy, teaching students with ASD sign language has yielded mixed results (see Bonvillian & Blackburn, 1991; Layton, 1987). Nevertheless, research appears to indicate sign language help students with ASD acquire functional language skills.

MAX'S SCENARIO

Since the time of Max's diagnosis, he has experienced a variety of low-tech and high-tech devices. While at the time they were being implemented, I was not sure I should have considered them as technology or support. This scenario will focus on video games and supports for writing.

Since the age of 3, Max has had a love for video games. I often saw these as a waste of time and believed they did not positively impact his academic, social, emotional, or behavioral needs. However, when Max was 11 years old my perspective changed after an appointment with the neurologist who explained the benefits of playing video games.

According to the doctor, playing games allowed Max the opportunity to relate with his peers at school. For example, he was able to converse on a topic that was age and grade appropriate with his classmates. He would also be able to invite friends over to play games (more conversation) which would then assist with turn taking. As Max has gotten older, I have seen the benefits video games have offered. Unfortunately his time playing games is still somewhat limited.

In addition to the typical Wii® and Play Station® games Max enjoys, his teachers throughout the years have often provided computer games or internet resources to support learning content, concepts, and skills. He has been able to use these both at school and home to enhance his learning. The continuity across environments has and continues to provide Max several positive outcomes including but not limited to: (a) knowing the expectations both at home and at school, (b) feeling successful while progressing through different levels, and (c) allowing seamless and meaningful conversations between the two different settings.

Writing has always been and continues to be difficult for Max. Max faces two challenges with writing (a) the physical task of writing (handwriting) and (b) the formulating and organization of ideas. Both of these factors have a significant impact on academics. Max is not alone. Simpson (2007) reported that handwriting is one of the most significant and serious impediment to academic participation for students with ASD. Similarly, Mayes and Calhoun (2003) went on to find graphomotor skills were significantly lower for students with ASD compared to peers regardless of age or IQ. They also reported this finding had a serious impact on written expression. When writing is a labor-intensive task, students may focus more on handwriting rather than the content of the product, limit the words they write to lessen the handwriting process, and begin thinking in fewer words which can have an impact on academic success (Broun, 2009).

To assist Max with the physical task of handwriting, he received occupational therapy, where they introduced a variety of activities to strengthen his hand muscles (i.e., Play-Doh and stringing beads) and low-tech devices (i.e., pencil grips, fatter pencils and crayons, and special scissors). While the muscles in his hands gain strength, handwriting continues to take effort and letters and numbers look like those made by younger students. He still puts a lot of thought into his writing and seeks ways to meet minimum writing requirements. Teachers have put word limits on sentences and sentences on paragraphs. For example, in 7th grade, Max had a writing assignment that was to include an introduction, body, and conclusion. Max's response, *Mom, I had no idea this meant more than three paragraphs*. This story helps to illustrate that Max continues to think minimally when it comes to what he is writing.

In 4th grade, writing assignments became lengthier and more of a challenge for Max. To help with the content and organizing his thoughts, his teachers put a great deal of effort into teaching him how to use and apply graphic organizers in his writing. For helping with handwriting, his teachers introduced typing. There is a growing body of neurological research on motor skills of students with ASD. There are also anecdotal reports from individuals with ASD that should not be dismissed. These reports show the value of having an alternative to pencil and paper writing (Broun, 2009). In the beginning, I must say Max was more skilled than I was expecting at using a keyboard. He understood basic concepts like how to capitalize letters. I think this was largely because the computerized games teachers had introduced. While he had the basic skills, we started out with Max typing some and dictating for me to type. His assignments and language has greatly improved from being able to type his assignments, so has his typing skills.

Assistive technology has made completing assignments easier for Max, aided with learning and socialization skills. In addition, it has reduced a tremendous amount of his stress and anxiety both at home and at school.

PROFESSIONAL ANALYSIS

A Perspective on Best & Promising Assistive Technology Practices for Children and Youth with Autism Spectrum Disorder

By

Dr. Earle Knowlton, Morningside College

If your lifetime perspective spans more than a few decades you will realize that it actually has been a relatively brief period of time since autism was first reported clinically by Hans Asperger in the late 1930s, Leo Kanner in the early 1940s, and others who soon followed their lead. In the 1950s and early 1960s, the prevailing explanatory theory for autism was psychoanalytic in nature, fueled initially by Kanner himself who, despite adhering for the most part to causal theories that featured innate neuro developmental factors, observed on more than one occasion that maternal warmth appeared to be lacking in some mothers of children with autism (Kanner, 1949). University of Chicago professor Bruno Bettelheim propelled the notion of deficits in maternal affection and bonding (i.e., *refrigerator mother* theory) into public prominence until alternative explanations attributing autism to neurobiological factors began taking hold in the scientific community during the mid to late 1960s and 1970s (see Rimland, 1964).

In the 40+ years since, scientific inquiry and practices in the education and treatment of autism have evolved rapidly and significantly. The Centers for Disease Control (CDC) now indicate a probable incidence rate of about 1 in 68, reporting that, "ASD is almost five times more common among boys than girls: 1-in-42 boys versus 1-in-189 girls. White children are more likely to be identified as having ASD than are black or Hispanic children" (CDC, 2014, paragraph 1). Notably, the CDC reported considerable interstate variability. "The number of children identified with ASD ranged from 1-in-175 children in Alabama to 1-in-45 children in New Jersey" (CDC, 2014, paragraph 1). The NIH's National Institute of Neurological Disorders and Stroke (NINDS) stated that, although there is no single, certain cause of ASD, the condition is neurogenic and "the theory that parental practices are responsible for ASD has long been disproved" (NINDS, 2014). This is clearly more (and more reliable and valid) demographic and epidemiological information than Bettelheim and others had available to them a mere half century ago.

Moreover, technologies relevant to education and treatment practices for children and youth with ASD have been advancing at a similarly fast clip. This Chapter devoted most of its discussion to four general application areas in which various digital media technologies have played starring roles in the emergence of evidence-based instructional practices for PK-12 education as well as job-related and post-secondary training for individuals with ASD: (a) assistive technology, (b) video modeling, (c) VR, and (d) augmentative/alternate communication.

Assistive & Instructional Technology

As discussed above, *The Technology Related Assistance Act* defines an assistive device as "any item, piece of equipment, or product …used to increase, maintain, or improve the functional capabilities of individuals with disabilities." It is certainly fair to say that the use of assistive technology is not by any means limited to applications toward the meeting of learning and performance needs of students with ASD. However, as is the case with all four technology application areas, the various technology products as well as the research utilizing them are clearly applicable across the autism spectrum.

As but one example, consider the popularity of and emergent evidence base for the use of visual representation systems (i.e., visual supports) with students along the autism spectrum (Jaime & Knowlton, 2007; Sherer et al., 2001; Simpson et al., 2005). Visual supports consist of objects, photos, drawings, and words/phrases that are mediated in a manner that supports the students' access to curriculum and instruction. Although the mediation of these supports can be as simple as a poster board display, several vendors provide higher-teach forms of mediated visual supports.

The Meyer-Johnson company offers the authoring software, Boardmaker (see http://www.mayer johnson.com/boardmakersoftware/?gclid=CP6StZS2wL4CFe07OgodkkMA7w), enabling teachers to create personalized visual supports such as schedules, menus, functional sequences (e.g., preparing a meal), and many others. Thus via a personal computer or tablet, visual supports are personalized and delivered to tens of thousands of students daily using assistive technology tools.

Whereas AT can be thought of as a set of tools that assist the learner in overcoming or circumventing conditions that interfere with learning, instructional technology is a broader concept no less beneficial to the learner but much more focused on enhancement of the act of instruction for teaching and training purposes.

For example, consider the recent body of work examining an instructional procedure that features covert prompting using telecommunications technology over distance. Several investigators have used this instructional technology to train high school students and young adults with ASD various job-related skills. Bennett, Ramasamy, and Honsberger (2012, 2013) used what they termed, *covert audio coaching* to train clerical and other employment skills. Essentially, verbal prompts are transmitted by trainers from a remote site to workers at the job site through hidden earpieces as they perform job tasks (e.g., filing). This prompting procedure is as effective as it is unobtrusive in shaping job task accuracy and efficiency.

Similar technologies and procedures have been used to facilitate job skill training in adolescents through audio cuing (see Allen et al., 2012) and to enhance access to the general education curriculum for students with emotional and behavior disorders through tele-coaching (see Knowlton et al., 2014). Functionally, the audio coaching, audio cuing, and tele-coaching procedures are quite similar and utilize identical telecommunications technology (i.e., remote bug-in-ear audio transmission).

Video Modeling

As with visual supports (and VR, discussed below), video modeling for students with ASD rests on the premise that a significant proportion of these students learn efficiently through the visual system (Ganz, Earles-Vollrath, & Cook, 2011). Video modeling involves the use of video recordings as models on the basis of which student behavior is shaped through imitation, prompting, and reinforcement (Wilson, 2013). These recordings often feature a person demonstrating the task being taught in terms of a sequence of its salient components.

Moreover, the learner can be the person on video who demonstrates the task requiring more video development time of course. This off-shoot is termed, video self-modeling, and has some support in the research literature. Hitchcock, Dowrick, and Prater (2003) reviewed 18 video self-modeling studies and concluded that the procedure is effective though specific conditions and learner characteristics varied across the studies reviewed. Comparative studies that examined the relative effectiveness of video modeling and video self-modeling have produced equivocal results (Sherer et al., 2001).

Another variation of video modeling involves the perspective or point-of-view the video model depicts. Here, the video can show the task from a third-person viewpoint or from the model's viewpoint, for example a *Go-Pro®* camera might be worn by the model, strapped around the forehead, as he demonstrates how to wring out a mop using bucket-mounted rollers; alternatively, the video camera might be perched on table or bookshelf recording this same task. Each video represents a different point-of-view, and several researchers have shown the first-person view may possibly be more effective than the third-person view for certain tasks (Tetreault & Lerman, 2010).

Virtual Reality

As advancement in virtualization technology continues its rapid ascent, educational uses of this technology are expanding as well. Nowhere is this expansion more evident than in the education and training of individuals with ASD. In a recent study by Smith et al. (2014), VR software was used to present training sessions to adults with ASD designed to improve their job interview skills. Results indicated VR-based role-play training was superior to standard training in interview behaviors for these individuals.

Similar work by other researchers has yielded similarly promising results in other areas of social performance by individuals with ASD. Laffy et al. (2010) investigated social competence in adolescents with Asperger syndrome. The authors used the iSocial VR environment to increase participants' social skills. Similarly, Ehrlich and Miller (2009) reported the effectiveness of VR software in training adolescents with ASD appropriate social behavior in a variety of potentially sensitive school-based contexts such as how to respond to a bully, riding the school bus, how to use the restroom, and other socio-behavioral competencies.

Augmentative/Alternate Communication

Once again the premise that many students with ASD learn with primary reliance on the visual modality is foundational to the proliferation of communication systems that primarily utilize visual stimuli. It is beyond the scope of this perspective on technology and the instruction of ASD students to review all such systems. Instead, it might be useful to consider the most prominent of these, the PECS (Bondy & Frost (1994, 2002)), which was developed by the authors in an attempt to ameliorate the dismal clinical communication outcomes apparent in children with autism. Its underlying notion is that communicative exchanges between a child with autism and a peer without a disability can be facilitated with pictures physically exchanged between the two children and initiated by the child with autism (Bondy & Frost, 1994).

PECS training was designed to proceed along six fairly distinct phases that begin with the topography of the exchange (child expresses communicative intent by giving the pictorial representation of this intent to the peer), moving on to word discrimination training and simple sentence structure, and culminating with answering questions such as, what do you want? Although, with respect to fidelity, the training phases can vary considerably in terms of their implementation, PECS has been scrutinized in numerous research studies and research views, and has been shown to be effective (Simpson et al., 2005). In the 20 years since its original publication, digitized forms of PECS content have emerged; however, practitioners still have the option to teach using actual picture cards. Little if any research has been conducted comparing the training effects of digitized vs. actual picture cards.

FIRST PERSON TESTIMONIAL

Max & Electronics

By

Amanda Neild

From a very early age, Max loves to use electronics. This has been beneficial to him at school and also to our family. When Max was 4 years old, he was already able to easily beat most of his video games. He seemed to intrinsically know which buttons to push to make the cars go or the people jump and his understanding of the strategies needed and purpose of each game appeared to be fairly advanced.

His knowledge of electronics has helped him at school. He is able to play computer based educational games with little direction from the teacher. So, games were used as rewards during his early years. As he has gotten older, he has been able to generalize these skills to learning how to develop software. For example, this year in high school Max is taking *How to Make Video Games as* an elective.

Finally, Max's familiarity of electronics has also benefited our family. Max purchased a Playstation® at a garage sale. It did not work, but he was able to watch YouTube videos and take it apart and put it back together. The Playstation® worked and he gave it as a gift to his cousins. Once, I needed to install Netflix® using our Wii®. I called Max and he was able to walk me through how to download it. Now, my family is able to watch a variety of movies from home.

SUMMARY & CONCLUSION

This chapter presented an overview of the Tech Act and provided a foundation regarding the benefits of incorporating AT and I/ET hardware and software devices into the classroom setting to enhance the learning outcomes for students with ASD. A truncated summary of video modeling, virtual reality, augmentative, and alternative communication devices were included because of the positive impact these technologies have had for students with ASD.

References

20 U.S.C. § 1400 et seq. (1990). Individuals with disabilities education act.

20 U.S.C. § 1400 et seq. (2004). Individuals with disabilities education improvement act.

Allen, K., Burke, R., Howard, M., Wallace, D., & Bowen, S. (2012). Use of audio cuing to expand employment opportunities for adolescents with autism spectrum disorders and intellectual disabilities. *Journal of Autism and Developmental Disorders*, Americans with Disabilities Act (1990). PL 105-220, 42 U.S.C. § 12101 et seq.

Bandura, A. (1969). *Principles of behavior modification*. New York: Holt, Rinchart & Winston.

Bandura, A., (1977). *Social learning theory*. Upper Saddle River, NJ: Prentice Hall.

Bennett, K., Ramasamy, R., & Honsberger, T. (2012). The effects of covert audio coaching on teaching clerical skills to adolescents with autism spectrum disorder. *Journal of Autism and Developmental Disorders*, *43*, 585–593.

Bennett, K., Ramasamy, R., & Honsberger, T. (2013). Further examination of covert audio coaching on improving employment skills among secondary students with autism. *Journal of Behavioral Education*, *22*, 103–119.

Bondy, A. S., & Frost, L. A. (1994). The picture exchange communication system [Electronic version]. *Focus on Autistic Behavior*, 9, 1–19.

Bondy, A. S., & Frost, L. A. (2002). *A picture's worth: PECS and other visual communication strategies in autism*. Bethesda, MD: Woodbine House.

Bonvillian, J. D., & Blackburn, D. W. (1991). Manual communication and factors and autism: factors relating to sign language acquisition. In P. Siple, & S. Fischer (Eds.). Theoretical issues in sign language research: Vol. 2, Psychology (pp. 255–277). Chicago, IL:, University of Chicago Press.

Bonvillian, J. D., & Nelson, K. (1976). Sign language acquisition in a mute autistic boy [Electronic version]. *Journal of Speech and Hearing Disorders*, *41*, 339–347.

Boser, K. I., Goodwin, M. S., & Wayland, S. C. (2014). Technology tools for students with disabilities: Innovations that enhance independence and learning. Baltimore, MD: Bookes.

Broun, L. (2009). Take the pencil out of the process. *Teaching Exceptional Children, 42*(1), 14–21.

Brown, M. R., & Fitzpatrick, M. (2010). Digital Equity: Understanding the Divide as it Relates to Culture and Disability. In S. Seok (Ed.). Research on human cognition and assistive technology: Design, accessibility, and transdisciplinary perspectives. Hershey, PA: IGI Global (CH 26).

Bryant, D. P., & Bryant, B. R. (1998). Using assistive technology adaptations to include students with learning disabilities in cooperative learning activities [Electronic version]. *Journal of Learning Disabilities*, *31*, 41–54.

Carr, E. G. (1979). Teaching autistic children to use sign language: Some research issues [Electronic version]. *Journal of Autism and Developmental Disorders*, *9*, 345–359.

Carr, E. G., Binkoff, J., Kologinsky, E., & Eddy, M. (1978). Acquisition of language by autistic children I: Expressive labeling [Electronic version]. *Journal of Applied Behavior Analysis*, *1*, 489–501.

Centers for Disease Control (2014). Press release: CDC estimates 1 in 68 children has been identified with ASD. Retrieved May 22, 2014 from: http://www.cdc.gov/

Chiang, H., & Carter, M. (2008). Spontaneity of communication in individuals with autism [Electronic version]. *Journal of Autism and Developmental Disorders*, *38*, 693–705.

Duhaney, L. M. G., & Duhaney, D. C. (2000). Assistive technology: Meeting the needs of learners with disabilities. *International Journal of Instructional Media*, *27*(4), 393–401.

Education of All Handicapped Children Act of 1975. P.L 94–142.

Edyburn, D. L. (2000). Assistive technology and students with mild disabilities [Electronic version]. *Focus on Exceptional Children, 32*(9), 1–24.

Ehrlich, J. A., & Miller, J. R. (2009). A virtual environment for teaching social skills: AViSSS. *Computer Graphics and Applications, IEEE*, *29*(4), 10–16.

Fairbanks, A. M. (2013). **1-to-1** building blocks [Electronic version]. *Education Week*, *32*(25), 12–15.

Fein, J. (1996). A history of legislative support for assistive technology. *Journal of Special Education Technology*, *13*, 1–3.

Fitzpatrick, M., & Theoharis, R. (2010). Assistive technology for deaf and hard of hearing students. In S. Seok (Ed.). Research on Human Cognition and Assistive Technology: Design, Accessibility and Transdisciplinary Perspectives. Hershey, PA: IGI Global (CH 12).

Fitzpatrick, M. (2005). Emergence of e-learning for middle school students with specific learning disabilities: Comparing e-learning with face-to-face instruction. (Doctoral Dissertation, University of Kansas, 2005). Dissertations Abstracts International, *67*, 465.

Fitzpatrick, M. (2010). Operation mindcrime: An era of globalized media consumers. Educating Youth for Citizenship*: East and West.*

Fitzpatrick, M., & Brown, M. (2008). Assistive technology access and use: Considerations for culturally and linguistically diverse students and their families. *Journal of Special Education Technology*, *23*(4) 47–52.

Flippin, M., Reszka, S., & Watson, L. R. (2010). Effectiveness of the picture exchange communication system (PECS) on communication and speech for children with autism spectrum disorders: A meta-analysis [Electronic version]. *American Journal of Speech-Language Pathology*, *19*(2), 178–195.

Gaines, R., Leaper, C., Monahan, C., & Weickgenant, A. (1988). Language and retention in young language-disordered children [Electronic version]. *Journal of Autism and Developmental Disorders*, *18*, 218–296.

Ganz, J., Earles-Vollrath, T., & Cook, K. (2011). Video modeling: A visually based intervention for children with autism spectrum disorder. *Teaching Exceptional Children*, *43*(6), 8–19.

Glabicki, M. (1996). Virtual reality. From *Remember* (CD). New York, NY: Mercury Records.

Hitchcock, C. H., Dowrick, P. W., & Prater, M. A. (2003). Video self-modeling intervention in school-based settings. *Remedial and Special Education*, *24*, 36–45. http://www.cdc.gov/media/releases/2014/p0327-autism-spectrum-disorder.html

Jaime, K., & Knowlton, H. E. (2007). Visual supports for students with cognitive and behavioral challenges. *Intervention in School and Clinic*, *42*, 259–270.

Jones, A., Kirkup, G., & Kirkwood, A. (1993). *Personal computers for distance education*. New York: St. Martin's Press.

Kanner, L. (1949). Problems of nosology and psychodynamics in early childhood autism. *American Journal of Orthopsychiatry*, *19*, 416–426. Doi: 10.1111/j.1939-0025.1949.tb05441.x

Knowlton, H. E., Elford, M., Wolf, H., Nutt, A., Carter, R., McNiff, M., Jones, J., & Williamson, M. (2014). Assuring access to the general curriculum using tele-coaching as a mechanism for remote delivery of verbal prompts and cues to students in general education classrooms. Manuscript in preparation.

Laffey, J., Schmidt, M., Stichter, J., Schmidt, C., Oprean, D., Herzog, M., & Babiuch, R. (2010). Designing for social interaction and social competence in a 3D-VLE. *Cases on Collaboration in Virtual Learning Environments: Processes and Interactions*, 154–168.

Layton, T. L. (1987). Manual communication. In T. L. Layton (Ed.), Language treatment of autistic and development when disordered children (pp. 189–213). Springfield, IL: Charles C. Tomas.

Lewis, R. B. (1998). Assistive technology and learning disabilities: Today's realities and tomorrow's promises [Electronic version]. *Journal of Learning Disabilities*, *31*, 16–26.

Mayes, S., & Calhoun, S. (2003). Ability profiles in children with autism: Influence of age and IQ. *Autism, 7*, 65.

McDonald, K. K., & Hannafin, R. D. (2003). Using web-based computer games to meet the demands of today's high-stakes testing: A mixed method inquiry [Electronic version]. *Journal of Research on Technology in Education*, *35*(4), 459–472.

Mechling, L., & Ayres, K. (2012). A comprehensive study: Completion of fine motor office related tasks by high school students with autism using video models on large and small screen sizes [Electronic version]. *Journal of Autism & Developmental Disorders*, *42*(11), 2364–2373.

Moore, D. J., & Taylor, J. (2000). Interactive multimedia systems for people with autism [Electronic version]. *Journal of Educational Media, 25*, 169–177.

Moore, D. J., McGrath, P., & Thorpe, J. (2000). Computer aided learning for people with autism: A framework for research and development [Electronic version]. *Innovations in Education and Training International, 37*, 218–228.

Moore, D., Cheng, Y., & McGrath, P. (2005). Collaborative virtual environment technology for people with autism [Electronic version]. *Focus on Autism & other Developmental Disabilities, 20*(4), 231–243.

National Institute of Neurological Disorders and Stroke (2014). Autism fact sheet (paragraph 10). Retrieved 5/8/14 from: http://www.ninds.nih.gov/disorders/autism/detail_autism.htm

Preston, D., & Carter, M. (2009). A review of the efficacy of the picture exchange communication intervention [Electronic version]. *Journal of Autism & Developmental Disorders, 39*(10), 1471–1486.

Quenneville, J. (2001). Tech tools for students with learning disabilities: Infusion into inclusive classrooms. *Preventing School Failure,* 45(4), 167–170.

Raskind, M. H., & Higgins, E. L. (1999). Speaking to read: the effects of speech recognition technology on the reading and spelling performance of children with learning disabilities [Electronic version]. *Annals of Dyslexia, 49*, 251–281.

Reichow, B., &Volkmar, F. R. (2010). Social skills interventions for individuals with autism: Evaluation for evidence-based practices within a best evidence synthesis framework [Electronic version]. *Journal of Autism & Developmental Disorders, 40*(2), 149–166.

Rimland, B. (1964). *Infantile autism: The syndrome and its implications for a neural theory of behavior.* Englewood Cliffs, NJ: Prentice Hall.

Roblyer, D. M. (2006). *Integrating educational technology into teaching* (4th ed.). Pearson Prentice Hall, NJ.

Sandholtz, J. H., Ringstaff, C., & Dwyer, D. C. (2000). The evolution of instruction in technology-rich classrooms. In *The Jossey-Bass reader on technology and learning* (pp. 225–276). San Francisco: Jossey-Bass, Inc.

Schneider, E. L., Glass, S., Henke, M., & Overton, J. (1997). Distance learning in gerontology: The future is here. *Generations, 21,* 46–49.

Seal, B., & Bonvillian, J. D. (1997). Sign language and motor functioning and students with autistic disorder [Electronic version]. *Journal of Autism and Developmental Disorders, 27*, 437–466.

Shane, H., Laubscher, E., Schlosser, R., & Flynn, S., (2012). Applying technology to visually support language and communication in individuals with autism spectrum disorders [Electronic version]. *Journal of Autism & Developmental Disorders, 42*(6), 1228–1235.

Sherer, M., Pierce, K., Paredes, S., Kisacky, K., Ingersoll, B., & Schreibman, L. (2001). Enhancing conversation skills in children with autism via video technology: Which is better, "self" or "other" as model? [Electronic version]. *Behavior Modification, 25*, 140–158.

Simpson, R. (2006, February 2–4). *Issues, trends, and scientifically-based practices for children and youth with Asperger syndrome.* Presented at The Applied Behavioral Analysis Conference on Autism, Boston, MA.

Simpson, R. and others (2005). *Autism spectrum disorders.* Thousand Oaks, CA: Corwin Press.

Smith, K. (1996). Virtual insanity. From *Traveling Without Moving* (CD). Santa Monica, CA: Sony Music Entertainment.

Storz, M. G., & Hoffman, A. R. (2012). Examining response to a one-to-one computer initiative: student and teacher voices [Electronic version]. *Research in Middle Level Education Online, 36*(6), 1–18.

Tetreault, A. S., & Lerman, D. C. (2010). Teaching social skills to children with autism using point-of-view video modeling [Electronic version]. *Education & Treatment of Children, 33*(3), 395–419.

Tonks, D., Weston, S., Wiley, D., & Barbour, M. K. (2013). Opening a new kind of high school: The story of the open high school of Utah [Electronic version]. *International Review of Research in Open & Distance Learning, 14*(1), 255–271.

Wang, P., & Spillane, A. (2009). Evidence-based social skills interventions for children with autism: A meta-analysis [Electronic version]. *Education & Training in Developmental Disabilities, 44*(3), 318–342.

Wehmeyer, M. L., Palmer, S. B., Smith, S. J., Davies, D. K., & Stock, S. (2009). The efficacy of technology use by people with intellectual disability: A single-subject design meta-analysis [Electronic version]. *Journal of Special Education Technology, 23*(3), 21–30.

Wilson, K. P. (2013). Incorporating video modeling into a school-based intervention for students with autism spectrum disorders [Electronic version]. *Language, Speech & Hearing Services in Schools, 44*(1), 105–117.

Yoder, P. L., & Layton, T. L. (1988). Speech following sign language training in autistic children with minimal verbal language [Electronic version]. *Journal of Autism and Developmental Disorders, 18*, 217–228.

11 Intervention Strategies

Chapter Objectives

After studying this chapter readers should be able to:

- Discuss how strategies, methods, and interventions can positively impact the educational and social outcomes of students with ASD.
- Compare and contrast the similarities and differences between Picture Exchange Communication System, Social Stories™, and power cards.
- Explain why it is important for students with ASD to have the ability to generalize skills, concepts, and knowledge from one setting to another.
- Identify the hidden curriculum of various educational and environmental settings.

Chapter 11 Subject Index:

1. Applied Behavior Analysis
2. Asperger's Syndrome
3. Augmentative Communication Systems
4. Autism
5. Autism Spectrum Disorder
6. Cartooning/Comic Strips
7. Circle of Friends
8. Direct Instruction
9. Evaluation
10. Generalization
11. Graphic Organizers
12. Hidden Curriculum
13. Modeling
14. Picture Exchange Communication System
15. Planned Ignoring
16. Power Cards
17. Presentation
18. Rationale
19. Redirection

20. SOCCSS
21. Social Stories™
22. Special Education
23. Universal Design for Learning
24. Verification
25. Video Modeling
26. Visual Schedules

INTRODUCTION

Teaching and learning strategies and environmental supports provide students on the **autism spectrum disorder** (ASD) with lifelong, individualized arrangements that facilitate understanding, learning, and adaptive functioning that can be generalized to home, school, and their community. Visual supports, references, organizers, and stories are a critical part of any program for individuals with **autism**. The use of visual systems and strategies are proven to reduce stress and support students when learning new content and skills.

DIRECT INSTRUCTION

Children with autism often do not innately develop the social and behavioral skills necessary to be successful at school, home, and in their community. As a result, teachers need to provide effective instructional sequences that facilitate student skill acquisition—often this includes **direct instruction**. The term *direct instruction* has been used by researchers to refer to a pattern of teaching that consists of the teacher explaining the new concept or skill to the students, having the students assess their comprehension by practicing under teacher supervision (i.e., controlled practice), and encouraging the students to continue to practice under teacher guidance (i.e., guided practice) (Joyce, Weil, & Calhoun, 2004). Before presenting and explaining new information, it is helpful to build a framework for the concepts being taught. Structuring statements at the start of the lesson are designed to clarify for the students the purpose, procedure, and specific content of the learning experience. Such comments are related to improved student outcomes, engagement, and participation during the learning activity (Block, 1980; Joyce et al., 2004; Medley, 1977).

After the context for learning has been established, instruction can be initiated with the presentation of the new concept, task, or skill. Students' success in learning the new material has a lot to do with the thoroughness and quality of the teacher's preliminary explanation. Effective use of direct instruction depends on spending significant time on explaining and demonstrating the new material (Rosenshine, 1985). Effective presentation practices that appear to facilitate learning in direct instruction include: (a) presenting material in small steps so that one concept can be mastered before moving to the next, (b) providing multiple examples, (c) modeling or providing narrated demonstrations for completing the tasks, (d) staying on the topic (i.e., avoiding digressions), and (e) reexplaining difficult pieces of information (Rosenshine, 1985). Finally, it is important to provide a visual representation of the concept or skill along with the verbal explanation to assists students in being able to understand the information. Later, at other points in the learning process (such as generalization) the visual representation can serve as a cue or a prompt (Joyce et al., 2004).

Following the presentation, teachers need to check the students' understanding and provide feedback on the new concept or skill. Research has shown that effective teachers do a better job providing feedback compared to noneffective teachers (Rosenshine, 1985). Effective teachers do not let errors go, nor do they give answers to students who have responded incorrectly. These teachers use techniques for correcting incorrect responses or they reteach the content. When the incorrect responses indicate a lack of understanding, the teacher should provide cues or prompts, such as referring back to the visual representation (Joyce et al., 2004).

One key for providing immediate and quality feedback to students during direct instruction has much to do with later achievement and outcomes. Feedback assists students in their ability to gauge their own understanding of the new material. To be effective, feedback must be corrective, respectful, and deserved. For students with autism, direct instruction needs to include: (a) a **rationale**, (b) **presentation**, (c) **modeling**, (d) **verification**, (e) **evaluation**, and (f) **generalization** in order to better help them develop social and behavioral skills.

Rationale. Many students with autism need to understand how and why concepts are required. Therefore teachers must share (a) why the information is useful, (b) how the student can use the information, and (c) how the concepts fit in with what they already know (Myles & Southwick, 1999). It is important the rationale include visual task analysis demonstrating the components of the lesson, which should also incorporate the amount of time that will be spent on the lesson, task, concept, or activity. Similar to students with other disabilities, students with autism need to understand the lesson rationale or objectives before they can or will learn. The rationale can be simple and does not need to be lengthy.

Presentation. The teacher tells and shows the student the goals for the presented content, task, or activity and states exactly what the student is expected to learn. Through a direct instruction format, material should be taught using visual and auditory methods (Myles & Southwick, 1999). Information is presented in small segments. This method of instruction is active, with the teacher serving as the primary focus while presenting information, asking questions, and offering feedback.

Modeling. When modeling, the teacher needs to ensure she has the student's attention before showing him what he is supposed to do. The teacher demonstrates the expectations. This could include how to participate in a cooperative group activity or how to use a language strategy. When modeling, it is important to demonstrate how to complete the task or activity correctly verses telling the student what they should not do (Myles & Southwick, 1999). Students with autism may know what not to do but may not know what to do or have a clear understanding of the expectations.

Verification. When teaching children with autism, the teacher must closely monitor the student's emotional state. It is often difficult for teachers to read the emotions of students with autism, since they often display a flat and sometimes seemingly negative effect. Therefore, it may be difficult to know when the student is stressed as a result of not understanding the new content or skill. The teacher must learn how to decipher how each student communicates emotional distress and meet that student's needs as necessary, through additional instruction, modeling or individual work sessions.

When the student is at a level to understand their emotional distress signals, the teacher and student can work together to set a system that will best meet the student's needs. Failure to engage in this step could result in the student "tuning out" or having a meltdown (Myles & Southwick, 1999). It is important to keep the student with autism actively engaged throughout the direct instruction process. This can be more difficult since many children with autism are easily distracted or focused on a specific interest area. Teachers may use physical prompts and cues to help students attend to the lesson at hand—these could include proximity control or pointing to an item.

Evaluation. The teacher needs to incorporate a variety of methods to assess the student's knowledge, understanding, and use of the new skill. To the extent possible, students should participate in this process. Self-evaluating their skills and understanding of concepts helps with their achievement, performance, setting goals, skill maintenance, and generalization (Myles & Southwick, 1999).

Generalization. A challenge facing children with ASD relates to their difficulty generalizing knowledge and skills from one activity to another. This means it is often a challenge to apply information and skills in different environments and with different individuals. While children with autism may be able to memorize facts, the facts often remain disconnected. For example, a student may be able to state a classroom rule for a specific situation, but they are unable to apply this rule to another setting such as classroom, hallway, or cafeteria. Therefore, teachers and families are often expressing concern over the inability to generalize. Effective collaboration with families enhances generalization abilities. Moreover, collaborating with families strengthens the effectiveness of an intervention by ensuring that strategies are implemented in a variety of contexts including home and community (Buron & Wolfberg, 2008).

In addition, generalization may be hindered during stressful situations. Myles and Southwick (1999) used the analogy of the brain to a computer to help explain how a learned behavior is *filed* in the brain to be retrieved at a later time. When a child is under stress, they are less likely to be able to access the thinking area of the brain. This causes them not to be able to act in a manner others would perceive to be a logical or rationally—and are unable to generalize what worked in another situation. Typically, children will retrieve an established behavior pattern under stressful circumstances rather than generalizing a newly learned behavior (Myles & Southwick, 1999).

Generalization of interventions and skills children with ASD learn needs to be a planned component of any program (Simpson, 2005). The lack of generalization skills taught to children with autism is a serious concern (Buron & Wolfberg, 2008), as many students have the ability to learn and use a specific strategy in one environment (i.e., the setting where it is taught and used), but fail to generalize to other similar contexts or environments.

USING EFFECTIVE INSTRUCTIONAL STRATEGIES

The practice of using unfounded interventions and strategies in the field of **special education** has always been a pervasive problem (Jacobson, Foxx, & Mulick, 2005). Due to the broad range of challenges children with ASD experience and families longing for solutions and anything that might help (Maurice & Taylor, 2005), the diagnosis of autism has opened the door to numerous fads, cures, and exaggerated claims. The Interactive Autism Network (2011) found that families were using 381 treatments for autism and some were using multiple at the same time (an average of five). Many of these claims (e.g., brushing skin, radical diets, or weighted vests) continue to be unsupported by evidence or research (Schrebman, 2005).

Families of children with autism seem to be easy targets for promises of fast and significant improvements and ultimately remediating the disability. Therefore, it is important for educators to be aware of the claims and false promises. They are equally at-risk for buying into the false hopes. Schools that use interventions that are not research-based run the risk of depleting budgets and financial resources, promoting families' unrealistic expectations, and hindering a child's progress (Zane, Davis, & Rosswurm, 2008).

Research suggests interventions that work best for students with ASD are those that target specific areas of need, such as social skills, language acquisition, nonverbal communication, and behavior management (Arnett, Fitzpatrick, & Theoharis, 2013). When teachers focus on these areas, they can greatly improve achievement and independence for their students (National Research Council, 2001). Two key issues seem to define the debate around effective programs for children with autism: (a) the amount of intervention a child should receive (time) and (b) what approach or methodology is best.

In 2001, the National Research Center, as part of a review of the research and proposed recommendations, established the benchmark of 25 hours per week of intervention. These hours combined services received at home, centers, and community-based resources that provide multidisciplinary instruction in the core deficit areas. Another way to consider the appropriate amount of time is to review model programs that have shown positive outcomes for children with ASD (Strain & Cordisco, 1993). Model programs have indicated a range from 16-to-40 hours per week of intervention.

In answering the second question, what approach is best, there are numerous educational interventions that have proven effective and have demonstrated improved outcomes for children with autism and their families (Buron & Wolfberg, 2008). The majority of both specific interventions and comprehensive programs for ASD come from the field of **applied behavior analysis** (ABA) (Smith, Groen, & Wynn, 2000). However, there is currently growing agreement among both professionals and researchers that there is no single educational strategy best for all children with ASD (National Research Council, 2001).

Researchers have reported that explicit connections between visual and auditory information need to be created for children with ASD. ABA, **Picture Exchange Communication System** (PECS), **Social Stories™**, **power cards**, **cartooning/comic strips**, **visual schedules**, **SOCCSS**, **graphic organizers**, and **video modeling** are research based strategies that are visual, support communication, and promote independence. It is important to remember that when using any of these strategies, students with autism must be taught how to use the strategy. Students will not be able to be shown the information one time and a change in social or behavioral skill or understanding of a concept be seen, but rather the student will need to have access to the material and be shown how to use the strategy repeatedly in order to be successful.

MAX'S SCENARIO

Through the years Max has used a variety of strategies to help him be successful socially, behaviorally, and academically. The supports had to be used consistently. Using them once or twice and then *throwing-in the towel* on the strategy and moving to the next one would never work for Max. He needed to use the same strategy over and over and over again. Sometimes, I would wonder if it made a difference, it did not seem any progress was being made. Then all of a sudden something would happen to let me know he was using the strategy and they did matter.

With my school schedule—taking classes, supervising student teachers, doing homework, etc.—was unpredictable. Sometimes, I could put Max on the bus, but not be home in time to get him off of the bus and sometimes it was the opposite. My mom or sister would sometimes be able to help out. It was very confusing to Max that whoever put him on the bus in the mornings might not be the same person who would get him off the bus in the afternoons. I made cards and stuck them in his backpack. The cards had a picture of whoever would be getting him off the bus in the afternoon (and they had words that read, *When I get home from school, I will see* _____.) Then all day at school, he would not have to stress about who would or would not be home and in the event something would cause a change in our schedule, I could call the school and they could tell him and change the card. This provided Max a visual with what he could expect during the day. Using visuals greatly reduced the amount of meltdowns significantly related to getting off of the bus and being surprised by who was there to greet him.

When Max was younger, he also had difficulty waiting. Waiting for anything! One of his teachers suggested we use a red, yellow, green system. I took a piece of paper with three pieces of Velcro and three circles one red, one yellow, and one green. When we would go out, I would explain, it is red we are waiting. It is not time to leave yet (or whatever the situation). Ok, its yellow—we are almost finished. Now, its green we are leaving the restaurant. This system took a lot longer for him to fully understand—there was not as much visual (compared to a picture) but it was visual and it was simple to make and implement and for a busy mom that was key (sometimes my frustration would increase with teachers wanting me to make and implement these crazy systems—sometimes simple is best). He also had a power card (discussed below) to help him with waiting his turn.

Max and I have used a lot of visual timers to help us keep track of what we need to be doing. Mostly, to let him know when it is time to finish playing video games and time to move on to something else. We have used both the timers that beep and an hour glass. The visual hour glass works best, because he can see how much time he has left. For a kid that can lose track of time this worked great (otherwise he was always saying it had been five minutes, when really an hour had passed—he could lose track of so much time).

Max has often participated in lunch bunch and activities that provide social supports. There were struggles and miscommunications during these times, but what was so nice was there was an adult there to provide support and help the kids work through the situation. Had it been a less structured environment such as the cafeteria, Max would have misinterpreted the situation or miscommunicated what he really wanted to say. Participating in these activities helped him to know what to do when he was in the situation and there was not an adult present.

As Max continues into high school, he still uses the supports—some to a lesser degree and others have just taken on a different format because now he can read and write, so pictures are less necessary. They are not displayed for everyone to see but are now more private and are just for him. Max has a schedule he keeps in a binder and a teacher has helped him to organize and he uses graphic organizers for his written assignments. Sometimes, Max can select an organizer that would be appropriate and other times the teacher teaches him how to use the organizer and tells him to use it. He also has strategies for reading and answering questions. Max continues to receive social supports from school. All of these strategies and services continue to be a part of Max's IEP. The teachers are aware and help him to generalize these strategies so that he is able to use them at home and in his community activities.

STRATEGIES, METHODS, & INTERVENTIONS

Applied Behavioral Analysis. ABA has a long-standing and rich tradition that extends beyond the field of autism (Buron & Wolfberg, 2008). This includes the technology of positive behavior supports. The technology of ABA should be a part of any teaching environment for students with and without autism. ABA has proven to be effective direct instruction that is highly structured and focuses on teaching functional skills with continuous monitoring of progress.

Applied Behavioral Analysis uses a positive reinforcement behavior approach to teach skills systematically. Children are provided with repeated opportunities to practice what they have learned and generalize the skills across environments and with other individuals. ABA has a tremendous amount of evidence (more than any other treatment for children with autism) stating its effectiveness for individuals with disabilities (Simpson, deBoer-Ott, Griswold, Myles, Byrd, & Adams, 2005).

ABA strategies include a discrete trial format, chaining and prompting, and shaping. It should be noted there are many other strategies that also include ABA. Shaping of a preferred behavior is particularly useful for children with ASD, who may become anxious if they are unable to complete a task with immediate perfection (Buron & Wolfberg, 2008). In addition, individuals may have learned inappropriate behaviors through years of practice, however, are able to use with success with others in different environments. Therefore, it is important to recognize and reinforce successive approximations of the preferred behavior.

Another approach, using ABA, involves the use of extinction or **planned ignoring**. Implementing this strategy, professionals and family members ignore the negative behaviors and respond only to the positive behaviors. It is important to continue to ignore the behavior even with the student's behavior is out of control (making sure the behavior will not harm themselves or others). If a professional or family member gives into the misconduct, the student has learned the level of behavior that must be achieved in order to gain attention, receive an item, or desired outcome in the future.

Redirection and consequences are two other approaches that use ABA. Sometimes it is better to redirect students with they begin to engage in a challenging behavior. When you notice a student is beginning to become anxious, e.g., redirect them to a more preferred activity. Consequences should be assessed in terms of what motivates an individual. Each student is different—what works for one will not work for all. Observe fixations as possible consequences or motivators—what serves as a reward may differ person to person (Buron & Wolfberg, 2008).

Picture Exchange Communication System. **Augmentative Communication Systems** have proven benefits with nonverbal children (Zangari, Lloyd, & Vicker, 1994). However, instructional strategies pose challenges. They rely on the over use of verbal and or physical prompts such as *what do you want*?

or *point to what you want*. This results in some children becoming dependent on prompts causing them to lack spontaneous communication (Mirenda & Daltil, 1987). PECS is an instructional intervention with augmentative communication systems developed by Bondy and Frost (2001).

PECS is frequently used with children with autism as a way for them to communicate without spoken language. It is a way to teach functional communication to children with limited language (Bondy, 2012; Yamall, 2000). It allows them to share their wants and needs using pictures. The system promotes self-initiated communication (Malandraki & Okalidou, 2007). While PECS was originally developed for use with young children, it has been proven beneficial for varying ages and developmental levels (Malandraki & Okalidou, 2007).

PECS was developed to provide an effective augmentative communication system for nonverbal children minimizing the prompt dependency by teaching children to spontaneously initiating their wants and needs through an exchange of a picture for the corresponding item or activity. For example, PECS helps the student learn how to interact with others by exchanging the picture of the desired item for the actual item. This process teaches the student how to initiate spontaneous communication in different environments and allows them to participate in cause-effect conversations (Malandraki & Okalido, 2007). The process is structured so that it resembles a naturalistic approach to teaching in that communication by the student is initiated, rather than controlled by adults' verbal and physical prompting cues.

PECS also attempts to provide verbal models of language with the use of the picture exchange to encourage spoken language. In addition, PECS combines previously researched procedures into the teaching protocol in order to encourage the child to initiate and be motivated by including a child choice, waiting, structure of the environment, and differential reinforcement (Reichle, York, & Sigafoos, 1991).

Social Stories™. The first step in teaching any new social skill or solving a social problem is to provide careful explanation of the social situation (Janzen, 2003). **Social Stories™** developed by Carol Gray (1993) have proven to be an effective tool with children with autism (Simpson, et al., 2005). By providing concrete information about social expectations in specific contexts, Social Stories™ encourages appropriate behaviors and social skills. They are short simple stories (typically between 5-10 sentences), that use a specific formula (descriptive, perspective, directive, affirmative, & partial sentences) (Gray, 2000). These short stories describe relevant social and environmental cues, the perspective of others who share the space in that setting, and a direct solution the student can employ to create a more positive response to the problem (Janzen, 2003). Through text and pictures, Social Stories™ describes a social situation duration (e.g., greetings, turn-taking, or standing in line) and provide instruction on positive and appropriate social behaviors (Gray & Garland, 1993). Presenting Social Stories™ before a specific event can reduce anxiety, improve behavior, and increase awareness of others (Xin & Sutman, 2011).

Power Cards. The power card strategy is a visual support that incorporates the child's special interest into teaching appropriate social skills, routines, and parts of the **hidden curriculum**. One of the benefits to the power card strategy is that it uses the interest of the child. The power card strategy presents information on a single sheet of paper. This is a short scenario told in first person—told from the perspective of the child's hero. It describes how their hero would solve the problem. A small card, the Power Card, recaps what the child could do in that same situation using short manageable steps. Max had difficulty waiting his turn and I developed a power card using his special interest—Buzz Lightyear (see below).

Cartooning/Comic Strips. Gray (1994) expanded the use of Social Story™ to include comic strip conversations. This strategy helps individuals with ASD understand what is happening in a given situation and how they can/should respond. This is a way for them to visualize the meaning of abstract social concepts and rules (Janzen, 2003).

You do not need to be an artist to develop comic strips—they are simple stick figures. Speech and thought bubbles are added to show what individuals are thinking or saying. One benefit of comic strips, they can be implemented quickly to provide immediate clarification for a social situation, the meaning to a piece of the hidden curriculum, or the steps to solve a social problem.

Visual Schedules. A schedule of the plans and activities for the day is a fundamental component of structured teaching. The students' day is filled with planned activities in designated locations. Further, each child's schedule should be individualized in terms of content and form so that it meets their individual needs (Buron & Wolfberg, 2008). It is not typical two or more students would have the same learning styles, communication systems, and interests, therefore it is important that their visual schedules reflect their individuality.

Schedules should be visual and accurately represent the events. Life is not always predictable, especially in schools, so predetermined schedules need to be created in a format that allows for quick changes to be displayed easily. Students will need to be shown and made aware of the changes that are being removed or substituted.

Research has shown visual schedules are an effective tool for children with autism (Goodman & Williams, 2007; Spriggs, Gast, & Ayres, 2007). Difficulty with transitions can greatly impede a child's ability to independently complete tasks across environments (Scheuermann & Webber, 2002). Visual schedules assist children in transitioning independently from one activity to another to provide them with structure and predictability (Bryan & Gast, 2000). Additionally, they can be used in a variety of ways to meet the needs of individual students or groups of students. Using real objects, drawings, or words they illustrate a sequence of events or the steps that complete an activity. By providing a visual of the day or the task to be completed, it enables children to predict what will happen next, reduce anxiety, and promote peaceful and smooth transitions.

When considering developing a visual schedule for a student, it is important that it be individualized to match the student's needs. To help ensure that the schedule will be accepted and used, the symbols must be meaningful and must be constructed in a way that is clear and easy to manipulate.

Students can move from schedules that include concrete objects to photographs, pictures, symbols, and finally words. As they become more independent, more responsibility related to their schedule can be given to the student. Students can start with a schedule that shares what will happen during an hour as they become more comfortable from the time they arrive at school until lunch and finally a schedule that is for the entire school day. As you consider which way is the best to structure the visual schedule (i.e., objects, photographs, pictures, symbols, or words), it is also important to consider if it would be best for the schedule to be displayed horizontally or vertically. Both ways serve a purpose, for non-readers visual schedules that are horizontal help to promote emergent reading skills.

Having a chart or visual schedule of expectations and events provides some security to students and ease anxiety. This strategy can be used in advance to prepare children with autism for changes in routine. Informing children of schedule alterations not only lessens anxiety, but also saves the teacher and the class from disruption (Myles & Southwick, 1999). The student who is showing signs of frustration may have their attention directed to the schedule to remind him when he completes the first activity they will move to an activity of interest.

SOCCSS. SOCCSS stands for the situation, options, consequences, choices, strategies, stimulation strategy. Social situations occurs daily and sometimes even hourly. These situations can make little or no sense to students with ASD. These children can end up in trouble or being teased because they did not and could not understand the direction or the intent behind the social interaction. SOCCSS is a strategy that can help students with autism turn seemingly random actions into a meaningful interaction (Myles & Southwick, 1999).

The SOCCSS strategy was created to help students with delays in social skills put social and behavioral issues into a sequential form (Myles & Southwick, 1999). The strategy helps students understand the problem and lets them see that they have options and a choice to make about the given situation. Then, the strategy helps them to work through the choices and see that each decision has a consequence. Myles and Southwick (1999) outlined the following procedures for the SOCCSS strategy:

- **Situation**. When a social issue arises or poses a problem, the teacher steps in and works with the student to identify the situation. Together they work to define the problem and state the goal. This stage can include discussion, writing, and drawings.

- **Options**. After identifying the situation and stating the goal, the teacher helps the student brainstorm several options for behavior. The teacher accepts all of the student's ideas for possible options—these are not evaluated. Each option could be displayed in picture or written format. It is important that multiple solutions are provided. Research shows this is a critical step in problem solving (Spivak, Platt, & Shure, 1976). Creating multiple solutions reduces student frustration and anxiety. It also helps students with ASD to begin to see multiple perspectives.
- **Consequences**. In this step, the teacher and student work together to evaluate each of the options generated during the step above. During this step, the teacher acts as the facilitator using questions to help the student develop the consequences for each option. Kaplan and Carter (1995) suggest evaluating on the criteria: (a) *will I get the solution I want?* and (b) *is it feasible, will I be able to see it through*? The consequences could be labeled "E" for efficacy or F for feasibility.
- **Choices**. With the guidance of the teacher facilitating, the student prioritizes the options and consequences and selects one of the solutions from the list of options generated.
- **Strategies**. The teacher and student work together to create a plan of action for the option selected. While the teacher can provide guidance by asking leading questions and facilitating the discussion, the student should be the one to develop the plan. This helps to ensure the student has a feeling of ownership.
- **Simulation**: The student is given an opportunity to turn the abstract strategy and the process of the SOCCSS strategy into something more concrete. This can be done either through role-play, discussion with a peer about the process and the plan, or writing or drawing out the plan.

Graphic Organizers. Graphic organizers provide students with autism a visual holistic representation of facts and concepts along with their relationship within an organized framework. This means, graphic organizers are a strategy that arrange key vocabulary and terms to show their relationship to each other, present abstract or implicit information through a more concrete and visual means. Graphic organizers can be used within any content areas and can be useful before, during or after students are presented with the content information. Examples of graphic organizers include but are not limited to semantic maps, Venn diagrams, outlines, and compare and contrast charts.

Video Modeling. For students with autism it is a challenge to initiate, maintain, and generalize skills across environments and with different individuals. Video modeling is another way students with autism can be presented with a visual that shows the contexts, content, skill, and steps required for the desired behavior or task (Bellini, Akullian, & Hopf, 2007). It has been proven effective for individuals of all ages with autism. It is a procedure that enables individuals to see and review a perfect example of themselves or others as the task or skill is performed. There are two ways this procedure is used: (a) self-modeling (i.e., by watching themselves perform the task perfectly on a carefully edited video) and (b) peer-modeling (i.e., watching a competent peer model complete the task—sometimes adult models can also be effective).

For students with autism, video modeling provides them with the benefit of the combination of both auditory and visual information. Students with autism also have difficulty focusing on relevant cues needed in order to learn, because they are unable to ignore the irrelevant stimuli occurring in the environment. Sometimes, the student has difficulty choosing which information is important and which is not. Carefully staged and edited videos can provide consistent, highly focused information that is attractive and holds the attention of the student with ASD.

Video models have been used to teach academic, social, communication, and behavior skills (Hitchcock, Prather, & Dowrick, 2004). They offer a way to provide multiple ways of representing information with concrete real-life examples and support resulting in increased independence. The children are shown a video of an ideal scenario of a situation or behavior, and then prompted to imitate the model.

Research has shown video modeling to have promise with children with ASD as being an effective tool. One reason they are believed to be effective is because videos are an engaging medium that do not require social interaction for learning (Daneshvar, Charlop-Christy, Morris, & Lancaster, 2003). Videos lesson confusion, as directions, information, responses, and consequences become more predictable. They also allow for feedback and prompts to be included (Janzen, 2003). It should be noted that video modeling reduces the needs for more intrusive prompts (Janzen, 2003). Daneshvar et al. (2003) research suggested video modeling may result in the faster generalization of skills. For example, one 13 year-old girl was having difficulty getting ready for school and completing her morning routine in a timely manner. After reviewing the video once, the student was able to decrease the time it took to get ready for school. With continual review of the video, the skills were maintained (Janzen, 2003). In addition, Janzen (2003) noted the following benefits of video modeling for students with autism:

- Seeing themselves on video performing the task correctly increases self-confidence and the willingness to try.
- Videos can be created for different environments to help support generalization of skills.
- Videos can be reviewed anytime and anywhere, so students can practice several times throughout the day or over the course of several days.

HIDDEN CURRICULUM

Every aspect of our society including schools has a hidden curriculum. The rules that are not spelled out and are not shared, but somehow everyone knows what they are (Bieber, 1994). Everyone is clued into the unspoken rules known as the hidden curriculum except for the children with autism spectrum disorders. Students who do not have an understanding of the hidden curriculum are at a disadvantage. They may inadvertently break rules of the hidden curriculum and then get in trouble (because they should have known) or are teased and further ostracized by their peers (Myles & Southwick, 1999). Consider some of these scenarios:

- All of the students know, it is ok to get out of your seat to sharpen your pencil in Ms. Smith's classroom and you must raise your hand in Mr. Jones' classroom.
- All of the students know, Mrs. Tall allows you to take the balls on to the woodchips during recess, but Mrs. Brown only allows on the blacktop.
- During lunch, if you only want milk you may head to the front of the lunch line.

Each of these school scenarios can be complicated for students with ASD to understand because they are unspoken rules and do not offer predictability, the hidden curriculum in society is even more complex and difficult for them to negotiate.

For example, attending parties of friends and birthday parties for family members have different rules. Going to a nice restaurant verses fast food has different procedures. Waiting to be seated is something we do at a nice restaurant, but we would think about if we were going to eat at McDonalds? Rules for using the bathroom, for girls this is a social trip and a time to touch up makeup—if a girl with ASD is asked to go to the restroom with a group of her peers it is important she know not to say no just because she does not need to use the restroom. Individuals with ASD need to be explicitly taught (a) teacher expectations, (b) students to interact with and those to stay away from, (c) teacher pleasing behaviors, and (d) behaviors that attract positive and negative attention (Myles & Southwick, 1999).

Understanding and being able to navigate the hidden curriculum can have a huge impact on students with ASD. It can keep them out of trouble and can assist with making friends. Thinking about the above scenarios, many teachers voice concern about teaching specific elements of culture. There are many other elements of the hidden curriculum that teachers can teach comfortably—and should the same as they would any other content area (Myles & Southwick, 1999).

For some areas, it may be more appropriate to enlist the help of peer models. It would not be appropriate for a teacher to share some of the hidden curriculum about what happens in the classroom, but a student could easily share Mrs. Walker allows us to whisper when our work is finished. This process of sharing and teaching the hidden curriculum needs to be well thought-out and presented carefully. It is recommended that peers identify hidden curriculum items and discuss them with the teachers and student's parents before sharing them with the student with ASD. As a group, they can decide the logistics for sharing the information and providing instruction for the hidden curriculum items (Myles & Southwick, 1999).

COMMUNITY ENGAGEMENT

Like all other children, individuals with ASD participate in activities outside of their home and school and will one day transition into the work environment. It is important they have an opportunity to participate in these activities in meaningful ways and that they feel successful in the experience. Environmental supports can enhance the student's ability to function more effectively.

Students may find organizations or clubs related to a specific area of interest; participate in church activities, or sports. They may require the supports described above in order for them to be able to participate. For example, in order for a student to participate in 4-H, they may need a visual schedule to help them be able to process the next activity at the meeting.

Adults in these different environments may have little or no experience working with students with autism. It is important for parents and teachers to share what works and provide strategies that may help in environment outside of home and school. Adults working with these children need to be constantly asking, "what can be done to make the environment more understandable?" (Myles & Southwick, 1999, p. 90).

Many individuals with ASD want to fit in (this is especially true for individuals with **Asperger's syndrome**). They want to be socially involved and have meaningful relationships with others. Many individuals with ASD are baffled by the way others think, talk, and manage social situations, by the way they use words, change topics, and make decisions quickly (Janzen, 2003). Teachers and parents need to be aware and guide individuals with ASD through the social situations they find difficult. Since, these can happen at home, school, and in the community, it is important everyone is sharing the information.

CIRCLE OF FRIENDS

Children with ASD often face significant challenges and it is easy to see how developing friendships could be difficult and a support network would be necessary for school success. **Circle of friends** provides an excellent venue for students to practice the social skills they have been learning from adults in a more direct instruction setting and apply it to really life with peers. Teachers and parents need to carefully select who the student should be paired with. This should be a social astute group and compliant buddies. Those who are selected to be in the circle of friends group need to value the person with autism, not merely dictate the activities.

For example, establishing a *lunch bunch* is a way to encourage a circle of friends gathering. The child with autism may bring a card with conversation starters that she could ask the other children in the group. The peers can then interact with her as a friend, helping her to participate in meaningful lunch room conversation. Recess games could then be incorporated. If the children participate in the same activities after school, they could watch for each other at these events. When the parents know their child is participating in circle of friends, they can call each other (or help their child call) to schedule play dates, shopping outings, or bike rides together to encourage social outings within the community.

MAX'S SCENARIO

Buzz Lightyear is a very busy space ranger. He works hard to make planet Earth a safe place for all of us. He uses his lasers to fight off invaders. When he is not fighting evil, he likes to play games with his friends. He knows in order for his friends to like playing with him, they all have to take turns. Buzz Lightyear wants you to have fun playing games with your friends, too. He wants you to remember his five steps for taking turns.

1. Sometimes, you will get to go first. Other times you might be second, third, or last.
2. Wait quietly with your hands in your lap until it is your turn to play.
3. When it is your turn, follow the game directions and take your turn.
4. After your turn is finished, sit quietly and wait for your turn again.
5. If you follow Buzz Lightyear's steps for taking turns, you will have fun playing games with your friends.

The four steps were placed on a small card with Buzz Lightyear's picture on it. While he could not read, this was a special card, and Max wanted to be like Buzz Lightyear. His teachers and I had read him the scenario many times and reminded him of the card whenever there was an activity that required turn taking.

FIRST-PERSON TESTIMONIAL

About Max

By

JacksonPenner, 9th Grader

Kids in my school are treated in class as if they had no disabilities. In school the teachers will most likely keep kids with minor disabilities in the same classes as everybody else. The teachers keep them with other people to make more friends. Most of the time you cannot tell whether someone has disabilities.

Personally, I like having people with disabilities in classes, because I like talking to them. About every morning, Max and I go to the cafeteria before school starts and talk about funny videos he found the night before. Then later when I get home from my sports and school I watch the videos he tells me I should see. Occasionally, I see him at swim meets, because his sister is on the same team as me.

I think it is a great idea to have people with disabilities to play sports. On the swim team there is a high schooler with Down syndrome who is probably better than most people. She is encouraged to swim and cheered on. Also in track there is another kid who is occasionally picked on by people videotaping him doing stupid stuff and posting it online.

PROFESSIONAL ANALYSIS

Making the Classroom Environment Accessible to *ALL*

By

Julie Mitchiner, Ph.D., Early Childhood Education, Gallaudet University

The classroom environment can either support or discourage children's learning experiences and growth. A positive classroom environment nurtures young children not only physically but also emotionally, intellectually, and aesthetically. According to Reggio Emilia, a leading early childhood philosopher, the environment acts as a third teacher whereas children learn and thrive by interacting with materials and using the space in creative ways (Gandini, 1988). A typical space in an Emilia classroom is thoughtfully designed to promote educational provocation for exploration and meaningful interactions among children and adults (Curtis & Carter, 2007; Strong-Wilson & Ellis, 2007).

Carefully planning on designing the classroom is one of many important tasks that an educator performs. Not only ensuring that the classroom is engaging and stimulating, but establishing the classroom to be fully accessible and equitable to *all* children is also crucial. In a classroom that is fully accessible, children can develop a sense of ownership, independence, and being valued as equal members of the class.

Children who engage in an accessible classroom also have the ability to demonstrate their individual strengths and unique learning styles which will lead to a successful learning experience (Darrah, 2007). A fully accessible classroom involves providing multiple and varied learning experiences and materials for all children including learners who are culturally, linguistically, and/or ability-diverse.

In recent years, experts proposed to integrate the principles of **Universal Design for Learning** (UDL) in early childhood settings in order to have a successful and equitable classroom for all children (Bertling, Darrah, Lyon, & Jackson, 2011; Conn-Powers, Cross, Traub, & Hutter-Pishgahi, 2006; Darragh, 2007). The basic principle in UDL is instead of waiting until a child with disability arrives in your classroom to make accommodation and adaptations, the classroom should be proactively designed to accommodate all kinds of learners.

In addition to making the classroom accessible to *all* children, considerations on creating an anti-bias environment are also important. In an anti-bias classroom, children learn about self and others' identity development such as race, culture, gender, economic class, and abilities (Derman-Sparks & Edwards, 2010). The children also learn about fairness and recognizing unfairness to advocate for self and others. It involves creating a space that promotes appreciation and respect towards diverse cultures and experiences. Setting up a classroom that is anti-bias will require careful selection of learning materials and classroom decorations.

PRINCIPLES OF UDL IN EARLY CHILDHOOD

The principles of UDL began in the architecture field with redesigning the public spaces like buildings, physical spaces, and materials to make it accessible for all people including individuals with disabilities. Some of the examples were installing curb cuts, entrance ramps, and automatic doors to make it possible for individuals with disabilities to have equitable access in the public space (Conn-Powers et al., 2006).

In result, not only people with disabilities benefitted from it, but everyone else too. For instance, families with young children and babies can now easily push their strollers across the street with curb cuts. A similar principle is applied in educational settings. UDL requires reframing societal perspectives towards individuals with disabilities from a deficit perspective to a more positive perspective that celebrates differences in abilities among individuals. Drawing from the established seven principles of UDL, educators need to ensure that the classroom is (a) equitable, (b) flexible, (c) simple and intuitive, (d) promotes perceptible information, (e) has a low tolerance for error, (f) requires low physical effort, and (g) varied in size and space for approach and use. Cunconan-Lahr and Stifel (2007) provided several examples of UDL in early childhood classrooms including but are not limited to:

- Incorporating a variety of manipulatives (e.g., in size, colors, texture, shapes, etc.).
- Using varied seating options (e.g., wheelchairs, mat, cushion, specialized seating, etc.).
- Consideration in sensory stimulation (e.g., visual noise, lighting, over visual simulation on walls, etc.).
- Ensuring that the space is safe and accessible to activities, space, and equipment.
- A balanced environment that hold spaces where children can become active or quiet.

- A multitude of technology made available involving assistive devices, software, computers, mobile devices, etc.
- Multiple ways to express self (writing, signing, singing, talking, gesturing, using assistive technology).

AN ANTI-BIAS CLASSROOM

Now that learners are more diverse in America, teachers need to create an environment in classroom that demonstrates a value in respecting and appreciating diverse cultures and experiences. The visual material environment includes books, toys, manipulatives, materials, posters, pictures, and the equipment. Careful selection of books involves in assuring that the images and information in the book accurately represent a range of diverse experiences, addresses social justice issues, and reflects different languages. Dramatic play areas should include diversity of gender play, diverse cultural life experiences like cooking, working, and celebrating.

FIRST PERSON TESTIMONIAL

Early Intervention is Critical

By

Nicole Hutchinson, The River School in Washington, DC

It is a Monday morning and you step into my preschool classroom. Everywhere you look children are moving, talking, and playing. In the book corner there are two children looking at stories together, piles of discarded books strewn all over the rug. At the sensory table, three children are scooping and pouring water with different sized measuring cups, splashing, and laughing together. In the corner a boy is crawling through an elaborate house made out of cardboard and fabric. At one table a girl is scribbling with crayons and at another a boy is building towers with blocks and knocking them over with a loud crash. At the easel two children are painting a big piece of paper. In the dramatic play area a girl is playing with puppets and making various animal sounds. One boy chases another around the room with a frog puppet pretending to tickle his peer. To an outsider this might look like chaos, but to a preschool teacher this is a regular day.

Amongst the commotion something magical is happening; all the children are exploring, discovering, and learning. At first glance, one might think my preschool classroom is just for play, but behind the scenes there is an elaborate and well thought-out plan for each child's individual success. My job is making preschool fun and helping all of the children become active participants in their own learning. What may look like just painting might be exploration of color or practice with specific motor skills. What may seem like just splashing in water is not only exploration of early science concepts but also an opportunity to develop social emotional skills while interacting with friends. What looks like pandemonium is actually an extraordinary place designed especially for young children to learn and explore. There is more to my preschool classroom than meets the eye.

The experience of preschool is different for every child. No two children are the same, and they come to school with a variety of background experiences, unique family and home environments, and different strengths and styles of learning. Each child who enters my classroom is unique, and it is my job to figure out how to best help them learn and grow. Partnering with families is a key component of teaching preschool. I can share with a family about how things are going at school, what we have been learning about and focusing on, and where their child might need additional support. Families can also share with me about how their child functions in environments outside of the school setting, what their favorite activities are currently, and share any changes in their home environment. I am much more successful at my job as a preschool teacher when I can collaborate with families to discover how their child learns best and work together to support their child's growth and development.

Teaching a class of preschoolers can be a juggling act. Meeting the diverse needs of each child in my classroom can be a challenge, and it requires flexibility, creativity, and patience. It is the art of embedding developmental goals into a hands-on active learning environment driven by the children's passions, interests, and their need to explore. Adapting instruction for each child's individual skill levels, interests, and areas of strength and weakness comes more easily when the lesson plans are dynamic, imaginative, and full of opportunities for the children to discover, create, and explore.

Every day in my preschool classroom I am tasked with the challenge of figuring out how to make it all work: designing lesson plans, targeting developmental goals, collaborating with families, and partnering with other professionals. Every day I walk into the classroom to another day of exploring and learning alongside a group of sweet, funny, and energetic preschoolers. To an outsider it might seem crazy, but amongst the chaos I have the joy of watching it all come together, and seeing the magic that is young children excited to learn.

SUMMARY & CONCLUSION

Students with ASD have difficulty processing, understanding, and organizing information from their environment. It is also clear that providing the information in a visual format is strength for the learners and allows them to have a permanent aid for reference. Systematic organization with a visual structure for events, time, and content provides support with teaching and learning new tasks including those that are social or behavioral. There is still a need to visually clarify ideas, concepts, sequences, and processes to help promote greater independence. Students with ASD may need more details and information compared to their peers, but to ensure understanding, it must be carefully organized and presented both visually and concretely. Using these strategies goes beyond the classroom and should be incorporated into home and community activities.

References

Arnett, S., Fitzpatrick, M., & Theoharis, R. (2013). *Foundations of special education: Understanding students with exceptionalities*. Dubuque, IA: Kendall Hunt.

Bellini, S., Akullian, J., & Hopf, A. (2007). Increasing social engagement in young children with autism spectrum disorders using video self-modeling. *School Psychology Review*, *36*(1), 80–90.

Bertling, J, Darrah, M., Lyon, D., & Jackson, S. (2011). Early childhood building blocks: Universal design for learning in early childhood inclusive classroom. (Research Brief).

Bieber, J. (1994). *Learning disabilities and social skills with Richard LaVoie: Last one picked ... first one picked on*. Washington, DC: Public Broadcasting Service.

Block, J. W. (1980). Success rate. In C. Denham & A. Lieberman (Eds.), *Time to learn*. Washington, D.C.: Program on Teaching and Learning, National Institute on Education.

Bondy, A., & Frost, L. (2001). The picture exchange communication system. *Focus on Autistic Behavior*, *9*, 1–19.

Bondy, A. (2012). The unusual suspects: Myths and misconceptions associated with PECS. *The Psychological Record*, *62*, 789–816.

Bryan, L. C., & Gast, D. (2000). Teaching on-task and on-schedule behaviors to high functioning children with autism via picture activity schedules. *Journal of Autism and Developmental Disorders*, *30*, 553–567.

Buron, K. D., & Wolfberg, P. (2008). *Learners on the autism spectrum: Preparing highly qualified educators*. Shawnee Mission, KS: Autism Asperger Publishing Co.

Cunconan-Lahr, R.L., & Stifel, S. (2007). Questions to consider in UDL observations of early childhood environment. Building inclusive child care project (BICC). Retrieved September 22, 2014, from http://www.pakeys.org/

uploadedContent/Docs/Higher%20Ed/CunconanLahr%20Kennedy%20Stifel%20Universal%20Design%20for%20Learning%20handout%202.pdf

Curtis, D., & Carter, M. (2003). *Designs for living and learning*. St Paul: Redleaf Press.

Daneshvar, S., Charlop-Christy, M. H., Morris, C., & Lancaster, B. M. (2003). Using video modeling and reinforcement to teach perspective-taking skills to children with autism. *Journal of Applied Behavior Analysis, 36*(2), 253–257.

Darrah, J. (2007). Universal design for early childhood education: ensuring access and equity for all. *Early Childhood Education Journal, 35*(2), 167–171.

Derman-Sparks, L., & Edwards, J. O. (2010). *Anti-bias education for young children and ourselves*. Washington, DC: National Association for the Education of Young Children.

Gandini, L. 1998. "Education and caring spaces" In Edwards, C., Gandini, L., & Forman, G. *The Hundred Languages of Children*. Greenwich, CT: Ablex.

Goodman, C., & Williams, C. M. (2007). Interventions for increasing the academic engagement of students with autism spectrum disorders in inclusive classrooms. *Teaching Exceptional Children, 39*(6), 53–61.

Gray, C. (2000). Writing social stories with Carol Gray: Accompanying workbook to video. The Gray Center for social learning and understanding. Jenizon, MI: Future Horizons.

Gray, C. (2003). Social stories. Retrieved October 3, 2014, from http://www.thegraycenter.org

Gray, C., & Garland, J. (1993). Social stories: Improving responses of students with autism with accurate social information. *Focus on Autistic Behavior, 8*, 1–10.

Hitchcock, C., Prather, M., & Dowrick, P. (2004). Reading comprehension and fluency: Examining effects of tutoring and video self-modeling on first-grade students with reading difficulties. *Learning Disability Quarterly, 27*, 89–103.

Interactive Autism Network. (2011). IAN research findings: Treatment series. Retrieved August 14, 2014 from http://www.iancommunity.org/cs/oam_treatment_reports/overview

Jacobson, J. W., Foxx, R. M., & Mulick, J. (2005). *Controversial therapies for developmental disabilities: Fads, fashion, and science in professional practice*. Mahwah, NJ: Erbaum.

Janzen, J. E. (2003). *Understanding the nature of autism: A guide to the autism spectrum disorders* (2nd ed.). San Antonio, TX: PsychCorp.

Joyce, B., Weil, M., & Calhoun, E. (2004). *Models of teaching* (7th ed.). Boston, MA: Pearson.

Kaplan, J. S., & Carter, J. (1995). *Beyond behavior modifications: A cognitive-behavioral approach to management in the school* (3rd ed.). Austin, TX: Pro-Ed.

Malandraki, G., & Okalidou, A. (2007). The application of PECS in a deaf child with autism: A case study. *Focus on Autism and Other Developmental Disabilities, 22*(1), 23–32.

Maurice, C., & Taylor, B. A. (2005). Early intensive behavioral intervention of autism. In W. L. Herward, T. E. Heron, N. A. Neef, S. M. Peterson, D. M. Dainato, G. Cartledge, R. Gardner III, L. D. Peterson, S. B. Hersh, & J. C. Dardig (Eds.). *Focus on behavior analysis in education: Achievements, challenges, and opportunities* (pp. 31–52). Upper Saddle River, NJ: Merril, Peterson.

Medley, D. M. (1977). *Teacher competence and teacher effectiveness*. Washington, D.C.: American Association of Colleges of Teacher Education.

Mirenda, P., & Dattilo, J. (1987). Instructional techniques in alternative communication for students with severe intellectual handicaps. *Augmentative and Alternative Communication, 3*, 143–152.

Myles, B. S., & Southwick, J. (1999). *Asperger syndrome and difficult moments: Practical solutions for tantrums, rage, and meltdowns*. Shawnee Mission, KS: Autism Asperger Publishing Co.

National Research Council. (2001). *Educating children with autism*. Washington, DC: National Academy Press.

Reichle, J., York, S. S., & Sigafoos, J. (1991). *Implementing augmentative and alternative communication*. Baltimore, MD: Paul H. Brookes.

Rosenshine, B. (1985). Direct International Encyclopedia of Education. In T. Husen & T. N. Postlethwaite (Eds.) (Vol. 3, 1395–1400). Oxford: Pergamon Press.

Scheuermann, B., & Webber, J. (2002). *Autism: Teaching DOES make a difference*. Belmont, CA: Wadsworth-Thompson Learning.

Schreibman, L. (2005). *The science and fiction of autism*. Cambridge, MA: Harvard University Press.

Simpson, R. (2005). *Autism spectrum disorders: Interventions and treatments for children and youth*. Thousand Oaks, CA: Corwin Press.

Simpson, R. L., deBoer-Ott, S. R., Griswold, D. E., Myles, B. S., Byrd, S. E., & Adams, L. G. (2005). *Autism spectrum disorders: Interventions and treatments for children and youth.* Thousand Oaks, CA: Corwin Press.

Smith, T., Groen, A. D., & Wynn, J. W. (2000). Randomized trial of intensive early intervention for children with pervasive developmental disorder. *American Journal on Mental, 105*(4), 269–226.

Spivack, G., Platt, J. J., & Shure, M. (1976). *The problem-solving approach to adjustment.* San Francisco: Jossey-Bass.

Spriggs, A. D., Gast, D. L., & Ayres, K. M. (2007). Using picture activity schedules to increase on-schedule and on-task behaviors. *Education and Training in Developmental Disabilities, 42*, 209–223.

Strain, P. S., & Cordisco, L. (1993). LEAP preschool. In S. L. Harris & J. S. Handelman (Eds.), *Preschool education programs for children with autism* (pp. 127–162). Austin, TX: Pro-Ed.

Strong-Wilson, T. & Ellis, J. (2007). Children and place: Reggio Emilia's environment as third teacher. *Theory into Practice, 46*(1), 40–47.

Xin, J. F., & Sutman, F. X. (2011). Using the smart board in teaching social stories to students with autism. *Teaching Exceptional Children, 43*(4), 18–24.

Yamall, P. (2000). Current interventions in autism: A brief analysis. *The Advocate, 33*, 25–27.

Zane, T., Davis, C., & Rosswurm, M. (2008). The cost of fad treatments in autism. *Journal of Early and Intensive Behavior Interventions, 5*(2), 44–51.

Zangari, C. Lloyd, L. L., & Vicker, B. (1994). Augmentative and alternative communication: An historic perspective. *Augmentative and Alternative Communication, 10*, 27–59.

SUBJECT INDEX

End of Book Subject Index:

Chapter 1 Subject Index:

Chapter 2 Subject Index:

Chapter 3 Subject Index:

Chapter 4 Subject Index:

Chapter 5 Subject Index:

Chapter 6 Subject Index:

Chapter 7 Subject Index:

Chapter 8 Subject Index:

Chapter 9 Subject Index:

Chapter 10 Subject Index:

UNITALICS

Chapter 11 Subject Index:

www.ingramcontent.com/pod-product-compliance
Lightning Source LLC
LaVergne TN
LVHW080656011026
849160LV00014B/1447